Joshua Tree

SUPPLEMENT

S U P P L E M E N T

RANDY VOGEL / ALAN BARTLETT

CHOCKSTONE PRESS
Evergreen, Colorado
1989

Published by
Chockstone Press, Inc.
Post Office Box 3505
Evergreen, Colorado 80439

ISBN 0-934641-14-5

All uncredited photos by Alan Bartlett.

FOREWORD
TO THE SUPPLEMENT

When Joshua Tree Rock Climbs was finally completed in the Spring of 1986, I let out a sigh of relief. John Wolfe's guidebook to Joshua Tree had lasted seven years before it was replaced, so with any luck it would be a number of years before I would have to undertake a new guide to Joshua Tree.

However, within months, it became painfully obvious that some sort of revamping or at least a supplement would become necessary. New route activity, which has always been a bit frenzied, accelerated at an unbelievable pace. Even the climbing magazines are unable to keep up with this prodigious production.

So, there I was, only two seasons since the appearance of the Guidebook, and looking at a pile of new routes which I estimated to approach nine hundred (900). Several alternatives came to mind: (1) do nothing about it, (2) re-do the entire Guidebook, or (3) somehow package this new material, for those who are interested in it, and at the same time correct some of the errors that crept into the last guide. This Supplement is the result of the decision to choose the last alternative.

The nightmarish task of organizing this material was not a pleasant thought. Of course, I did the only logical thing, procrastinate. Fortunately, Alan Bartlett came to the rescue. He spent two weeks digesting, checking and translating this information into a workable format. Todd Gordon graciously provided his living room as a work space for Alan. Alan's experience as a guidebook writer *(Rock Climbs of the Sierra East Side)* and intimate knowledge of Joshua Tree should be given credit for much of what is right about this Supplement.

As with the last guide it is completely impossible for one (or two) person(s) to keep track of all the climbs being done in Joshua Tree National Monument. Without the effort of dozens of people who have submitted route information, this Supplement would have never been possible. However, even with the cooperation of all of these people, the Supplement, I am sure, is still far from complete. Some climbers choose, for whatever reasons, not to provide route information, and unless this information is available from other sources, it did not find its way in here by some means of sorcery.

Of the many people who have assisted, I would like to also extend a special thanks to: Todd Battey, Scott Cosgrove, Dave Evans, Craig Fry, Bob Gaines, Mari Gingery, Todd Gordon, Tom Herbert, Vaino Kodas, Herb Laeger, Randy Leavitt, Troy Mayr, Alan Nelson, Mike Paul, Vicki Pelton, Alan Roberts, Todd Swain, and Jonny Woodward.

Randy Vogel, January, 1989

CONTENTS

INTRODUCTION
TO THE SUPPLEMENT

HOW TO USE THIS BOOK

This Supplement is intended to be used in conjunction with *Joshua Tree Rock Climbing Guide* (1986). Although some of the route information herein is sufficiently complete in and of itself, in many cases, maps, photographs or other routes located in the Guidebook are referred to in locating climbs in this Supplement. Page references made in this supplement usually refer to pages in the Guidebook, but this is not always the case; hopefully it will be obvious. When viewing any map, north is always straight up.

In order to make the use of the Supplement/Guide easier, the index in this Supplement contains a complete index to both the Supplement and the Guidebook. Page numbers opposite route names will be followed by an "S" or a "G", indicating where the information will be found. In some cases, routes may be listed or referred to in both the Supplement and Guide, and there will be two page numbers, one followed by an "S" and one by a "G". Therefore, if you are looking for a particular route, refer to the Supplement index, and it will let you know whether it's in the Supplement or the Guidebook and on what page to find it. Hopefully, this will avoid unnecessary flip-flopping from one book to the other.

Since many climbers feel that the most valuable aspects of a guidebook is having a place to check off routes, a complete Route By Rating index for both the Guide and the Supplement is also contained in the Supplement. This Route By Rating index lists every route in the Supplement and Guide by rating (from 5.0 to 5.13, etc.). A check-off "box" will be found in front of each route in the Route By Rating index, so that routes can be conveniently "checked off".

NEW ROUTES AND CORRECTIONS

This Supplement contains both routes which were not listed in the Guidebook as well as corrections to information contained in the Guide. All new routes or corrections are listed in numerical order, following the format of the Guidebook.

New routes will be assigned a number which corresponds to the nearest existing route, followed by an alphabetical suffix (e.g.: route numbers 78A, etc.). In many cases, if a new route lies immediately adjacent to an existing climb, the Supplement may provide no further information than: "Climb the offwidth 50' right of *Psychokenesis.*" In this case, you should refer to *Psychokenesis* in the Guide and determine the location of the new route accordingly. Because this Supplement follows standard guidebook procedure of listing routes left to right, the new routes with alphabetical suffixes are generally found to the right of the route with the number their alphabetical suffix has been added to (e.g. route 45A is right of route 45). There are a few exceptions to this rule, and they are noted where they appear in the text. All routes have at least a brief route description anyway, so it is hoped that these identifying numbers will only help clarify a route's location, rather than add to the confusion.

Corrected routes from the Guidebook will retain their original numbers.

RATINGS

Most of the corrections to the Guidebook involve changes in ratings. Since no one climber has done all the routes in the Monument (including the authors), the rating reported by other climbers (most often the first ascent party) must be used. For new routes in this Supplement, numerical ratings are given in the more than familiar Yosemite (Tahquitz) Decimal System (YDS). Due to the lack of complete information, new routes are not given quality (star) ratings, as was done in the Guide. When a new Guide is compiled, perhaps there will be enough of a consensus to give all routes star ratings.

Other corrections involve locations of routes, freeing of former aid routes (very few of these), and the leading of former top-rope routes. We didn't worry too much about this last group, and tended to only report it if the lead involved the placing of fixed gear (bolts or pitons). It seems safe to assume that any top-rope route from the Guide with a rating of 5.9 or below has probably been led, if not soloed.

ENTRANCE FEES

As all regular climbers of Joshua Tree are aware, in 1987 Joshua Tree National Monument instituted an entrance fee (user fee). As of the date of this writing, these fees are as follows:

$2.00 Per walk-in/rider on bus/or motorcycle [(Good for seven (7) days]
$5.00 Per vehicle [no limit on occupants and good for seven (7) days]
$15.00 "Joshua Tree" Yearly Pass [Good for one (1) calendar year, Jan. 1 to Dec. 31, only at Joshua Tree National Monument]
$25.00 Golden Eagle Pass. The Golden Eagle Pass may be used at all National Parks/Monuments [Good for one (1) calendar year, Jan. 1 to Dec. 31]

There is no charge for camping in the Monument, with the exception of Black Rock and Cottonwood. However, since neither Black Rock or Cottonwood campgrounds are frequented by climbers, camping is essentially free. Please be advised that there is a fourteen (14) day camping limit per year in the Monument.

ABOUT TRASH, ETC.

Climbers have become one of the largest users of Joshua Tree National Monument. There are certain areas of the Monument which were once rarely visited by humans, but are now heavily used, almost entirely by climbers. Climbers have a very real and often negative impact on the delicate desert environment at Joshua Tree. The responsibility for lessening this impact rests with each and every climber.

One of the most tangible forms of environmental impact which climbers have on the Monument is the refuse they leave behind. This trash takes many forms, however, the three most common and serious forms of trash pollution being discarded (used) tape, improperly disposed of human waste (including toilet paper) and "poot slings".

While there is absolutely no excuse for ever leaving used tape behind (this will easily fit into your pack or pocket), convenient restroom facilities are not available in most areas of the Monument. Climbers must use common sense and care when using the "facilities", *ala natural*. A few rules should be observed. Do not ever leave human waste anywhere near waterways (i.e., dry stream beds). When it rains in the Monument, this waste will pollute the valuable and scarce rain water which is relied upon by many animals of the Monument. Human waste should also not be left on or near the many informal trails which climbers use. Although many climbers make a habit of burying their waste, the fact remains that human waste decomposes the quickest when not buried. Soiled paper should be carried out in a small plastic Ziploc bag; this is the only way to ensure that the dry desert environment does not have to struggle for years to decompose it on its own.

"Poot" slings (runners left on fixed protection) are often an unsightly and unnecessary form of pollution. Additionally, when climbers, for some unknown reason, tie slings directly into bolts, it may be impossible for subsequent climbers to clip into the hangers. There is very little reason for ever tying directly into a bolt with a runner. Looping a sling through a bolt works just as effectively, and means that subsequent parties can easily remove the sling. Furthermore, climbers should familiarize themselves with ways of retrieving slings after rapping off fixed protection when they are close to the ground (this is almost always possible in Joshua Tree).

When plastered on the rock, chalk can be a form of visual pollution. Although the majority of the routes in the Monument will "wash clean" after a good rain, overhanging climbs (e.g.: **Leave it to Beaver**) are so protected from the rain that they never get clean. In an effort to alleviate this problem, climbers are requested to use "rock-colored" chalk. This is available at most climbing shops.

Mountain Bikes are frequently used by climbers as a quick and easy way of getting from one climb to another. However, climbers should be aware that use of mountain bikes (or any vehicle) off established roads is prohibited. Bicycles also cause accelerated damage to the fragile desert environment. In order to encourage compliance with Monument policy, the Monument has purchased several bike racks which will be placed at convenient locations.

QUAIL SPRINGS

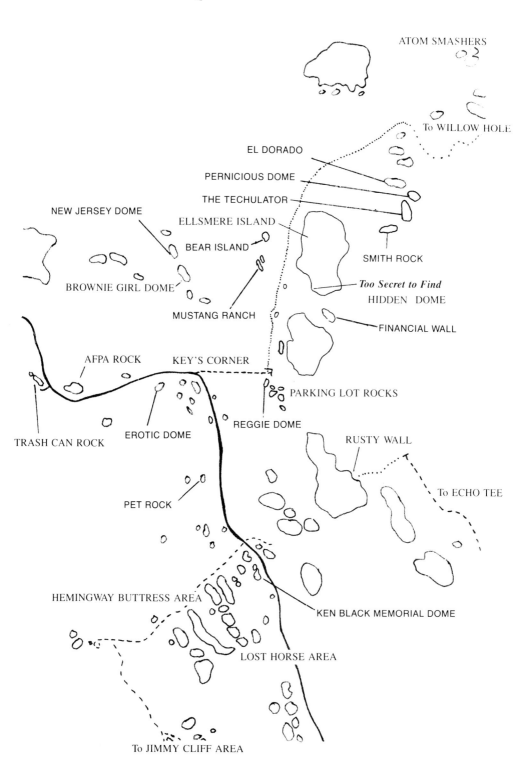

ATOM SMASHERS

To WILLOW HOLE

EL DORADO

PERNICIOUS DOME

THE TECHULATOR

NEW JERSEY DOME

ELLSMERE ISLAND

BEAR ISLAND

SMITH ROCK

BROWNIE GIRL DOME

MUSTANG RANCH

Too Secret to Find
HIDDEN DOME

FINANCIAL WALL

AFPA ROCK

KEY'S CORNER

PARKING LOT ROCKS

TRASH CAN ROCK

EROTIC DOME

REGGIE DOME

RUSTY WALL

To ECHO TEE

PET ROCK

HEMINGWAY BUTTRESS AREA

KEN BLACK MEMORIAL DOME

LOST HORSE AREA

To JIMMY CLIFF AREA

THE NEGROPOLIS

This is the brown buttress which lies upon a large hill on the left (east) side of Quail Springs Road approximately 3.3 miles past the Joshua Tree Entrance to the Monument and 2.4 miles before you get to **Trash Can Rock.** Three routes are known.

4A DANCE ON FIRE   5.11a   This is the three bolt face climb on the left side of the buttress. FA: Mike Lechlinski and Mari Gingery, December 1987.

4B TAP DANCING   5.11a   Start just right of **Dance On Fire** and climb face and thin crack past three fixed pins. FA: (TR) Bob Gaines and Pat Nay, October 1986. (Lead) Lechlinski and Gingery, December 1987.

4C B FOR BEERS   5.10b   Approximately 100 feet right of **Tap Dancing** climb a dike system past three bolts. FA: Todd Gordon, Mike Brown and Craig Fry, October 1985.

VAGMARKEN BUTTRESS

Approximately 5.5 miles past the Joshua Tree Entrance to the Monument and 1.2 miles before you get to **Trash Can Rock** is a large hill on the left (east) side of the road. The following route lies on the largest (obvious) buttress on the hillside.

4D VAGMARKEN BUTTRESS   5.7   Climb the middle of the buttress past one bolt. FA: Herb Laeger, Eve Laeger and Dave Houser, June 1980.

TRASHCAN ROCK- WEST FACE

16A HISTORY   5.11a (TR)   Climb the face between **Cranny** and **Eschar.** FA: Todd Gordon, Brian Sillasen and Frank Bentwood, February 1988.

18 BIMBO   This route should be rated 5.10a.

27 KARPKWITZ   This route should be rated 5.6.

WHITE CLIFFS OF DOVER

45A SCIENTIFIC AMERICANS   5.8   Climb the arete right of **Jack Of Hearts** past two bolts. FA: Todd Swain and Peggy Buckey.

48A AN OFFICER AND A POODLE   5.8   50 yards right of **Popular Mechanics** and on the right side of a large buttress, climb a crack then up the face past one bolt. FA: unknown.

48B SEARCH FOR CHINESE MORSELS   5.10b   To the right of **An Officer And A Poodle** is a brown wall. Climb past two bolts then up cracks to top. FA: Pinson, Scott and Saltzer, January 1987.

48C SHIBUMI   5.10d   Right of and across a gully from **Search For Chinese Morsels** is this thin, straight-in crack that steepens at the top. FA: Mark Dubé, Alan Roberts and Darrel Hensel, January 1986.

49A DOVER SOLE   5.6   Climb a left facing dihedral with a crack on the left wall lying midway between **Voice Buddy** and **Red Snapper.** FA: Alan Roberts, January 1986.

AFPA ROCK

52A BOULDER FACE   5.7   Just right of **Boulder Crack** climb a face and short crack. FA: Todd Swain, April 1986.

52B BITCH, BITCH   5.7   This is the leftmost obvious line on the main face of **Afpa Rock.** Follow cracks and grooves up and slightly left, then straight up. FA: Dave Evans and Margie Floyd.

52C WHICH BITCH   5.8   Climb cracks right of **Bitch, Bitch** and left of **Route #53.** FA: unknown.

53 UNKNOWN   This route should be rated 5.10c and is poorly protected.

56A SPAGHETTI SAUCE SUNSET   5.10c   This route climbs the crack between **Which Witch** and **Two Our Surprise** passing a bolt at the top. FA: Tom Weldon et al, March 1981.

57A SHELTERED   5.8   This route is on the back side of **AFPA Rock,** near its right side. It is a crack that starts fingers and progressively widens. FA: Alan Roberts and Kristin Laird.

EROTIC DOME

This formation is located 50 yards south of Quail Springs Road approximately .3 miles past **AFPA Rock.** Both known routes face the road. Map, supplement page 4.

57A EROTIC CITY   5.11   Climb a thin crack until possible (necessary) to traverse right to a crack which leads to the top. FA: Mike Paul, John Mallory and Mike Fogerty, December 1985.

57B VOLGA BOAT MEN   5.8   Climbs the hand crack on the narrow rib to the right of *Erotic City.* FA: Brian Sillasen, Todd Gordon and Dave Wright, October 1987.

PARKING LOT ROCKS

BUBBA ROCK

This formation is located approximately 100 yards southeast of the parking lot. The north face is heavily huecoed and faces the parking lot. Map, supplement page 4.

58A BUBBA TAKES A SIESTA   5.10a   Follow huecos on the good rock on the north face of **Bubba Rock** past one bolt to an arching crack. FA: Don Wilson and Jack Marshall, February 1988.

REGGIE DOME

This is the western-most formation of the **Parking Lot Rocks.** The first two of the following routes are on the northeast face, directly off the parking area. Map, supplement page 4.

58B THOMSON ROOF   5.8   Climb up and right, then step left and climb a finger crack over a roof. FA: Reggie Thomson, Todd Gordon, Scott Gordon, Mike Brown and Howard Boyd, December 1985.

58C REGGIE ON A POODLE   5.10a   Up and to the right of *Thomson Roof* climb an incipient crack to a bolt and loose face climbing to the top. FA: T. Gordon, S. Gordon, Thomson, Rick McKay, Brown and Boyd, December 1985.

Routes 58D through 58F lie on the west face of **Reggie Dome** to the right of a low angle slab which is plainly visible on the drive to the parking lot.

58D NINNY'S REVENGE   5.10a   Climb the short flaring crack just left of a chimney/gully. Walk off left. FA: Don and Karen Wilson, March 1986.

58E POPS GOES HAWAIIAN   5.8   To the right of *Ninny's Revenge* follow a steep dike in brown rock past a bolt to a flake, then move right to rejoin the dike. FA: Don and Karen Wilson, March 1986.

58F THE CHIEF   5.5   Climb a fine crack in excellent rock to the right of *Pops Goes Hawaiian.* FA: Don and Karen Wilson, March 1986.

FINANCIAL WALL

The best way to find **The Financial Wall** is to follow the approach for *Breaking Away,* but rather than turning back south to that route, walk east into a broad valley. Go east until you can turn south to a formation with an overhanging east face. This is **The Financial Wall.** Map, page 4. .

59A TAXED TO THE LIMIT   5.12a   This is the left-slanting crack on the left side of the wall. FA: Herb Laeger and Bob Yoho, February 1986.

59B HIGH INTEREST   5.11a   Slightly left of center of the wall is an obvious hand crack. Climb this, but take the jog right at the top. FA: Laeger and Yoho, February 1986.

59C THE SPECULATOR   5.11+   This route follows the obvious central crack which leads up into a body slot. FA: Laeger and Yoho, February 1986.

59D THE CRASH   5.12+   *The Crash* follows the left leaning corner which leads to a finger crack just right of *The Speculator.* FA: Laeger, Yoho, February 1986.

59E HIGHER YIELD   5.10d   Climbs obvious line on the right side of the wall. FA: Herb and Eve Laeger and Rich Perch, November 1986.

THE BACKSTREETS

The Backstreets lies about 100 yards south of **The Financial Wall.** The only known route is on the east face.

59F JUST A SKOSH   5.9   To the left of a break in the east face climb over a small roof then continue up a more moderate crack. FA: Don and Karen Wilson, April 1986.

OUTWARD BOUND SLAB

Approach the **Outward Bound Slab** as for **Ellsmere Island.** Before you get the approach gully for **Hidden Dome** you will see an obvious south-facing slab to your right (east). The **Slab** more or less faces **The Financial Wall.**

59G PAINT ME GIGI   5.7   Ascend the left-most crack on the face (no pro); slants left. FA: unknown.

59H OUTWARD BOUND SLAB ROUTE   5.8   Climb past three bolts to the right of **Paint Me Gigi.** FA: Mike Brown, Reggie Thomson, Howard Boyd, Scott Gordon and Todd Gordon, December 1985.

59I MASTERING 5.2   5.2   Easy gully right of **Outward Bound Slab Route.** FA: unknown.

59J LOOK MOM NO HANDS   5.7   Follows crack to face right of **Mastering 5.2.** FA: unknown.

59K ONE FOR THE ROAD   5.10a   This route is located on the far right side of the **Outward Bound Slab,** 200 feet right of **Look Mom No Hands.** Climb a finger crack just right of a left facing book capped by a roof. FA: Roger Linfield and Dennis Yates, December 1986.

COOL DOME

As you make the approach to **Hidden Dome, Cool Dome** is the formation on your left about ⅓ the way up the approach gully. It is plainly visible in the top photograph on page 39 of the guide about ¾" above the word "approach".

59L BANK NOTE BLUES   5.9   This route follows the obvious offwidth crack on the west side of the dome which starts in a right facing dihedral. FA: Alan Roberts and Todd Gordon, December 1985.

59M BEDTIME FOR DEMOCRACY   5.10b   Start around the corner and right of **Bank Note Blues.** This route follows a right slanting crack which is reached by a traverse left from the top of a small dihedral. Originally climbed with no fixed gear, two bolts and two fixed pins were added by a later party mistakenly thinking theirs the first ascent. FA: Tom Addison and Scott Pond, March 1987.

59N STARDUST MEMORIES   5.9 +   Start around and right of **Bedtime For Democracy** on **Cool Dome's** east face. Face climb past five bolts. FA: Troy Mahr, Steve Anderson, Ed Hunsaker and Steve Axthelm, February 1988.

59O TOO SILLY TO CLIMB   5.5   Ascend the left facing book just right of **Stardust Memories.** FA: Addison and Pond, March 1987.

59P FINGER STACKS OR PLASTIC SACKS   5.10b   This is the double thin cracks right of **Too Silly To Climb** and left of a tree. Start in a "pit". FA: Addison and Pond, March 1987.

59Q RICKETS AND SCURVY   5.10b   Climb a thin crack leading to twin hand cracks right of **Finger Stacks or Plastic Sacks.** FA: Mayr, Anderson and Axthelm, February 1988.

59R CLAMMING AT THE BEACH   5.9   Across the canyon and opposite **Stardust Memories** is this 3" crack. FA: Addison and Pond, March 1987.

HIDDEN DOME

60A TUCSON BOUND   5.8   Climb cracks just right of **Calgary Stampede**. FA: Todd Gordon and Alan Roberts, December 1985.

60B THE SCREAMING WOMAN   5.10a   This climb lies just right of **Tucson Bound,** and passes a bolt at the top. FA: Dave Evans, Jim Angione, Herb Laeger and Dave Bruckman, December 1986.

60C THE SCREAMING POODLE   5.10c (TR)   Discontinuous cracks immediately left of **Too Secret To Find**. FA: unknown.

60D BALANCE DUE   5.10d   Follow thin cracks and face climbing past two bolts to the right of **Too Secret To Find**. FA: Laeger, Bruckman and Evans, December 1986.

60E MAJOR CREATIVE EFFORT   5.10   About 30 feet right of **Balance Due** is a left slanting hand crack which leads to easier face climbing. FA: Greg Murphy and Dave Houghton, February 1987.

ELLSMERE ISLAND

61A GO WITH THE FLOE   5.9+   This route is located in the gully right (south) of the **Ellsmere Island** routes. It is a vertical crack on a steep wall leading to a left-slanting traverse crack. FA: Pete Charkin, Alan Roberts and Bruce Howatt.

62A FUN IN THE SUN   5.9+ (TR)   This route ascends the front of the buttress right of **Made in the Shade**. FA: Todd Swain and John Thackray, March 1987.

62B FRIGHT NIGHT   5.4   Climb the crack to the right of **Fun in the Sun**. FA: Swain, March 1987.

62C ABLE WAS I ERE I SAW ELLSMERE   5.7   This route lies on the face of the block below and to the right of **Made In The Shade**. FA: Randy Vogel, Darrel Hensel and Alan Roberts, January 1986.

63A THE HOUDINI ARETE   5.11c (TR)   Follows face climbing to an arete left of **The Great Escape**. FA: Troy Mayr, John Mallory and Bob Gaines, January 1988.

64A MATH   5.10b   This is the left facing overhanging crack/corner right of **Aftermath**. FA: Robert Alexander and Eric Fogel, October 1986.

65A GEOMETRY   5.11a   To the left of **Aftermath** climb this left facing roof/crack system. FA: Alexander, Fogel, Nick Beer and Ruth Galler, October 1986.

65B BABY FACE   5.7   This route is located 50 feet right of **Baby Roof** and just right of the descent. Face climb past two bolts. FA: Thackray and Swain, March 1987.

65C GAIL WINDS   5.9   This is a three-bolt face climb just right of **Baby Roof**. FA: Don and Karen Wilson, January 1987.

66A HIT IT ETHEL   5.8   This is the hand crack leading to face climbing past three bolts just right of **Route 66** (route #67). FA: Don and Karen Wilson and Jack Marshall, March 1988.

67A APE MAN HOP   5.10a   Just left of **Route 66** (route #67) climb the face past two bolts. FA: Ron White, Marshall and Don and Karen Wilson, February 1988.

67B CHOCOLATE DECADENCE   5.7   This is the dogleg dihedral 50 feet left of **Ape Man Hop**. FA: Karen Wilson and Julie White, March 1988.

68A GUN FOR THE SUN   5.10a   This route is on the face to the left of **As The Wind Blows;** two bolts. FA: Marshall, Don and Karen Wilson, March 1988.

MUSTANG RANCH

The Mustang Ranch consist of two rocks to the left (west) of the road, due west from the approach for **Hidden Dome**. The first three routes are on the larger western formation.

68B BLUE VELVET   5.11d (TR)   This route follows a right slanting crack/seam on the left side of the formation. FA: Dick Cilley, 1987.

68C PRETTY IN PINK   5.11b (TR)   To the right of **Blue Velvet** and past a break in the wall are two thin crack/seams. This route is the left one. FA: Mike Paul and Dick Cilley, 1986.

68D WOMEN IN CAGES   5.11c (TR)   This route is the right hand crack/seam mentioned above. FA: Paul and Cilley, 1986.

The next three routes are located on the right side of the smaller eastern formation. They are about 25 feet long and it is possible to boulder as well as top-rope them.

68E STABLE GIRL 5.11 (TR) This is the left of two thin cracks/seams. FA: Paul and Cilley, 1986.

68F VIVA LAS VEGAS 5.11 (TR) The right thin crack/seam. FA: Paul and Cilley, 1986.

68G MUSTANG RANCH 5.10 (TR) Climb protruding dike to the right of *Viva Las Vegas*. FA: Paul and Cilley, 1986.

BEAR ISLAND

This formation lies directly west of **Ellsmere Island** and to the north of **Mustang Ranch.** Map, supplement page 4.

68H SHARDIK 5.3 Climb the crack on the arete at the north end of the formation. FA: Todd Swain, March 1987.

68I POLAR BEARS IN BONDAGE 5.7 Climb a short crack through a bulge then up the easy gray face 15 feet left of *Kodiak*. FA: Swain, March 1987.

68J KODIAK 5.5 Climb the face and varnished crack on the right side of the west face. FA: Swain, March 1987.

Routes 69 – 72 (**High and Dry, Wren's Nest, Red Eye** and **Jah Loo**) are all mismarked in the guide, and the photos on page 42 are not applicable. They are apparently on **Pernicious Dome** and **The Techulator** (see section below), though no more information than that is given here. It is possible that some of the newer routes listed on those formations may indeed be these routes. There are also at least two more top-ropes to the right of **Jah Loo.**

BROWNIE GIRL DOME

73A TIGE 5.8 Climb the dike to the right of **Buster Brown** past one bolt. FA: Alan Roberts and Alan Bartlett, January 1988.

73B WHERE BROWNIES DARE 5.10a On the north face of **Brownie Girl Dome,** 10 feet left of the main crack system, lieback a crack up to a patina face then follow a crack above to the top. FA: Ernie Ale, Bruce Burns and Kevin Millis, June 1988.

NEW JERSEY DOME

This formation lies just northwest of **Brownie Girl Dome.** Map, supplement page 4.

73C JERSEY GIRL 5.10a On the southwest corner of the dome, climb easy, but loose rock up and left to an overhanging face. Small brass/steel nuts mandatory. FA: Karen and Don Wilson, December 1985.

THE MIDDLE KINGDOM

The following routes are located in an area termed **The Middle Kingdom.** It is comprised of various formations, mostly undeveloped, which lie north and east of **Ellsmere Island** and south of **The Atom Smashers.** To reach these climbs, continue past **Ellsmere Island** on the Willow Hole approach trail until a broad valley is seen to the east (right). The north-most obvious formation to the east is called **El Dorado.** It is a brown square-shaped crag. **Pernicious Dome** is the pointed brown formation southeast and back in a wash from **El Dorado.** Several other formations are located nearby. Map, supplement page 4.

EL DORADO

Routes 73D, 73E and 73F are located on the north face of **El Dorado.** Route 73G is located on the west face (the one seen on the approach).

73D MARY DECKER 5.11 (TR) This is the smooth left side of the north face. FA: Kevin Powell and Darrel Hensel, January 1985.

73E ZOLA BUDD 5.10d (TR) To the right of **Mary Decker,** climb up and right to reach a seam which reaches the top. FA: (TR) Alan Roberts, Powell, Tim Powell and Hensel, January 1985.

73F ROB'N THE CRADLE 5.10c Just right of **Zola Budd** is a left-leaning offwidth. Start to the left of this crack and climb up and right into it, and follow the crack to a horizontal break (meeting **Zola Budd** briefly). Go right, then up a crack. FA: Hensel, Roberts, Greg Epperson, December 1985.

73G WIDE WORLD OF SPORTS   5.10c   On the west face of **El Dorado,** climb an overhanging hand crack, then jog right to a hand/fist crack in the summit block. FA: Roberts, K. Powell, Dan Ahlborn, Hensel, T. Powell, Bob Kessenger, January 1985.

PERNICIOUS DOME
The following routes are located on the west face of **Pernicious Dome.**

73H UNDERCLING BYPASS   5.8   This route ascends a smooth slab beneath a left-slanting roof on the lower left side of the west face. FA: Dennis Yates, Roger Linfield, December 1986.

73I A LITTLE BIT OF MAGIC   5.10c   This is the left-arching crack high on the west face. FA: Linfield and Yates, December 1986.

73J DREAMS OF RED ROCKS   5.7   This climb is located on a knobby face just right of a left-facing flake. The climb finishes about 30 feet right of *A Little Bit Of Magic.* FA: Yates and Linfield, December 1986.

73K FRIENDLY FISTS   5.9   Opposite the west face of **Pernicious Dome** is this short left arching corner with a fist crack. This is actually the northeast side of **The Techulator.** FA: Linfield and Yates, December 1986.

73L TANNING SALON   5.6   On the south face of a small formation west of **Pernicious Dome** is this open book. FA: Yates and Linfield, December 1986.

THE TECHULATOR
The Techulator is the large massif south of **Pernicious Dome.** Map, supplement page 4.

73M SHORT BUT FLARED   5.10b   Climb the crack in a shallow dihedral on the northwest face of **The Techulator.** This route somewhat faces *Tanning Salon.* FA: Linfield and Yates, December 1986.

73N MUFFIN BANDITS   5.10b   Below and to the right of *Short but Flared* is this prominent left-facing book which doesn't quite reach the bottom. FA: Yates and Linfield, December 1986.

73O TCHALK IS CHEAP   5.10d   Several hundred feet right of *Muffin Bandits* and higher up climb past one bolt then follow cracks above a Gothic arch. FA: Yates, December 1986.

73P GARDEN PATH   5.10a   70 feet right of *Tchalk Is Cheap* climb a gully behind an oak tree. FA: Linfield and Yates, March 1987.

73Q CHUTE TO KILL   5.11a   Right of *Garden Path* lieback a large flake, then follow three bolts up a waterchute. FA: Yates and Linfield, March 1987.

73R UNDER A RAGING MOON   5.10b   This is the short right-facing corner above *Chute to Kill.* FA: Linfield and Yates, December 1986.

73S TOO THIN FOR POODLES   5.10c   150 feet right of *Under a Raging Moon* and *Chute to Kill* climb a thin crack until it forks. Take the left fork, then head up past two bolts. FA: Linfield and Yates, December 1986.

73T PILLAR OF DAWN   5.10a   Several hundred feet right and around the corner from the previous routes is a large pillar. This route follows a dihedral on the south face of the pillar. FA: Linfield and Yates, December 1986.

SMITH ROCK
Smith Rock lies 100 yards south of *Too Thin For Poodles.* This formation is oriented in an east-west manner. Map, supplement page 4.

73U THE NUTS AND BOLTS OF CLIMBING   5.10c   This route is on the northeast corner of **Smith Rock.** Climb an overhanging hand crack to a flake, then go up a face past two bolts. FA: Linfield and Yates, December 1986.

73V BIGHORN HAND CRACK   5.7   This is the straight-in hand crack on the south face of **Smith Rock.** FA: Yates and Linfield, December 1986.

73W RIDERS ON THE STORM   5.10a   Above and east of *Bighorn Hand Crack* are a pair of clean, slightly overhanging offwidths facing west. This is the right crack. FA: Linfield and Yates, March 1987.

73X VULTURE'S ROOST   5.9   This route is west of **Smith Rock,** high on a hillside on the east side of the **Ellsmere Island** clump. The route is on a formation just left of the ones shown in the top photo on page 42 of the guide, where *High and Dry* is (mistakenly) shown as being. The route is north-facing, and climbs a crack above a large flake. FA: Yates and Linfield, December, 1986.

73Y CLEAN CRACK   5.10b   This route is on an obvious dome east of **El Dorado,** reached by continuing past that formation on the approach towards Willow Hole. It faces north (towards the approach road) and is a thin crack in flawless rock. FA: Alan Roberts and Bill Meyers.

THE ATOM SMASHERS – MAIN AREA (aka TIMBUKTU TOWERS)

77A THE BATES MOTEL   5.12a   This route follows the long obvious arete to the right of *Offshoot;* climb past six bolts. FA: Jonny Woodward and Darrel Hensel, February 1988.

78A NUCLEAR WASTE   5.9 +   This route is the offwidth crack about 50 feet left of *Psychokenesis.* FA: Tony Yaniro, 1983.

79 PSYCHOKENESIS   5.11b   There are no bolts leading to the upper dihedral, rather climb the overhanging ramp/dihedral. Also the route is a little harder than reported in the guide. FA: May have been aided, unknown. FFA: Either Tony Yaniro and Ron Carson, or A. Bell and Vaino Kodas, 1983.

79A PSYCHOTECHNICS   5.10c   This route allows for a better second pitch alternative when climbing Psychokenesis. Climb that route and belay where the upper dihedral eases in difficulty. Climb right, out of the dihedral, then up the exposed arete past a bolt to the top. FA: Woodward and Hensel, January 1988.

79B UNKNOWN   5.10d   This and the following route lie on the east face of the **Timbuktu Towers,** directly below the east side of the leaning pillar visible in the photo on page 45 of the guide. Climb the face route on the left past three bolts to the top of a left-leaning arch. FA: Kodas, etc.

79C UNKNOWN   5.10c   This is the two-bolt face route leading to the base of the left-leaning arch; belay as per the above route. FA: Kodas, etc.

THE IVORY TOWER

This is the leaning pillar containing the route *Famous Potatoes* on its east face. Three difficult routes have been done on its overhanging north face.

80A THE POWERS THAT BE   5.13a   This route has five bolts and is near the left edge of the face. FA: Randy Leavitt, April 1988.

80B CHAIN OF ADDICTION   5.13b   Climb the center of the face past nine bolts. FA: Leavitt, October 1988.

80C LA MACHINE   5.13c   This route is near the right edge and has six bolts. FA: Leavitt, August 1988.

80D TELEKINESIS   5.11c or 5.10a   The best approach for this route appears to be boulder-hopping up the gully left of *Sine Wave,* then proceeding north (left) in a gully between the two formations north of the main **Timbuktu Towers.** A large scoop-shaped boulder is perched at the top of the northwest end of the formation on your right (east). *Telekinesis* climbs the crack(s) directly below the scoop.
(Var.1) 5.10a Undercling the flake up and right to a thin crack.
(Var.2) 5.11c Start down and right of the above variation; climb up and left along double arching cracks to reach the top thin crack.
FA: Yaniro, Carson and Bret Maurer, 1983.

80E PUMPING HATE   5.13a   This route is a five-bolt climb on the east face of the first rock southeast of the main **Timbuktu Towers** formation. In the photo on page 45, it is on the back side of the rock above and right from the number 79. FA: Randy Leavitt, April 1988.

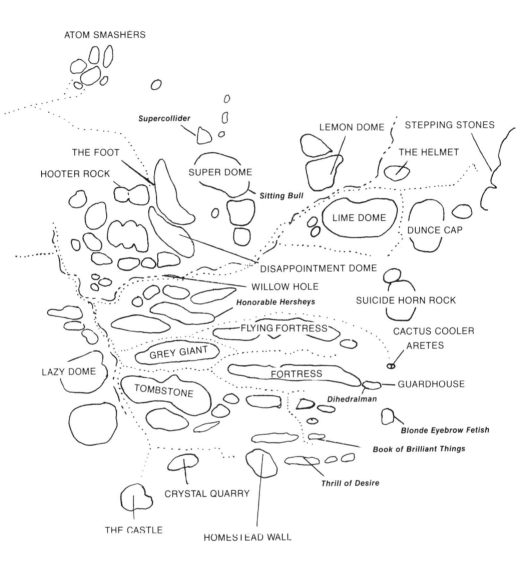

ATOM SMASHERS

Supercollider

LEMON DOME

STEPPING STONES

THE FOOT

THE HELMET

HOOTER ROCK

SUPER DOME

Sitting Bull

LIME DOME

DUNCE CAP

DISAPPOINTMENT DOME

WILLOW HOLE

SUICIDE HORN ROCK

Honorable Hersheys

FLYING FORTRESS

CACTUS COOLER
ARETES

GREY GIANT

LAZY DOME

FORTRESS

GUARDHOUSE

TOMBSTONE

Dihedralman

Blonde Eyebrow Fetish

Book of Brilliant Things

CRYSTAL QUARRY

Thrill of Desire

THE CASTLE

HOMESTEAD WALL

HOOTER ROCKS

Hooter Rocks can be seen in the lower left hand part of the photo on page 50 of the guide as three small formations starting about 45 degrees left and below of the "W" in "WILLOW HOLE" and continuing right under the word "HOLE". It is right and nearer the bottom of the photo from **The Foot** (see description below). The north faces are in shadow. The best approach is to head for the **Atom Smashers Area** but stay to the south (right) in the open basin. **Hooter Rock** lies just past **The Atom Smashers** on the right (south). Map, supplement page 12.

87A THE CROW'S NEST   5.11 +   This route is the overhanging face/crack which leads to a crack going through a roof near the summit of the middle formation's north face. FA: Mike Lechlinski, February 1988.

87B HOOTERVILLE TROLLEY   5.10 +   This route lies on the north face of the left-most (eastern) formation. Climb a clean crack to a face then past two bolts. FA: Dave Evans, Brian Sillasen and Dave Stahl, December 1986.

87C KP CORNER   5.10a   to the left of *Hooterville Trolley* and slightly around the corner climb a face up to a brown right-facing corner. FA: Kevin Powell and Alan Roberts.

THE FOOT

The Foot is an aptly named formation which lies approximately ¼ mile southeast of the **Atom Smashers Area. The Foot** can be seen on page 50 of the guide as three finger shaped formations just right of the words " TO SUPER DOME" in the lower left hand part of the photo. The best approach is to hike towards **Hooter Rocks,** but continue east past this formation, then head southeast in the canyon until you can see **The Foot** on your left. Map, supplement page 12.

87D DR. SCHOLL'S WILD RIDE   5.10a   This is the long "glassy clean" offwidth on **The Foot** formation; two pitches. FA: Dave Evans, Margie Floyd and Jim Angione, December 1986.

87E THE NEW SHOE REVIEW   5.10d   This is a six-bolt face route to the left of *Dr. Scholl's Wild Ride.* FA: Evans, Craig Fry, Todd Battey and Floyd, September 1987.

DISAPPOINTMENT DOME

This formation is the large southwest-facing face/dome which lies adjacent and south of **The Foot** and on the left side of a gully which starts between **Hooter Rock** and **The Foot.** Several routes have been done on the large face of **Disappointment Dome,** but information for all of these is incomplete. Map, supplement page 12.

87F UNKNOWN   ?   Bolted face route on the right hand part of the southwest face. FA: unknown.

87G THE LETDOWN   5.9   Climb thin cracks to the right of a brown left-leaning dihedral and right of the unknown bolted face route. FA: Powell and Roberts.

87H ROLLER COASTER   5.9   This is the short finger crack to the right of *The Letdown.* FA: Powell and Roberts.

87I UNKNOWN   ?   Face route to the right of *Roller Coaster* on a face separated from the southwest face. FA: unknown.

THE SUPER DOME

The next two routes are on a small formation north of the **Super Dome.** Map, supplement page 12.

88A SUPERCOLLIDER   5.8   This is a 150- foot finger crack on the west face. FA: Randy Leavitt and Doug Englekirk, October 1987.

88B SPANKING   5.11c (TR)   Left of *Supercollider,* near the northwest corner of the rock, this is a finger crack out a roof leading to a rounded arete. FA: Leavitt and Englekirk, October 1987.

88C STONE HINGE   5.11   This route lies on the north side of the **Super Dome** where several "terraces" can be seen. A large block is lying against the lower terrace which has a fingers to thin hands crack in its right side. FA: Tony Yaniro, Vaino Kodas and Dan Michael, 1983.

92 THE MOHAWK   5.12c   First pitch 5.12b; second pitch 5.12c.FFA: Randy Leavitt, January 1987.

93A SITTING BULL   5.10b   This is a classic finger to fist crack in a corner on the southeast side of the dome. FA: Leavitt and Rob Slater, September 1988.

LEMON DOME

Lemon Dome is located approx. ¼ mile east of **The Super Dome.** From Willow Hole proper, continue east, then northeast, following Rattlesnake Canyon for about 450 yards. The Canyon narrows and is filled with large boulders. At this point there are two large formations forming the sides of the canyon. The dome on the left (north) is **Lemon Dome.**

93A THE LEMON HEAD 5.10b This route lies on the large south face of **Lemon Dome.** Start on the left side of the face, climbing past four bolts up to the middle of the face. Above, slung plates and knobs protect the climbing to the top. FA: Todd Gordon, Craig Fry and Margie Floyd, January 1986.

LIME DOME

Lime Dome is the huge complex formation south of **Lemon Dome** and across the canyon.

93B THE LEMON SLICER 5.11a This perfect split crack lies directly across from *The Lemon Head,* low on **Lime Dome** and to the right. FA: Evans and Fry, December 1985.

93C LEMON LEMON 5.10a This two-pitch route lies about 150 feet to the left (east) from *The Lemon Slicer* on the north face of **Lime Dome.** FA: Evans and Fry, December 1985.

THE DUNCE CAP

The Dunce Cap lies ⅓ mile east of **Lime Dome** and is reached by continuing past **Lemon and Lime Domes** down Rattlesnake Canyon to an open area. The formation in the middle of the open area (on your right) is **The Helmet.** Continue right of **The Helmet** until to your right (south) you will see an imposing face/formation. This is the north face of **The Dunce Cap.**

93D THE DUNCE CAP 5.10c From the highest pillar on the north face, climb past a bolt to a crack which leads to the top. FA: Mike Lechlinski, Mari Gingery, John Bachar, Brenda Bachar and Craig Fry, 1982.

SUICIDE HORN ROCK

This dome lies about ¼ mile south of **The Dunce Cap.** It can be reached by going south along the west side of **The Dunce Cap,** or more easily from Willow Hole, by walking east towards **Lemon Dome,** but continuing east (south of **Lime Dome**) until a large north-south wash (½ mile from Willow Hole) is reached. Go south along a wash to **Suicide Horn Rock.**

93E BIGHORN DIHEDRAL 5.10b This route follows a classic steep flake leading to a thin corner on the west face of **Suicide Horn Rock.** FA: Mari Gingery, Mike Lechlinski and John Bachar, 1982.

93F COMPACT PHYSICAL 5.11c This is the 40-foot finger crack splitting the summit block above *Bighorn Dihedral.* It could be climbed as a second pitch to that route. FA: Randy Leavitt and Mike Geller, March 1985.

93G ROCK LYPSO 5.10a This route is located on the east face of **Suicide Horn Rock.** Climb a wide undercling protected by a bolt and large friends. FA: Fry and Dave Stahl, April 1986.

THE STEPPING STONES

This band of cliffs lie about 350 yards east and slightly north of **The Dunce Cap.** Approach as per **The Dunce Cap,** but after passing **The Helmet** on the north (left) side, head straight east to the cliffs on the hillside. Routes are described left to right. Map, supplement page 12.

93H STEPPING OUT OF BABYLON 5.9 This route lies just left of *Stepping Razor.* FA: Fry and Stahl, April 1986.

93I STEPPING RAZOR 5.10b This is the two-pitch perfect wide hand crack leading to a slightly overhanging corner near the left side of the cliff band. FA: Fry, Bob Roback and Stahl, April 1986.

93J STEPS AHEAD 5.10c, A1 Two pitches of mixed aid and free climbing to the right of *Stepping Razor.* FA: Stahl and Fry, April 1986.

93K FIRST STEPS 5.8 This crack climb lies to the right of *Steps Ahead.* FA: Fry and Stahl, April 1986.

CACTUS COOLER ARETES

This formation lies south of **Suicide Horn Rock** and roughly east of the **Fortress** area. If you are at the **Fortress,** head east out the valley, then somewhat south to this "split" formation. If you are near the **Duncecap/Suicide Horn Rock** area, head south. The "aretes" are formed by the north-south split of the formation. All of the routes are top-rope problems. See map page 12.

93L ARETE #1 5.10a (TR) This is the northwest arete of the eastern formation. FA: Randy Leavitt and Mike Geller, January 1985.

93M ARETE #2 5.11b (TR) This is the west side of the southwest arete of the eastern formation. FA: Leavitt and Geller, January 1985.

93N ARETE #3 5.11a (TR) The south side of the southwest arete of the eastern formation. FA: Leavitt and Geller, January 1985.

93O ARETE #4 5.11a (TR) This is the southeast arete of the western formation. FA: Leavitt and Geller, January 1985.

93P HONORABLE HERSHEYS 5.11a (TR) This route lies on the northeast arete, on brown-spotted rock, of a formation 300 yards north of the Grey Giant. There are two bolts on top. See map on page 12. FA: Randy Leavitt and Mike Geller, February 1985.

THE TOMBSTONE

101A TURTLE DAYS 5.8 This is a three-bolt face climb on a slab/buttress across from the **Grey Giant.** FA: Dave Evans, Kelly Carignan, Tom Smith and Crista Smith.

105A THE FUGITIVE 5.10d This is a five-bolt climb on the west face, 200 feet down and left from **Heaven Can Wait.** FA: Dave Evans, Spencer Lennard and Todd Gordon, November 1986.

THE FORTRESS AREA

107 BOOK OF BRILLIANT THINGS 5.13a The location of this route is incorrect in the guide. To get to it and the following two routes, walk east in the rock-filled gully on the back (south) side of the **Fortress.** The route is on the southeast face of a formation on the right side of this canyon. Near the east end of this formation, tunnel through (south) to the south face. See map, page 12.

The next seven routes are across the valley (**The Homestead**) south of the *Book of Brilliant Things.*

107A B.A.S.E. ARREST 5.10c This is a thin hand crack on the northwest face of a small formation 100 yards south of *Book of Brilliant Things.* FA: Randy Leavitt and Rob Slater, March 1985.

107B BAILEY'S FOSTER 5.10b This is on the north face of the formation left (east) of *B.A.S.E. Arrest.* Climb an offwidth leading to a hand crack in a corner. FA: Brian Bailey and Leavitt.

107C THE THRILL OF DESIRE 5.12c This route is about 100 yards right of *B.A.S.E. Arrest,* on a separate formation. It is a steep, left-facing corner with a very thin crack and some bolts in its lower section. FA: Leavitt, 1987.

THE HOMESTEAD WALL

This is the north face of the formation right (west) of *The Thrill of Desire.* See map, page 12.

107D MERCY ROAD 5.11a This is a steep bolted route on the left. FA: Leavitt and Glenn Svenson.

107E LOOKING FOR MERCY 5.11a Climb the face right of *Mercy Road.* The routes join for the last 15 feet. FA: Leavitt and Svenson.

107F EMPTY STREET 5.10c The face right of *Looking for Mercy.* FA: Leavitt and Svenson.

107G MOONSTRUCK 5.10b The rightmost route, this climbs face and a hairline fracture. FA: Leavitt and Svenson.

Randy Leavitt leading The Thrill of Desire

Photo: Brian Bailey

THE GUARDHOUSE

This is a formation on the east end of **The Fortress.** The following four routes can be approached from the **Cactus Cooler/Suicide Horn** area, but an easier approach directly to these routes is from Wonderland Valley by walking about 600 yards north along the Wonderland Wash from **The Cornerstone.** Coming that way, **The Guardhouse** will be on the left side of a broad valley after the wash has opened up. See map, page 12.

107H DIHEDRALMAN   5.13   On the south face of **The Guardhouse,** climb a left-facing dihedral with a thin crack. FA: Randy Leavitt, 1987.

107I AVANTE GUARD-DOG   5.11d   This is a double roof right of *Dihedralman.* FA: Leavitt and Svenson, December 1988.

The next two routes are on the east face of a formation south of **The Guardhouse.**

107J LUSTING CLH   5.8   Climb a flake/crack on the left side of the face. FA: Rob Slater.

107K BLONDE EYEBROW FETISH   5.10c   This is a 1¼" crack right of *Lusting CLH.* FA: Leavitt and Slater.

THE FORTRESS

113A PEAR-GRAPE ROUTE   5.10a   This is the crack right of *Natural Selection.* FA: Todd Gordon and Tom Michael, May 1987.

117A WHERESABOLT?   5.11+   (TR)   Direct start to *Catapult,* avoiding traverse in from the left. FA: Mark Robinson and Will Chen, October 1986.

121A GANADO   5.10b   First crack right of *Julius Seizure.* FA: Todd Gordon, Sharon Sadlier, Dave Evans, Craig Fry and Marge Floyd, March 1986.

THE FLYING FORTRESS

122A BOOGS' ROUTE   5.10b   The nice looking crack right of *No San Francisco.* FA: Dave Bruckman, Todd Gordon and Dave Evans, November 1987.

THE GREY GIANT – NORTH FACE

131 THE COLISEUM   5.10b   This climb was mistakenly called *The Maltese Falcon* in the guide. FA: Tony Yaniro, 1983.

131A DROP YOUR DRAWERS   5.9   Offwidth/chimney between *The Coliseum* and *Drop a Frog.* FA: Brian Povolny and Frith Yazzie, March 1986.

CRYSTAL QUARRY

This formation lies northeast of **The Castle,** roughly opposite and across the gulley/valley from it. Approach as for **The Castle** routes. Map, supplement page 12.

135A SACK IN THE WASH   5.10b   Approach this and the following route by third classing up slabs. This is a right-facing dihedral on the left side of the formation. FA: Rob Stahl, Dave Stahl, Craig Fry and Todd Battey.

135B HANDS OF FIRE   5.11c (TR)   The overhanging "wave-shaped" crack right of *Sack in the Wash.* FA: Dave Stahl, February 1987.

135C CRYSTAL DEVA   5.10c   This route climbs discontinuous cracks and face starting down low and right of the two previous routes. FA: Craig Fry and Dave Stahl, February 1987.

VOICE'S CRAG

136A C SHARP ROOF   5.10   This is a roof and thin crack 100 feet left of *War Crimes.* FA: Herb Laegar and Rich Smith, March 1979.

The next two routes are on a tower on the right end of **Voice's Crag.** Both routes face the road.

137A MUSH PUPPIES   5.8+   The left route, this connects several right-slanting cracks. FA: unknown.

137B ADAMS' HAPPY ACRES   5.5   The right route consists of steep flakes and cracks. FA: unknown.

PET ROCK

This is the small formation midway between **Voice's Crag** and **Lizard's Hangout.** The two routes are on the west face, away from the road. Map, supplement page 4.

140A EXCITABLE BOY   5.9   Climb the short, shallow left-facing corner on the left side of the face. FA: Todd Swain and Peggy Buckey, March 1986.

140B SHE'S SO UNUSUAL   5.7   A crack in brown rock 60 feet right of the preceding route. FA: Swain and Buckey, March 1986.

ROADSIDE ROCK

141A STAINS OF THE STARS   5.8+   Around the corner to the right of *Just Another Roadside Attraction* is this right-slanting undercling leading to an offwidth crack. FA: Todd Gordon, Todd Swain and Derrick, March 1986.

141B ROY'S SOLO   5.6   Right of the preceding route, on the backside of **Roadside Rock** is this short crack. FA: Roy McClenahan, March 1986.

LIZARD'S HANGOUT

142A RIGHT LIZARD CRACK   5.9   Between *Alligator Lizard* and *Progressive Lizard* are two cracks starting together and forming a vee. This is the right crack. FA: unknown.

142B LEFT LIZARD CRACK   5.10c   The left crack. FA: unknown.

142C ANOTHER CILLEY TOPROPE   5.11c (TR)   The bottomless groove just right of *Progressive Lizard.* FA: Dick Cilley.

 143 PROGRESSIVE LIZARD   This climb should be rated 5.9.

 144 CHICKEN LIZARD   This climb is easily leadable with RP's or brass nuts.

144A LIZARD TAYLOR   5.5   Climb the face left of a crack left of *Chicken Lizard.* FA: Todd Swain and Peggy Buckey, March 1986.

MEL'S DINER

150A I LOVE BRIAN PICCOLO   5.8+   This is a steep crack high on the formation, above and right from the *Mel Cracks.* FA: Todd Gordon, Quinn McCleod and Brian Sillasen, September 1986.

BUSH DOME

This dome is located behind and to the right of **Mel's Diner,** and is easily seen from the Quail Springs Road.

151A KATE'S BUSH   5.8   A long, obvious crack on the left side of the face which goes past a bush, then follows another crack up to the top. FA: Todd Gordon, Dave Evans, Margie Floyd, Deanne Gray, Jim Angione, Eric Charlton and Scott Gordon, September 1986.

151B CHESTWIG   5.10a   Improbable-looking thin crack left of the center of the crag. FA: Dave Evans, Margie Floyd, Jim Angione, Scott Gordon, Eric Charlton and Todd Gordon, September 1986.

LEFT HAND OF DARKNESS – EAST FACE

155A TO AIR IS HUMAN   5.10d   This is a three-bolt climb on the left arete of the block left of the upper (easy) section of *Uncle Fester.* It can easily be done in a single pitch with the *Uncle Fester* start. FA: Herb Laegar, Eve Laegar and Rich Perch, November 1987.

156A JANE PAULEY   5.8   This is the left of two double cracks right of *Uncle Fester.* FA: Tom Michael and Todd Gordon, October 1986.

156B BRYANT GUMBEL   5.8   The right of the two double cracks. FA: Todd Gordon and Cody Dolnick, October 1986.

156C GRANDPA GANDER   5.10c   Three bolt face left of *Granny Goose.* FA: Herb Laegar, Andy Brown and Lotus Brown, October 1986.

LEFT HAND OF DARKNESS – WEST FACE

159A POTATO MASHER 5.12b Seam with one bolt right of *Anti-Gravity Boots*. FA: Tom Herbert (TR), December 1987. Kurt Smith (lead), January 1988.

KEN BLACK MEMORIAL DOME

This is the first formation southeast of **Left Hand of Darkness.** Two routes are known, both facing the road. Map, supplement page 4.

159B HOLIDAY IN THE SUN 5.10 Start beneath a small roof and pass it on its right, then move left onto a rounded arete and climb past one bolt to the top. FA: Ken Black, 1983.

159C CHICKEN MECHANICS 5.9 Crack line starting down and right from *Holiday in the Sun.* FA: Brian Sillasen and Todd Gordon, May 1986.

HEMINGWAY BUTTRESS – EAST FACE

171A SPOODLE 5.9 First crack left of *Importance of Being Ernest.* FA: Brian Povolny, Steve Strong, Tom Michael and Todd Gordon, October 1986.

174A POODLE-OIDS FROM THE DEEP 5.10b The first crack left of *On the Nob.* The route goes up and left, then back up and right in an obvious steep ramp/corner. FA: Dave Evans and Todd Gordon, May 1986.

174B MOVEABLE FEAST 5.10c Start on *Poodle-oids from the Deep,* then work up and right past bolts and fixed pins to the right edge of the formation. Cut back left across a steep face, then up to the true summit, where rappel bolts will be found. FA: Roy McClenahan and Helga Brown, March 1988.

176 THE OLD MAN AND THE POODLE This route is mismarked in the guide; it starts left of where shown, and traverses right to reach the main upper crack, which is drawn in correctly.

179A ASTROPOODLE 5.10c Do the *Head Over Heels* roof, then continue straight up to a bolt at the next roof. Work right past another bolt to meet *Space Walk*. FA: Herb Laegar, Bob Kamps and Kevin Wright, October 1988.

179B SPACE WALK 5.8 Start 15-20 feet right of *Head Over Heels* and climb a hand crack which leads left around a corner to a large ledge. FA: Herb Laegar, Eve Laegar, Mike Jaffe and Rich Smith, January 1980.

180A PUZZLIN' EVIDENCE 5.11a This climb is just left of *Fusion Without Integrity* and has several bolts and a fixed pin. FA: Dave Evans, Todd Gordon and Craig Fry, October 1987.

182A RAVENS DO NASTY THINGS TO MY BOTTOM 5.9 The crack left of *Easy as Pi.* FA: Dave Evans and Todd Gordon, May 1986.

The following two routes are on the extreme right side of **Hemingway Buttress,** several hundred feet right of *Easy as Pi,* and best approached from the Lost Horse Road.

183A MARCOS 5.9/10a As seen from the Lost Horse Road, this is a high right-facing dihedral. FA: Dave Evans and Todd Gordon, February 1986.

183B AQUINO 5.8 A hand crack which splits a pear-shaped buttress, down and left from the *Marcos* dihedral. FA: Gordon and Evans, February 1986.

HEMINGWAY BUTTRESS – WEST FACE

184 AMERICAN EXPRESS The photo is mismarked in the guide. This follows the left line, marked #185.

185 LAYAWAY PLAN This is misdrawn in the guide. It starts just right of *American Express* and goes up and right via a thin lieback seam, before going back up and left, following the upper part of the marked line. The lower part of the drawn line, which goes right, then back left, is a 5.9 variation to this route.

BANANA CRACKS FORMATION

185A DON'T THINK TWICE 5.9 About 175 feet left of the *Banana Cracks* and slightly farther back is this dihedral leading to a roof. FA: Herb Laegar, Eve Laegar, Patrick Paul and Rich Smith, November 1982.

185B PAPAYA CRACK 5.11b/c The steep thin crack just left of *Left Banana Crack.* FA: Tom Michael, March 1987.

188A BABY BANANA 5.7 On the northeast side of the **Banana Cracks** formation (facing Quail Springs Road) is a left slanting crack. Start behind a tree and climb up into a left-facing book, then traverse right to reach the upper part of the left-slanting crack. FA: Don Wilson and Karen Wilson, November 1986.

THE IRS WALL – EAST FACE

189A ALF'S ARETE 5.11a Arete/face right of **Squatter's Right** with seven bolts. FA: Alan Nelson and Alfred Randell, December 1987.

191A COMMANDER CODY 5.7 Cracks and plated face midway between **Atomic Pile** and **Tax Free.** FA: Todd Gordon and Cody Dolnick, November 1986.

195A MR. BUNNY'S TAX SHELTER 5.5 Start at the same place as **Mr. Bunny vrs. Six Unknown Agents** and follow a crack up and left which turns into a chimney near the top. FA: Alan Bartlett, May 1988.

COPENHAGEN WALL

197A IT SATISFIES 5.7 The crack left of **Quantum Jump,** which goes over an arch at the bottom. FA: Alan Bartlett and Katie Wilkinson, May 1988.

199 THE SCHRODINGER EQUATION This route has been led, with one bolt placed. Jonny Woodward, 1986.

200A PERHAPS THE SURGEON GENERAL 5.8 On the backside of the **Copenhagen Wall,** up and right through the tunnel from **Heavy Water** is this face climb with one bolt. FA: Alan Bartlett and Todd Gordon, October 1988.

200B DIAL-A-PILE 5.5 On the small formation right (north) of the **Copenhagen Wall,** climb a crack right of a tree, then traverse right to another crack leading to the top. FA: Alan Bartlett and Katie Wilkinson, May 1988.

DAIRY QUEEN WALL

201A BLIZZARD 5.9 This is a loose wide crack on the wall left of **Pat Adams Dihedral.** FA: unknown.

201B LEAP YEAR FLAKE 5.7 Climb cracks to a left-facing flake directly below **Pat Adams Dihedral.** FA: Todd Gordon and Cyndie Bransford, February 1988.

201C DOUBLE DELIGHT 5.7 This is a right-slanting crack right of **Pat Adams Dihedral.** FA: unknown.

201D CHILI DOG 5.6 A left-facing corner just right of **Double Delight.** FA: unknown.

201E SLUSHIE 5.10a A bolted face climb right of **Leap Year Flake** that goes to a rap station. FA: unknown.

201F ADAMS FAMILY 5.9 This is a long thin crack right of **Slushie.** FA: Dave Evans and Margie Floyd.

201G LURCH 5.8 The next crack right of **Adams Family.** FA: unknown.

201H I FORGOT TO HAVE BABIES 5.10b (TR) Climb cracks left of **Scrumdillishus** and go over a roof at the top. FA: Darrel Hensel, Dave Evans, Kate Duke and Todd Gordon, May 1988.

203A HOT FUDGE 5.9 Climb the bucketed face to the right of **Frosty Cone.** FA: Dave Wonderly and Jack Marshall, December 1986.

206A NUTS AND CHERRIES 5.6 The first crack right of **Double Decker.** FA: Wonderly and Marshall, December 1986.

206B DATE SHAKE 5.6 The crack right of **Nuts and Cherries.** FA: Wonderly and Marshall, December 1986.

206C BIOLOGICAL CLOCK 5.9+ This route is on the small wall right of **Dairy Queen Wall,** facing south. Climb a hand crack, then go over a roof and up plates past one bolt. FA: Todd Gordon, Dave Evans, Kate Duke, Darrel Hensel and Alan Bartlett, May 1988.

PLAYHOUSE ROCK

207A BREAK A LEG 5.9 Climb the face between *Final Act* and *Curtain Call,* going over a roof at the top. FA: Jack Marshall, Dave Wonderly and A. Avarado, November 1986.

208A PSYCHO GROOVE 5.9 The water groove right of *Curtain Call,* with one bolt. FA: Ken Black, 1983.

208B FIGHTING THE SLIME 5.9 Arete between *Psycho Groove* and *I'm So Embarrassed For You.* FA: Mike Law, 1983.

209A LEADING LADY 5.9 Left-leaning cracks just right of *I'm So Embarrassed For You.* FA: Jack Marshall, Dave Wonderly and A. Avarado, November 1986.

THE (LOWER) FREEWAY WALL – WEST FACE

210A FALSE SMOOTH AS SILK 5.7 About 100 feet left of *Smooth as Silk,* this is a crack in a knobby buttress that starts with a short headwall. FA: unknown.

211A STOP TRUNDLING 5.10a The crack left of *Start Trundling.* FA: Todd Gordon, March 1986.

212A START FUMBLING 5.10 The crack right of *Start Trundling.* FA: Roy McClenahan, 1987.

THE (UPPER) FREEWAY WALL – WEST FACE

214A CAST UP A HIGHWAY 5.11a (TR) Climb the face left of *Nobody Walks in L.A.* FA: Eric Rasmussen, Rob Segger and Matt Shubert, April 1988.

218A THE TALKING FISH 5.10d Bolted route between *Cake Walk* and *Junkyard God.* FA: Todd Gordon and Tom Beck, September 1988.

TINY TOTS ROCK

220A DATE RAPE 5.9 This is the crack left of *Tinker Toys.* FA: unknown.

221A WHO'DA THOUGHT 5.11c (TR) Face and thin cracks between *Dinkey Doinks* and *Cole- Lewis.* FA: Eric Rasmussen, Rob Segger and Matt Shubert, April 1988.

222A SPONTANEOUS HUMAN COMBUSTION 5.11 Bolted face right of *Cole-Lewis.* FA: Dave Evans and Jim Angione, October 1988.

ROCK GARDEN VALLEY

224A SILENT BUT DEADLY 5.9 This climbs the right arete of the *Pop Rocks* formation, starting in a low angle wide crack. FA: Alan Bartlett and Katie Wilkinson, May 1988.

224B HOLLY DEVICE 5.10c Ascend the center of the buttress left of *Spitwad* past four bolts. FA: Todd Gordon, Tom Michael, Mark Walters and Jeff Jarvi, March 1987

234A WHY DOES IT HURT WHEN I PEE? 5.10b Thin cracks just left of *What's Hannen.* FA: Todd Gordon and Dave Evans, May 1986.

235A MR. MICHAEL GOES TO WASHINGTON 5.8 Midway between *Swiss Cheese* and *Bolivian Freeze Job,* climb thin cracks up and right, and then back left. FA: Tom Michael and Alan Bartlett, April 1988.

235B BLUE SKY, BLACK DEATH 5.5 This is a left-slanting hand and fist crack just right of the preceding route and left of a chimney/break in the wall. FA: unknown.

235C BARN DOOR, LEFT 5.9 (TR) Left of two right-slanting cracks a short distance left of *Bolivian Freeze Job.* FA: unknown.

235D BARN DOOR, RIGHT 5.9/10 (TR) The right of the two cracks. FA: unknown.

LOST HORSE WALL – NORTH END

237 ENOS MILLS GLACIER This climb should be rated 5.11a and has fairly poor protection.

239A MEAT WAGON 5.9 This route climbs the right-facing, right-leaning dihedral with a wide crack, right of *Are You Experienced?.* FA: Kevin Powell and Alan Roberts, 1987.

239B HESITATION BLUES 5.10b Right of a bushy break in the wall, climb up to an alcove and jam the crack out its top. When the crack splits, take the right one. Rappel 75' from the stance above. FA: Alan Roberts and Eric Gompper, 1987.

239C HAPPY LANDINGS, LINDA 5.11b Start at the base of *Just Another Crack From L.A.* and follow thin cracks up and left, then straight up (crux). Continue up and right in checkerboard cracks. FA: Ken Black and Mike Law, 1983.

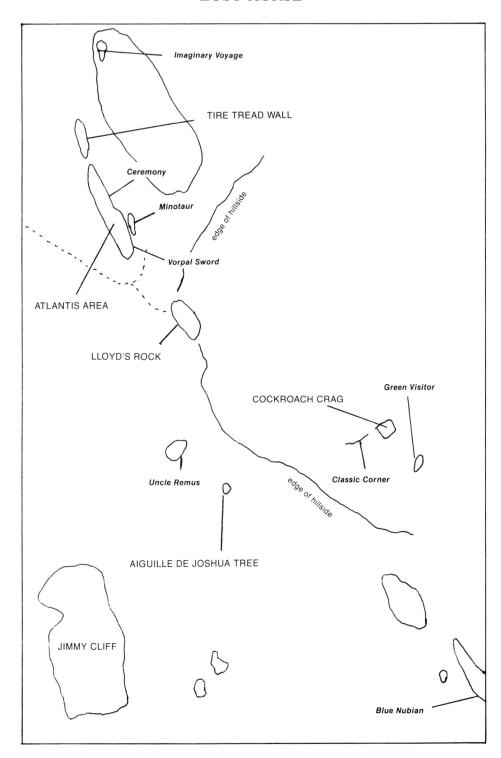

Imaginary Voyage

TIRE TREAD WALL

Ceremony

Minotaur

edge of hillside

Vorpal Sword

ATLANTIS AREA

LLOYD'S ROCK

Green Visitor

COCKROACH CRAG

Classic Corner

Uncle Remus

edge of hillside

AIGUILLE DE JOSHUA TREE

JIMMY CLIFF

Blue Nubian

LOST HORSE WALL – SOUTH END

240A GOSSAMER WINGS 5.10a This is a three-pitch route left of **Wilson Regular Route.** Start in a left-facing book with many plates, then head up and right to a belay in an alcove. Continue up steep plates to a large ledge. The final pitch zig-zags up slabs to the overhanging summit dihedral. FA: Alan Bartlett and Alan Roberts, April 1988.

241A ALTITUDE SICKNESS 5.8 Start on **The Swift,** then head left after passing the tongue of rock. Two pitches. FA: Tim Bombaci and Chet Wade, November 1987.

244A HEADBANGERS' BALL 5.11c This is a four-pitch climb right of **Dappled Mare.** Start just right of the easy approach pitch to that route, and climb a right-curving arch until one can cross it. Continue up to a belay at the base of **Mare's Tail.** Climb thin cracks left of **Mare's Tail,** then go past three bolts to a bolted belay. Go up and left past two bolts to a horizontal crack. Traverse left to the bolted **Dappled Mare** belay. Traverse back right and go up a thin crack to two bolts. From the upper one, traverse left to join **Roan Way.** FA: Roy McClenahan and Alan Bartlett, April 1988.

IMAGINARY VOYAGE FORMATION

251 BLACK PLASTIC STREETWALKER 5.10c This climb, formerly called **Route 251,** was mistakenly listed as a top-rope route in the guide. It had, however been led on the first ascent with minimal protection. Two bolts have been added by a party mistakenly thinking they were doing the first lead, giving decent protection to what was formerly a very bold venture.

252A GRAVEL SHOWER 5.10b (TR) Climb the face below **Imaginary Voyage.** FA: Hans Florine, Mike Lopez and Phil Requist, March 1988.

ATLANTIS AREA

This area is located in a hidden canyon behind and to the right of **Imaginary Voyage,** and is best approached by parking at the same place as for the **Super Creeps Wall.** Skirt right around the rocks below **Imaginary Voyage,** until one can turn left and enter the canyon from the south. The routes are all on the left side of the canyon, facing northeast. Map, supplement page 22.

256A VORPAL SWORD 5.9 This is on a tower on the left as you enter the canyon. It is a left-slanting thin crack with a diamond-shaped chockstone near its top. FA: Todd Gordon, Brian Sillasen and Tom Atherton, March 1988.

256B GRAIN SURPLUS 5.8 A grainy crack just right of **Vorpal Sword.** FA: Alan Bartlett, Brian Sillasen and Todd Gordon, March 1988.

256C MINOTAUR 5.7 The left of two cracks on a formation right and in front of the previous routes. It has a wide section near the top. FA: Gordon and Bartlett, March 1988.

256D FANTASY OF LIGHT 5.10a Thin crack just right of **Minotaur.** FA: Sillasen, Bartlett and Gordon, March 1988.

256E SELF ABUSE 5.6 The leftmost hand crack on the main **Atlantis** wall. FA: Bartlett and Gordon, March 1988.

256F HOT CRYSTALS 5.9 The next crack right of **Self Abuse.** FA: Sillasen, Gordon and Atherton, March 1988.

256G ANNOITED SEAGULL 5.8 The next crack right, which starts off a block. FA: Sillasen, Gordon and Atherton, March 1988.

256H CEREMONY 5.10c Right of **Annoited Seagull,** climb past a bolt and follow thin cracks to the top. FA: Dave Evans, Craig Fry, Jim Angione, Sillasen, Gordon and Bartlett, March 1988.

256I SOLAR TECHNOLOGY 5.6 The crack right of **Ceremony** splits a short way up; take the left branch. FA: Fry, Evans, Bartlett, Gordon, Angione, Sillasen and Cyndie Bransford, March 1988.

256J MEN WITH COW'S HEADS 5.5 The right branch of the previously mentioned crack. FA: Sillasen, Gordon and Atherton, March 1988.

256K WET PIGEON 5.8 Next crack right of **Men With Cow's Heads.** FA: Sillasen, Gordon, Angione, Evans and Bartlett, March 1988.

256L UNWIPED BUTT 5.8 The next crack right, an ugly offwidth. FA: Gordon, Bransford, Sillasen, Fry and Bartlett. FA: March 1988.

TIRE TREAD WALL

Up and right from the main **Atlantis** wall is this steep wall with a weird black tread-like stain on it. There are three obvious cracks on it. Map, supplement page 22.

   256M TREADMARK LEFT   5.8   The left crack. FA: Bartlett and Gordon, March 1988.

   256N TREADMARK RIGHT   5.8   The center crack FA: Gordon and Bartlett, March 1988.

   256O FLAT TIRE   5.8   The right crack. FA: Bartlett and Gordon, March 1988.

LLOYD'S ROCK

This rock is around and to the right of the entrance to the **Atlantis** canyon. It faces **Jimmy Cliff.** Map, supplement page 22.

   256P FLAWLESS FISSURE   5.9   This starts in a left-facing book on the left side of the rock. Lieback a wide crack, then step right into a perfect finger crack leading over a small roof. FA: Don Wilson and Karen Wilson, April 1986.

   256Q FRIEND EATER   5.8   On the main face of the crag are two curving cracks. This is the left one. FA: Wilson and Wilson, April 1986.

   256R RR DOES IT AGAIN   5.10+   (TR)   A thin tips crack between the two main cracks, leading into the left one. FA: Alan Roberts and Don Reid, January 1988.

   256S MICRONESIA   5.10d   The right curving crack. FA: Reid and Roberts, January 1988.

The next route is on a small boulder/pillar south of **Lloyd's Rock** and west of a finger of rock known as **Aiguille de Joshua Tree.** See map, page 22.

   256T UNCLE REMUS   5.11b   Climb the southeast face of the pillar past three bolts. Take a tie-off sling for a flake. FA: John Bacher (TR); Kurt Smith (lead).

COCKROACH CRAG

Several hundred yards right (southeast) from **Lloyd's Rock** and high on a hillside is this squat brown rock. Map, supplement page 22.

   256U CLASSIC CORNER   5.7   This is a handcrack in clean grey rock down and left from the main **Cockroach Crag.** FA: Scott Cosgrove, January 1988.

   256V ARMS FOR HOSTAGES   5.11   (TR)   A severely overhanging brown wall above **Classic Corner.** FA: Tom Gilje, Mike Lechlinski and Scott Cosgrove, January 1988.

   256W R.S. CHICKEN CHOKER   5.11b   On the far left side of **Cockroach Crag,** this is a finger crack which goes over a roof. FA: Mike Lechlinski, Tom Gilje, Todd Gordon, Mari Gingery and Scott Cosgrove, January 1988.

   256X THE FABULOUS T. GORDEX CRACKS   5.8   Double cracks to the right of **R.S. Chicken Choker.** FA: Gordon, January 1988.

   256Y ROACH MOTEL   5.10a   Around the corner to the right of the two previous routes, this ascends thin cracks passing several horizontals. FA: Gilje, January 1988.

   256Z CLIMB OF THE COCKROACHES   5.8   Ascend a big flake leading to face moves right of **Roach Motel.** FA: Gordon, Gingery, Lechlinski, Cyndie Bransford and Jennifer Wonderly, January 1988.

   256AA ROACH ROOF   5.6   The roof right of **Climb of the Cockroaches.** FA: Gordon and Lechlinski, January 1988.

Several hundred feet right of **Cockroach Crag** is a steep wall facing **Cockroach Crag** with two bolted face routes. Map, supplement page 22.

   256BB GREEN VISITOR   5.11+   The left bolted route. FA: Gilje, Gingery and Cosgrove, January 1988.

   256CC THIRD BOLT FROM THE SUN   5.11a   The right bolted route. FA: Lechlinski and Gingery, January 1988.

LOST HORSE RANGER STATION AREA

The following two routes are on a wall in front of and slightly right from **Wall of 10,000 Holds.** Rap from a bolt anchor on top.

   261A POLLY WANTS A CRACK   5.10a   Start off a pointed boulder and climb past three bolts to a left leaning crack. FA: Tad Welch, Peggy Buckey and Todd Swain, March 1986.

261B PIRATES OF THE CARABINER 5.10b Right of the preceding route climb past a bolt to a flake. From its top, go past two more bolts to a right-leaning offwidth. FA: Swain, Welch and Buckey, March 1986.

S CRACK FORMATION

264A JINGUS CON 5.11+ Start on the **Right S Crack** and climb out right passing two bolts. FA: John Yablonski, Mike Lechlinski, Mari Gingery and Tom Gilje, January 1988.

The next route is located about ¾ mi. northwest of the **S Crack Formation,** near the end of the service road.

264B MOSAR 5.10 A bouldering start leads to discontinuous cracks to horizontal slashes. FA: Mike Lechlinski, February 1988.

265A VOGELS ARE POODLES TOO 5.11b (TR) Left of **Android Lust,** climb over a roof then go left and up an arete. FA: Mark Robinson and Will Chen, October 1986.

HILL STREET BLUES

270A BLUE MONDAY 5.10b This is a thin crack just right of **Blues Brothers.** FA: Darrel Hensel, Alan Roberts and Dave Evans.

271 RHYTHM & BLUES This route is mismarked in the guide. It is a short distance left of where it is shown.

272 BLACK & BLUE This route is mismarked in the guide. It lies a good ways left of where it is shown, on a very short section of the cliff.

272A BABY BLUE EYES 5.10b In the picture on page 89 of the guide, this short quality climb is directly under the **CR** in **S CRACK FORMATION.** FA: Evans, Hensel and Roberts.

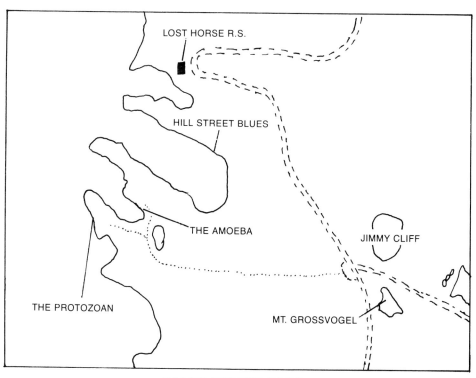

CANDLESTEIN PASS

CANDLESTEIN PASS

This is the canyon south of the **Hill Street Blues** area. It is best approached from the **Jimmy Cliff** parking area. Stay left of a small formation as you walk into the canyon. Farther, the main formation, **The Amoeba,** splits the canyon into two canyons. Two of the routes will be found on **The Protozoan,** a formation on the left side of the left canyon. The remaining seven routes are on **The Amoeba.** Map, supplement page 25.

THE PROTOZOAN

272B 13 YEAR OLD DEATH TRAP   5.7   This climb faces north and ascends cracks in a right-facing book. FA: Don Wilson, Karen Wilson, Chris Wilson and Doug Muñoz, October 1987.

272C THE TOOTHPICK   5.11c (TR)   A thin seam 100 feet right of the previous route. FA: Mike Lechlinski and Mari Gingery.

THE AMOEBA

272D HOLLOW DREAMS   5.11/12 (TR)   On the south side of the formation (facing **The Protozoan**), this ascends a difficult, friable flake. FA: Todd Battey, February 1988.

272E THE AMOEBA   5.10   Right of *Hollow Dreams,* facing southeast, this climb has two bolts and ascends a thin flake. FA: unknown.

272F CHAMBER OF COMMERCE   5.10c   Right of *The Amoeba* is this straight-in thin crack. FA: Craig Fry and Dave Bruckman, February 1988.

272G ILLICIT OPERATIONS   5.11c   Right of the previous route, this is a thin crack in a rust-colored wall. It starts with a wide lieback. FA: Fry and Bruckman, February 1988.

272H THE SKEPTIC   5.10c   On the north face of **The Amoeba,** this is the left of two arching cracks. FA: Jack Marshall, Ron White, Sam Owing and Robert Carrere, October 1987.

272I PERUVIAN PRINCESS   5.10b   The right arching crack. FA: Marshall, White, Owing and Carrere, October 1987.

272J LOWER LIFE FORMS   5.10b   This is a finger and hand crack right of the previous routes. FA: Don Wilson, Karen Wilson, Ron White, Doug Muñoz and Sam Owing, October 1987.

JIMMY CLIFF – WEST FACE

273A THE LONE RANGER   5.9   Climb the scuptured buttress right of *Grain of Truth* past three bolts. FA: Todd Swain, November 1988.

273B GS-5   5.9 (TR)   The face left of *The Lone Ranger,* joining that route at its last bolt. FA: Swain, November 1988.

273C TASGRAINIAN DEVIL   5.9   Start 100 feet left of *Live from Tasmania* in an alcove below a chimney. Climb a hidden finger crack to varnished lieback flakes. This climb is only visible from *Live from Tasmania.* FA: Todd Swain and Gary Garrett, November 1988.

275A PEANUT GALLERY   5.11a   This is a steep bolted climb on the backside of the large block right of *Lurleen Quits,* not visible from the road or the approach. FA: Alfred Randell and Dave Tucker.

JIMMY CLIFF – SOUTH FACE

275B THE VELVEETA RABBIT   5.7   This climb is located about midway between *Lurleen Quits* and *Downpour,* at the closest point of **Jimmy Cliff** to the road. It is a crack in a slab that goes over a small roof. FA: Kelly Carignan and Marge Floyd, April 1986.

275C SHORT STOP   5.10a   This climb is at ground level, below and left from *Downpour.* It is a straight-in thin crack leading to a roof which is passed on the right. This appeared in an old Joshua Tree supplement (mistakenly rated 5.8), but somehow didn't make it into the last guide. FA: unknown.

JIMMY CLIFF – EAST FACE

280A CHILLY WILLY   5.10c, A1   This bolted line just left of **Penalty Runout** awaits a free ascent. FA: Dave Evans, Brad Singer and Dale Chocker, February 1988.

281 PENALTY RUNOUT   This route should be rated 5.9, and is difficult to protect in its crux (starting the second pitch).

287A CLIFF HANGER   5.10b   Corner and face with one bolt just right of **Friendly Hands**. FA: Andy Brown and Lotus Steele, April 1987.

ARID PILES AREA

289A NICE AND STEEP AND ELBOW DEEP   5.10b   This is a north-facing overhanging fist crack 100 yards north of **The Outsiders**. FA: Dennis Yates and Roger Linfield, April 1986.

291A QUICKSTONE   5.12b   A bolted face left of **29 Palms**. FA: Jonny Woodward and Darrel Hensel, January 1988.

292A THE 39 SLAPS   5.11c   Climb the bolted outside arete right of **29 Palms**. FA: Hensel and Woodward, December 1987.

The next two routes lie on the outer (west) faces of the crags/boulders that form the west side of the **29 Palms** corridor.

292B JACKALOPE   5.11   This route is more or less in front of **29 Palms**, and climbs an undercling leading to face past one bolt. FA: Mike Lechlinski, Mari Gingery, John Yablonski and Tom Gilje, January 1988.

292C SECRET SAUCE   5.11   This is an undercling/lieback about 100 yards left of **Jackalope** and also west-facing. FA: Lechlinski, Gingery, Yablonski and Gilje, January 1988.

295A SPINNER   5.7   This route climbs the west face of a small boulder/spire 100 yards southwest of **29 Palms**. FA: Alan Nelson and Scott Loomis, 1981.

303A NIGHT GALLERY   5.9 +   This climbs the obvious crack system left of **Shooting Gallery**. FA: Todd Gordon, Marge Floyd, Jim Angione and Dave Evans, September 1986.

303B SHOOTING GALLERY DIRECT   5.10a   Climb straight up to the upper crack, left of the original start. FA: Dave Evans.

MT. GROSSVOGEL

305A DR. SEUSS VOGEL   5.7   Climb the crack right of **Ranger Danger**. FA: Todd Gordon and Kathy Boyd, April 1986.

306A BIG BIRD   5.7 +   This route climbs the crack right of **Iron Mantel**, and goes up and left on steep rock at the top. FA: Gordon and Boyd, April 1986.

306B ROBORANGER   5.5   Ascend the crack just left of **Robaxol** and finish up the obvious clean dihedral. FA: Todd Swain, November 1988.

307A OHM ON THE RANGE   5.4   Start in the chasm between the east and west faces of **Mt. Grossvogel**, on the back (east) side of the **Chaffe N' Up** summit block. Climb a short right-leaning finger crack, then move left and follow a vertical hand crack to the top. FA: Swain, November 1988.

310 CRAZY CLIMBER   This climb should be rated 5.11a and is misdrawn in the guide; it is actually farther right, near where the person is standing in the photo on page 99.

PEP BOYS CRAG

316A FINGERTIP TRAVERSE OF JOSH   5.8   This route is down low and on the right side of the **Pep Boys Crag** massif. It is close to the road and almost faces **The Milepost.** Climb up to and follow the left side of a short Gothic arch. Traverse right from its top, then go up. FA: Alan Roberts and John Hayward. Map, supplement page 31.

316B STRAIN GAUGE   5.10b/c   This is several hundred feet around and right from the previous route, facing away from the road. Climb out of an alcove via a finger crack which widens to thin hands. FA: Alan Roberts and Alex. Map, supplement page 31.

DIHEDRAL ROCK AREA

317A GLORY ROAD   5.12a   150 feet left of *Coarse and Buggy* is this 5-bolt climb up a deceptively low-angle face. FA: Mike Paul and Paul Borne, March 1988.

318 ROTS O' ROCK   5.13b   This climb has been freed and now has five bolts. FFA: Scott Cosgrove, September 1988.

The next five routes are on **The Road Block,** a block on the north side of **Dihedral Rock.**

321A MIDNIGHT OIL   5.11c   The leftmost line, with two bolts. FA: Mike Paul and Paul Borne, March 1988.

321B RAMMING SPEED   5.11d   The next line right, also with two bolts. FA: Borne, March 1988.

321C VANISHING POINT   5.12b   The next route right, with four bolts. FA: Borne, March 1988.

321D IMMACULATE CONCEPTION   5.9   Right of *Vanishing Point,* this climbs a dihedral to a roof. FA: Charles Cole, Dave Evans and Dave Wonderly.

321E FAR SIDE OF CRAZY   5.10b   The farthest right route, this ascends a low-angle face with seams and one bolt. Serious. FA: Paul Borne, February 1988.

WATTS TOWERS

323A SOUL RESEARCH   5.9   This is a straight crack directly opposite **The Aviary.** FA: Brian Sillasen and Todd Gordon, March 1987.

326A URBAN REDEVELOPMENT   5.8   This is a direct start to *Sole Food,* right of the regular start. FA: Dave Evans and Jim Angione, December 1986.

326B TALUS PHALLUS   5.6   There are two cracks right of *Sole Food.* This is the right one. FA: Todd Gordon and Cody Dolnick, June 1988.

326C BANDERSNATCH   5.10b   This is a steep, tricky climb right of *Talus Phallus,* with the crux near the bottom. FA: Gordon and Dolnick, June 1988.

X FACTOR DOME

331A CHARLES WHO?   5.11b   At the extreme south corner of the dome (50 yards north of **Labor Dome**) climb a thin flake leading to face climbing past three bolts. FA: Randy Vogel, Dave Evans and Rob Raker, February 1987.

FOUND IN THE DUFFLE CRAG

This is the crag immediately right of **Lost in the Shuffle Crag,** plainly visible in the photo on page 106.

334A THE MAGIC TOUCH   5.9   On the left side of the east face, this is a left-slanting crack with a fixed pin near the bottom. FA: Herb and Eve Laegar, November 1980.

334B BOOMERANG   5.7   This ascends a large right-slanting ramp on the west (back) side of the crag. FA: Alan Roberts and Alex, January 1988.

334C LIFE WITHOUT T.V.   5.9   This is a grainy right-slanting fist crack on the small formation right (north) of **Found in the Duffle Crag.** It is visible from the road. FA: Alan Bartlett, Tom Atherton, Vicki Pelton and Todd Gordon, March 1988.

JAM OR SLAM ROCK

335 CRANKING SKILLS OR HOSPITAL BILLS   This climb should be rated 5.10d.

336 FIRE OR RETIRE   This climb should be rated 5.10c.

336A FIRE OR RETIRE, DIRECT FINISH   5.11   Move left from the top of the crack, then stem up through a scoop and curving crack to the top. FA: Ken Black, 1983.

336B NO PERCH IS NECESSARY   5.10d   This climb is on the front side of **Jam or Slam Rock,** facing the road. Climb past two bolts, then up a thin crack. FA: Rich Perch, Vaino Kodas, Bob Yoho and Herb Laegar, November 1987.

SUMMIT OR PLUMMET ROCK

This rock is about 300 yards northwest of **Jam or Slam Rock.** It has two routes, both facing the road.

336C KODAS SILENCE   5.11d   The left route, with two bolts. FA: Kodas, Perch, Laegar and Yoho, November 1987.

336D LAEGAR DOMAIN   5.10d   The right route, with one bolt. FA: Laegar, Kodas, Yoho and Perch, November 1987.

WALL STREET

This low-angle slabby face is just west of **Slump Rock,** plainly visible from the road. It is actually the back side of **Elephant Dome.** Three routes are known.

338A WALL STREET   5.9   The left route, with a fixed knifeblade near the start. FA: Alan Roberts and John Hayward, February 1988.

338B INSIDER INFORMATION   5.7   The center route, which goes over a small roof. FA: Roy McClenahan.

338C LUNCH IS FOR WIMPS   5.9   The right route, with a bolt at the start. FA: Roberts and Hayward, February 1988.

The next three routes are on a short, steep brown wall above and to the right of **Wall Street.** This wall is actually the back side of **The Great Burrito.**

338D BEEF AND BEAN   5.10a   Climb the obvious central crack. FA: Roy McClenahan and Alan Roberts.

338E RED CHILE   5.11 (TR)   The face left of the crack. FA: unknown.

338F GREEN CHILE   5.11 (TR)   The face right of the crack. FA: unknown.

THE FOUNDRY

This is the formation directly behind the **JBMF** boulder. It is described as a "broken rock formation" in the guide. There are three routes on its northeast face, all ending together just right of a giant guano pile. These are referred to in the guide, although no information is given. There are also two routes on its southwest (backside) face, facing into Real Hidden Valley.

338G STAINLESS STEEL RAT   5.10   The leftmost crack on the northeast face. FA: unknown.

338H STEEP PULSE   5.12 (TR)   The center route. FA: Mike Paul.

338I VAINO'S CRACK   5.9   This is the left-leaning crack on the right. FA: Vaino Kodas.

338J JUMAR OF FLESH   5.9+   This is the left of two offwidth/chimney routes on the southwest face. FA: Todd Gordon, Alan Roberts, Brian Sillasen and Bob, January 1988.

338K SIX-PACK CRACK   5.10b   The right route. FA: Roberts, Gordon, Sillasen and Bob, January 1988.

338L LITTLE LIEBACK   5.10a   This is a wide lieback crack leading to a roof on a formation just right of the **JBMF** boulder. FA: unknown.

THREE PILE ISLAND

339A HOLD YOUR FIRE   5.13a   This is a bolted face route just right of *The Colossus of Rhoids.* FA: Kurt Smith, January 1988.

339B ACUPUNCTURE   5.8   This is an obvious hand crack facing the road on the small tower right (northeast) of **Three Pile Island.** FA: Earl Phillips, George Zelenz and Dean Rosnau, December 1986.

The next route is located a short distance up the canyon to the left of **Three Pile Island,** on an unnamed formation on the left.

339C VICKI THE VISITOR   5.10b   Climb thin cracks on the right side of the formation, with several traverses to the right. The route leads up into a cleft near the top. FA: Todd Gordon, Vicki Pelton and Alan Bartlett, February 1988.

GATEWAY ROCK AREA

342A PITFALL   5.11c   To the right of the trail leading into the Real Hidden Valley is this 4-bolt face climb on a steep block facing the parking area. FA: Herb Laegar, Rich Perch and Jim Beyer, November 1986.

345A PIT BULL ATTACK   5.10d   Climb a crack to an arete with one bolt left of *Semi Tough.* FA: Bob Gaines and Dwight Brooks, January 1988.

LOCOMOTION ROCK

348A GRAIN DANCE   5.10b (TR)   The crack/seam right of *Jumping Jehosaphat.* FA: Bob Gaines, 1987.

351A GUNKS WEST   5.10b   This route is just right of *Snnfchtt.* A hangerless bolt marks its start. FA: Todd Swain and Thom Scheuer, April 1984.

352A JUMP BACK LORETTA   5.5   Climb a hand crack in a right-facing corner at the far right end of **Locomotion Rock.** FA: Todd Swain, March 1985.

352B BETTY GRAVEL   5.7   Directly across from **Locomotion Rock** is this grainy left-leaning hand crack. FA: Todd Swain and Peggy Buckey, April 1985.

SPORTS CHALLENGE ROCK

356A SUNSET STRIP   5.9   This west-facing route is located on a small rock in front of the west face of **Sports Challenge Rock.** Climb a flake to enter a left-slanting crack, then go up and right on easy face to the top. FA: Alan Bartlett and Debbie Daigle, March 1988.

358A DON'T BE NOSEY   5.10d (TR)   Start just right of *Ride a Wild Bago* and climb up and right, joining *None of your Business* near the top. FA: Jonny Woodward and Maria Cranor, November 1987.

362A TRIATHLON   5.11c (TR)   Left of *Clean and Jerk,* surmount an overhang and continue up to meet a right-slanting crack. FA: Bob Gaines, April 1988.

The next two routes are on the west face of an unnamed tower just east of **Hidden Tower.**

374A MY FIRST FIRST   5.9   A smooth face with one bolt leads to a short crack near the top. FA: Alan Bartlett, Tom Atherton, Todd Gordon and Vicki Pelton, February 1988.

374B BIVVY AT GORDON'S   5.4   Rotten flakes and cracks right of *My First First.* FA: Alan Bartlett, February 1988.

SNAKE DOME

This is the small formation south of **Elephant Dome.** Three routes have been done, all on the southwest face.

382A HANDLIN' SNAKESKIN   5.10c   Thin RP cracks on the far left side of the face. FA: Alan Bartlett and Dave Evans, February 1988.

382B I LOVE SNAKES   5.9+   The central crack system, which leads up into a break in the summit. FA: Todd Gordon, Vicki Pelton and Marge Floyd, February 1988.

382C BLACK TODD   5.10   The rightmost route, which has one bolt midway up. Poor rock FA: Dave Evans and Alan Bartlett, February 1988.

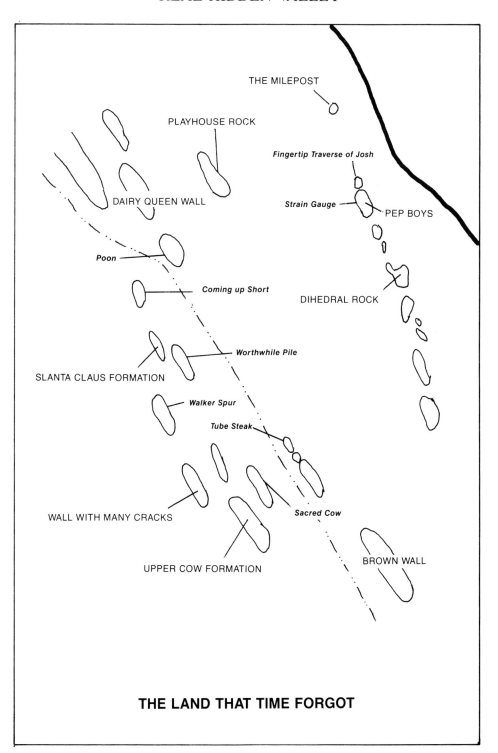

THE MILEPOST

PLAYHOUSE ROCK

Fingertip Traverse of Josh

Strain Gauge — PEP BOYS

DAIRY QUEEN WALL

Poon

Coming up Short

DIHEDRAL ROCK

Worthwhile Pile

SLANTA CLAUS FORMATION

Walker Spur

Tube Steak

WALL WITH MANY CRACKS

Sacred Cow

UPPER COW FORMATION

BROWN WALL

THE LAND THAT TIME FORGOT

THE BROWN WALL

385A JAMES BROWN   5.11b (TR)   This is the crack/corner between **Jerry Brown** and **Brown 25.** FA: Matt Dancy, December 1985.

388A SHAME   5.10c   Thin cracks to the right of **Savwafare ist Everywhere,** with one fixed pin. FA: Jonny Woodward and Darrel Hensel, January 1987.

THE LAND THAT TIME FORGOT

This is the canyon running northwest from the **Brown Wall.** Walking up it would eventually take one to the **Lost Horse Wall.** The following fourteen routes are described as though one is coming from **Real Hidden Valley,** but they could as easily be approached from the **Lost Horse Wall,** or from the Quail Springs Road by walking between **Dihedral Rock** and **Pep Boys Crag,** or from the vicinity of the **Dairy Queen Wall.** Map, supplement page 31.

388B TUBE STEAK   5.10c   This is on the small formation a short distance left of **Savwafare ist Everywhere.** It is a left-leaning tube with a finger and hand crack in its back. FA: Alan Roberts and John Hayward.

388C SACRED COW   5.10a   Walking from **Savwafare ist Everywhere,** this is on the first main formation on the left, almost directly opposite **Tube Steak.** It has a summit feature resembling a cow. The route climbs a crack leading to the 'cow' formation. FA: Alan Roberts and Todd Gordon, January 1988.

388D UPPER COW   5.10a   Above **Sacred Cow,** this is an obvious crack on the highest formation. FA: Gordon and Roberts, January 1988.

388E REACH FOR A PEACH   5.10b (TR)   Climb the face right of **Upper Cow.** FA: Roberts and Hayward.

388F COW PIE CORNER   5.6   This is the corner right of **Reach for a Peach.** FA: Roberts and Hayward.

Right of the formation with **Sacred Cow** is a wall with many cracks, resembling a loaf of sliced bread. The next two routes are on a wall right of this. Map, supplement page 31.

388G NORTH FACE OF THE EIGER   5.10a   This is the left of two cracks on the formation, and starts behind a pine tree. FA: Roberts and Gordon, January 1988.

388H WALKER SPUR   5.10a   This is the right of the two cracks. FA: Gordon and Roberts, January 1988.

Below and to the right of these routes is a formation with three cracks. It is identifiable by a phallic-shaped spire (**The Woody**) on its right side. Map, supplement page 31.

388I SLANTA CLAUS, LEFT   5.7   The left crack. FA: Roberts and Gordon, January 1988.

388J SLANTA CLAUS, CENTER   5.10a   The center crack. FA: Roberts and Gordon, January 1988.

388K SLANTA CLAUS, RIGHT   5.8   The right crack. FA: Roberts and Gordon, January 1988.

388L WORTHWHILE PILE   5.7   This is an incipient crack on the small formation left of the **Slanta Claus** routes. FA: Gordon and Roberts, January 1988.

388M COMING UP SHORT   5.10a   This is on a wall right of the previous routes. It climbs over a roof to a hand crack above. FA: Roberts and Hayward.

The next two routes are opposite the previous route, on the right side of the canyon as one approaches from the **Real Hidden Valley.** They are on a large, low-angle gray slab about ½ mile from the **Brown Wall.** Map, supplement page 31.

388N POON   5.10a   This is the left route, and has a difficult start. There is no protection. FA: Gordon and Roberts, January 1988.

388O TANG   5.5   The right route, in the middle of the formation. FA: Gordon and Roberts, January 1988.

THE THIN WALL – EAST FACE

391A COUNT ON YOUR FINGERS 5.9 Climb thin cracks just right of **No Calculators Allowed** and just left of a right-facing book. FA: Todd Swain and Ned Crossley, March 1986.

Just right of the previously mentioned right-facing book are three distinct closely-spaced crack systems.

391B CONSERVATIVE POLICIES 5.8 The left crack, which moves right at the top to avoid a loose section. FA: Alan Bartlett and Debbie Daigle, March 1988.

391C BUTTERFINGERS MAKE ME HORNY 5.8/9 The middle crack system. FA: Todd Gordon and Cyndie Bransford, May 1988.

391D CHOCOLATE IS BETTER THAN SEX 5.9+ The right of the three cracks. FA: Gordon and Bransford, May 1988.

Farther right are two more easier-appearing cracks.

391E ALMOST VERTICAL 5.7 The left crack. FA: Alan Roberts and Kristen Laird, December 1987.

391F HOLY ROLLER 5.6 The right crack. FA: Alan Bartlett and Debbie Daigle, March 1988.

THE THIN WALL – WEST FACE

392A KEITH'S WORK 5.11a (TR) Right of **Sandbag,** climb up to and follow the left of two V-cracks. FA: Hans Florine and Phil Requist, March 1988.

THE SENTINEL – EAST FACE

394A SENTINEL BEACH 5.8 Climb cracks and face just left of the tree 150 feet left of **Ball Bearing.** FA: Alan Bartlett and Katie Wilkinson, May 1988.

THE SENTINEL – WEST FACE

396A THE BUTT BUTTRESS 5.10b This is a 4-bolt climb on the far left side of the face, starting from ledges about 50 feet off the ground. FA: Dave Evans, Todd Gordon, Marge Floyd, Mike Brown and Terry Peterson, January 1988.

401A SACRED BEAR A3+ Start right of **Not For Loan** and nail thin cracks up and right to meet **Scared Bare.** Fixed rurps at the beginning and end of the climb mark the route. FA: Todd Gordon and Jim Murray, February 1986.

403A JUST A DREAM AWAY 5.10+ A2+ This is a mixed route left of **Illusion Dweller.** Eight bolts, two pitches. FA: Dave Evans and Charles Cole.

THE HIDDEN CLIFF

407 BIKINI WHALE This climb has been led, with bolts placed on the lead. Kurt Smith, December 1987.

407A RAILER 5.12c Climb **Bikini Whale** until it is possible to work out left in a horizontal crack, then up to the top. FA: Scott Cosgrove, December 1987.

407B BIKINI BEACH 5.12b (TR) Climb **Bikini Whale** to where **Railer** splits off left and move right in the horizontal crack, then up to the top. FA: Scott Cosgrove, October 1986.

TUMBLING RAINBOW FORMATION

408A TWO STAGE 5.10a About 75 feet left of **Run For Your Life,** climb a straight-in crack to a ledge, then continue up a right-facing dihedral. This climb is plainly visible in the photo on page 130. FA: Roger Linfield, November 1986.

408B RUN FROM YOUR WIFE 5.10c Climb the initial crack of **Two Stage,** then move right into a smaller crack and climb past a piton and two bolts. FA: Charles Cole and Troy Mayr, December 1987.

411A DON'T LOOK A GIFT FROG IN THE MOUTH 5.9 This is a right-facing corner about 40 feet left of **Fisticuffs,** which finishes by tunneling through a slot. FA: unknown.

411B TALES OF BRAVE ULYSSES 5.9 This is a finger crack which starts where **Don't Look a Gift Frog in the Mouth** finishes. It is a short distance right of the upper section of **Rainy Day, Dream Away.** FA: Tim Bluhm and Donald Wise, October 1987.

HOUSER BUTTRESS

438A SNAP ON DEMAND 5.11d A three-bolt climb on a large boulder left of **Houser Buttress.** FA: Darrel Hensel and Jonny Woodward, October 1986.

441 PUSS N' BOOTS 5.11+ Astute observers may have noticed that there was no route #441 in the guide; that's because this route was in progress at the time but hadn't been completed. Now it has, and is a steep bolted line just right of *Loose Lady.* FA: Bob Rotert and Kelly Carignan.

445A HERBIE'S HIDEAWAY 5.10d In a canyon to the right of *Dodo's Delight* is this thin finger crack leading up to the same belay as that route. FA: Herb Laegar, Eve Laegar and Bob Kamps, January 1987.

The next two routes are located on a north-facing wall more or less directly behind the **Solosby** face. They are approached by going up the rocky gully right of **Houser Buttress.** This gully soon becomes a corridor, and the wall is on your left. There are a couple of roof boulder problems on the right wall, opposite these routes.

445B THE ALBATROSS 5.10c This is a thin crack above an alcove that widens to hands. FA: Mike Lechlinski et al, 1981.

445C DAN'S PAPERBACKS 5.7 To the right of *The Albatross* is this nice hand crack in a right-facing corner. FA: Dan Michael, 1981.

MILES OF PILES ROCK

The following three routes are on the east face of **Miles of Piles Rock,** reached by walking around its south side, right of *Winds of Whoopee.*

449A CRUELTY TO ANIMALS 5.10a This is a hand crack in a left-facing book on the left side of the face. FA: Alan Bartlett, Dave Evans and Pat Nay, April 1988.

449B RAT BOY 5.10c Starting at the same place as *Cruelty to Animals,* climb a right-slanting crack, pass a yucca bush, and continue up a thin crack in a small corner. FA: Evans and Bartlett, April 1988.

449C CRIPPLE CRACK 5.10b This is a 2- pitch route in the center of the wall which starts with an overhanging thin crack and belays on a large ledge. The second pitch goes up over a small roof, then moves left into a chimney. FA: Alan Roberts, Tony Puppo and Alan Bartlett, March 1988.

449D LONG-NECKED GOOSE 5.9 This route is across the canyon and faces the three previous routes. It follows a left-slanting inverting corner and passes two bolts near the top. Poor rock. FA: Bartlett and Roberts, March 1988.

449E FASCIST GROOVE THING 5.11a (TR) This is on a west-facing wall behind and left from *Long-Necked Goose.* It could also easily be approached from **Wimp Tower.** The climb is a long right-slanting groove that starts with a small roof. Head left near the top. FA: Russ Walling et al.

BLUE NUBIAN WALL

451A MOMENTO MORI 5.11a This is a thin crack on the buttress right of *Conceptual Continuity.* There is a fixed pin at the start, and the route stays in the left-hand crack midway up. FA: Dave Evans, Pat Nay and Alan Bartlett, April 1988.

INTERSECTION ROCK

453A *TRAPEZE* 5.11/12 This route lies between *Left Ski Track* and *Right Ski Track* and starts off a block with difficult face moves past a bolt. Above, four variations have been done.
Variation: TRAPEZE LEFT 5.12c Climb up to a long roof, move left and go over its left side.
Variation: TRAPEZE CENTER 5.12a Climb over the center of the roof.
Variation: TRAPEZE RIGHT 5.11d Climb to the roof, move right to two fixed pins, then over the roof.
Variation: FAST TRACK 5.11d From the first bolt, climb right to meet *Lower Right Ski Track* near its roof. FA: Bob Gaines et al, January 1987.

460A *GAZ GIZ* 5.6 Start just left of *Zigzag* and climb up to double horizontal cracks. Follow these straight left to meet *Goldenbush Corner* above its roof. FA: Craig Fry.

465A *ELIJAH'S COMING* 5.10b Climb the face between *The Waterchute* and *Mike's Books* past one bolt. The second pitch stays right of *Mike's Books* with no protection. FA: Bob Gaines and Bruce Christie, October 1986.

473A *A QUESTION OF MASCULINITY* 5.12c (TR) Climb cracks and an arete right of the lower section of *Billabong*. FA: Kevin Thaw, February 1988.

THE OLD WOMAN

506 *IRON MAN TRAVERSE* 5.10c This route now goes free. FFA: Charles Cole and Randy Vogel, March 1986.

THE BLOB

508A *THE WONDERFUL WORLD OF ART* 5.10+ Climb a thin crack to an awkward bombay chimney just left of *Buissonier*. FA: Roy McClenahan and Todd Gordon, March 1988.

508B *JUNIOR* 5.10c The face right of *Buissonier*, with two bolts. FA: Alan Nelson and Sally Moser, November 1987.

515A *THE PERSIAN ROOM* 5.13 (TR) 100 feet right of *Zulu Dawn*, and starting down low is this overhanging thin crack. FA: Dick Cilley, 1988.

520A *DIALING FOR DUCATS* 5.10b Climb the face left of *Safety in Numbers* past two bolts. FA: Alan Nelson and Alfred Randell, December 1987.

521A *SAFETY IN SOLITUDE* 5.9 Face to flake to crack right of *Safety in Numbers*. FA: Alan Nelson, December 1987.

523A *BEGINNER'S LUCK* 5.9 Start at the base of *Beginner's One* and angle up and left to the top of *Berkeley Dyke*. FA: Alan Nelson, December 1985.

524A *REALITY CHECK* 5.9 Climb dikes between *Beginner's One* and *Beginner's Twenty-Six*. FA: Alan Nelson, December 1985.

STEVE CANYON

527A *YEI-BEI-CHEI CRACK* 5.9 This is the short steep crack right of *Watanobe Wall*. FA: Todd Gordon, Dave Evans and Kelly Carignan, April 1986.

527B *OPEN SEASON* 5.9+ Start as for *Season Opener*, then move left and climb past bolts to the top. FA: Brad Singer et al, March 1988.

528A *COME-N-DO ME* 5.10b This is a three-bolt climb right of *Season Opener* that goes over a roof at the start. FA: Herb Laegar and Kevin Wright, October 1988.

539A *SUPER MONSTER KILLER* 5.11a Climb a crack to a face with three bolts between *Grain Surgery* and *Fist Full of Crystals*. FA: Eric Andersen and Chris Clark, February 1987.

545A *INVISIBLE TOUCH* 5.10d The left of two bolted routes on the outer face of the *Skinny Dip* pillar. FA: Bob Gaines and Yvonne MacPherson, March 1987.

545B *KING PIN* 5.11a The right bolted route, which starts from the *Skinny Pin* chimney. FA: Alan Bartlett and Scott Cole, February 1988.

551A *LAND OF THE LONG WHITE CLOUD* 5.10b This the the green dihedral right of *Jack Grit*. Poor Rock. FA: Todd Gordon and John Madgwick, September 1987.

551B *KIWI ROUTE* 5.10d Climb steep thin cracks right of *Land of the Long White Cloud*. Go right in a horizontal crack at the top. Poor rock. FA: Roy McClenahan et al.

THE WALL – NORTH END

569A HANDS UP 5.10+ Climb an easy crack right of **Hands Off** leading to wild moves past a bolt on the highest summit block. FA: unknown.

THE WALL – MIDDLE SECTION

569B WALLFLOWER 5.10a The face left of **C.F.M.F.** with one bolt. FA: Alan Nelson and Shartel McVoy, January 1987.

570A LASERATOR 5.11b (TR) Steep thin flakes between **C.F.M.F.** and **Laid Back**. FA: Nelson, January 1988.

THE WALL – SOUTH END

571A BROWN SQUEEZE 5.10+ Climb the vertical dike left of **Good to the Last Drop** past two bolts. FA: Mike Law, Ferret and Chunder, 1983.

574A DON'T WALTZ WITH DICK 5.10d (TR) Climb the lower face left of **Damn Jam** to meet the **Don't Dik With Walt** traverse. FA: Mark Spencer and Shirley Spencer, April 1986.

CHIMNEY ROCK – WEST FACE

581A FEAR OF FLYING 5.10d Bolted route up dikes between **Ballet** and **Howard's Horror**. FA: Bob Gaines and Terry Ayers, October 1986.

582A BREAK DANCING 5.11a Three-bolt route right of **Howard's Horror**. FA: Bob Gaines, Todd Gordon, Mike Paul, Walt Shipley, Rondo Powell and Bill Micklish, April 1988.

582B DIRTY DANCING 5.10a Climb the right-facing flake just left of **Damper** and pass one bolt near the top. FA: Gene West and Bill Bloch (TR), March 1987. Bob Gaines and Yvonne MacPherson (lead), November 1987.

582C TWISTED CRYSTALS 5.11a This climbs a dike with three bolts above the finish of **Howard's Horror**. FA: David Estey and Alfred Randell, January 1987.

584 PINCHED RIB Many holds have broken off on this route and it is now rated 5.10b.

CHIMNEY ROCK – EAST FACE

584A CAMOUFLAGE 5.12c Just left of **The Flue**, climb past horizontal cracks and four bolts to the top. FA: Paul Borne, October 1988.

HVCG – BACK SIDE

The following three top-rope routes are on a steep wall behind campsite 42.

587A MOONLIGHT CRACK 5.10+ (TR) This is a shallow offwidth that doesn't quite reach the ground; it starts with mantel moves. FA: unknown.

587B MAJOR THREAT 5.12a (TR) Climb the face 12 feet left of **Moonlight Crack**. FA: Mark Wallace, December 1986.

587C MINOR THREAT 5.11d (TR) Climb the face six feet right of **Moonlight Crack**. FA: Wallace, December 1986.

CYCLOPS ROCK

598A STAIRWAY TO HEAVEN 5.12a (TR) Climb between **Telegram for Mongo** and **Leader's Fright,** going directly over the main roof. FA: Peter Wütlich and Thomas Kraus, November 1986.

601A SPAGHETTI & CHILI 5.7 Between **Are We Ourselves** and **Penelope's Walk,** climb up a left-facing flake to join **Penelope's Walk**. FA: Frank Avella and Jack Knox, May 1986.

602A GOLDILOCKS 5.7 Climb a gold seam to a roof right of **Penelope's Walk**. FA: unknown.

THE POTATO HEAD

606A FRIEND BENDER 5.11b This climb is located on the south wall at the northwest end of the central corridor of **The Potato Head.** Climb a finger crack up and right to overhanging face moves. Escape right above this. FA: Alan Nelson and Tom Herbert, January 1987.

606B TUBERS IN SPACE 5.4 Directly opposite **Overnight Sensation** on **Cyclops Rock,** this route ascends a slab leading to a hand crack. FA: Todd Swain March 1987.

HIT MAN ROCK

610A **BISCUIT EATER** 5.10a This is the first crack right of **The Enforcer.** FA: Dave Evans, Todd Gordon and Kelly Carignan, April 1986.

610B **SKINWALKER** 5.10c Climb a difficult crack to a V-slot left of **The Bruiser.** FA: Gordon and Evans, April 1986.

611A **ACUITY** 5.7 This is a large V-slot/corner on the northwest corner of **Hit Man Rock.** It is visible from the Quail Springs Road. FA: Alan Nelson, December 1987.

LABOR DOME

613A **TIME AND A HALF** 5.10d (TR) Climb the crack going directly over the roof right of **A Woman's Work is Never Done.** FA: Randy Leavitt, 1986.

PATAGONIA PILE – EAST FACE

619A **SHIRT HEADS** 5.11/12 (TR) Start right of **No Shirt Needed,** cross it at the ledge and go over the roof and up the face left of the upper part of that route. FA: Mark Robinson and Will Chen, October 1986.

620A **DEAD MAN'S EYES** 5.11b Start 50 feet right of **Wet T-Shirt Night** at the left margin of a cave. Climb a poorly-protected corner to a roof, then up an overhanging crack to a hole. Continue up and left to the top. FA: Rob Robinson and Dane Sorie, April 1988.

621 **THE FLYING DUTCHMAN** 5.12 This climb, formerly called **Fat Lip,** is mismarked in the guide. It is actually much farther right and is now a free climb. It starts on a stack of rocks and climbs straight up on pin scars. FFA: Mike Paul, October 1988.

621A **THE YARDARM** 5.11 This is the left of two bolted routes right of **The Flying Dutchman.** FA: Mike Paul, October 1988.

621B **WALK THE PLANK** 5.11 The right bolted route. FA: Mike Paul, October 1988.

WALL OF BIBLICAL FALLACIES

This is the overhanging northeast face of the formation northeast of **Patagonia Pile.** It faces the **Rollerball** formation; approach as for that formation. It is the formation between **Patagonia Pile** and **Rollerball** on the map on page 140 of the guide. Eight routes have been reported.

621C **FISSURE OF MEN** 5.1 The easy chimney on the left side of the wall. FA: Randy Leavitt and Doug Englekirk, January 1987.

621D **RESURRECTION** 5.11d Climb a steep crack past three pins right of **Fissure of Men.** Take the left crack in the upper headwall. FA: Randy Leavitt and Paul Schweizer, January 1987.

621E **MEDUSA** 5.12c Climb the lower section of **Resurrection** and take the right crack in the upper headwall. FA: Hidetaka Suzuki.

621F **NEW TESTAMENT** 5.9 The large left-facing book right of **Resurrection.** FA: Randy Leavitt and Glen Svenson, January 1987.

621G **WALK ON WATER** 5.12b Climb a seam right of **New Testament** past a pin and two fixed copperheads. FA: Randy Leavitt and Paul Schweizer, February 1987.

621H **BLOOD OF CHRIST** 5.11d Three-bolt climb right of **Walk on Water.** FA: Leavitt and Schweizer, February 1987.

621I **BURNING BUSH** 5.12c Two-bolt climb right of **Blood of Christ.** FA: Leavitt and Schweizer, February 1987.

621J **MANNA FROM HEAVEN** 5.9 Short inverting corners at the far right side of the wall. FA: Perry Beckham, January 1987.

ROLLERBALL FORMATION

622A **ROLLER COASTER** 5.11c (TR) Climb a thin crack to a face to a roof 20 feet left of **Rollerball.** FA: Vaino Kodas and Herb Laegar.

RUBBLE ROCKS

This "formation" lies just northwest of **Rock Hudson,** midway between that formation and the **Rollerball** formation. Two routes are known.

622B CARY GRANITE 5.3 Climb a water groove and finger crack on the northwest face of the formation. FA: Todd Swain, March 1987.

622C TOPROPE CONVERSION 5.11+ This is on the east face of a narrow corridor splitting **Rubble Rocks.** Bolts and other fixed pro mark this 40-foot route. FA: unknown.

DINOSAUR ROCK

625A DYNO-SOAR 5.10c A1 Climb the face left of **Negasaurus** to two bolts. Use the second one for aid, then continue up the face to the final **Negasaurus** crack. FA: Todd Swain and Peggy Buckey, April 1986.

625B GORGASAURUS 5.7 Left and around the corner from **Dyno-soar,** climb the left of two cracks, then friction right to reach the lower left end of a slanting ladge system. Follow this right, crossing **Dyno-soar** and **Negasaurus.** FA: Kevin Pogue and Elisa Weinman, March 1986.

DUTZI ROCK

627A PRETZEL LOGIC 5.10/11 Start at **Pinhead** and follow a horizontal crack left via underclings until it is possible to climb straight up to the top. FA: Dave Evans and Todd Gordon, November 1987.

631A TEQUILA 5.10d (TR) Follow a thin crack to face just left of **Shakin' the Shirts.** FA: Bob Gaines and Linh Nguyen, March 1988.

ROCK HUDSON

636A SPANISH BOMBS 5.11c The face between **Looney Tunes** and **Hot Rocks,** with eight bolts. FA: Francisco Blanco (TR), 1987; Paul Borne (lead), December 1988.

638A WHERE EES DE SANTA CLAUS? 5.10a On the left side of the northeast face of **Rock Hudson** is a small face with a right-slanting dike. Climb this to a steep flake/crack leading to a bolt. Traverse left from the bolt to the top. FA: Herb Laegar and Dave Ohlsen, December 1986.

THE PEYOTE CRACKS – WEST FACE

641A STAND BY ME 5.10a (TR) Start in the tree right of the **Left Peyote Crack** and climb the face above. FA: Peggy Buckey and Todd Swain, March 1987.

THE PEYOTE CRACKS – EAST FACE

645 DIMP FOR A CHIMP 5.11b This is the shortest, left-most line on the wall. It was mistakenly called **Pygmy Village** in the guide and very mistakenly rated 5.9.

648 THE WATUSI 5.12b This route has been led, with two bolts. Mike Lechlinski, Terry Ayers and Tom Gilje, December 1988.

649 DIAL AFRICA This route should be rated 5.12a (TR).

649A APARTHEID 5.12b Climb the lower section of **Dial Africa** then move right and up past four bolts. FA: Scott Cosgrove, November 1987.

649B BUFFALO SOLDIER 5.12c This climbs the line marked **Dimp for a Chimp** (route #650) past four bolts. No route existed here before this was put up, as **Dimp for a Chimp** is actually much farther left (see above). FA: Scott Cosgrove, November 1987.

The following route is found by driving northwest from Echo Tee towards Keys Ranch. After about ⅓ mi. an offwidth through a roof will be seen low down on the hillside to the left.

650A THE MANEATER 5.10d Climb the above-mentioned offwidth. FA: Mike Paul and Bill Russell.

ECHO COVE ROCKS – SOUTH FACE

ECHO COVE

653A RUBIK'S REVENGE 5.12b (TR) This climb is located on **The Toy Block,** a large boulder on the southeast side of the clump of rocks 100 yards northeast of the Echo Cove parking area. Climb the overhanging south face with a roof crack start. There is a 2- bolt anchor on top. FA: Alan Nelson, November 1987.

655A THE SOUND OF ONE SHOE TAPPING 5.8 This is a three-bolt climb left of **W.A.C..** FA: Larry Kuechlin Jr. and Cory Zinngrabe, November 1988.

664A SANTA'S LITTLE HELPERS 5.11a Climb the arete/face right of *Hang Ten* past five bolts. FA: Alfred Randell et al, December 1987.

664B THE ALIEN LIFE FORM ARETE 5.10/11 Just right of *Santa's Little Helpers* is this dangerous arete route with one bolt. FA: Mike Lechlinski, Mari Gingery, Dave Evans and Todd Gordon, May 1988.

669A DEATH ON THE NILE 5.10a Between *Deceptive Corner* and *Out to Grunge* is this face climb with one bolt. FA: Alan Bartlett, Mike Lechlinski, Mari Gingery, Tom Atherton, Dave Evans, Todd Gordon, Josh and Otis, May 1988.

670A BUCKET BRIGADE 5.7 Starting off a ledge up and left from *Out to Grunge* climb steep buckets to a left-slanting crack. Move back right from the crack's top. FA: Alan Bartlett and Katie Wilkinson, May 1988.

ECHO COVE ROCKS – SOUTH FACE

671A THE RIDDLER 5.12a This is the farthest left route on the face. It climbs up to a roof and follows the thin crack above it past a bolt. FA: Mike Paul, February 1988.

671B TM'S TERROR 5.10b Just right of *The Riddler* climb up to and follow a right-slanting crack out a roof. FA: Alan Nelson, Tom Herbert and TM Herbert, December 1987.

674A SABRETOOTH 5.7 Start behind the tree just right of *Axe of Dog* and climb to the top of a flake. Continue up via cracks and face. FA: Alan Nelson, December 1987.

674B SICKER THAN JEZOUIN 5.11b 30 feet right of *Sabretooth* is a right-facing corner with two bolts on the left wall. FA: Jean-Luc Jezouin, Bill Herzog, Rob Mulligan et al, February 1987.

674C CHIPS AHOY 5.7 This climbs a loose face past several small bushes right of the preceding route. FA: Alan Nelson, December, 1987.

674D WILD EAST 5.9 Right of *Chips Ahoy* and a short distance left of *R.M.L.* is this one-bolt route leading into a brown right-facing corner. FA: Bill Herzog and Ernie Ale, January 1987.

674E *HORNY CORNER* 5.9 Climb the crack and corner immediately left of *R.M.L.* until one can clip a bolt and step right onto the arete leading to the top. FA: Ale and Herzog, January 1987.

676A *F.U.N.* 5.10c (TR) Start with the opening moves of *C.S. Special* then climb the face to the left of that route. FA: Alan Nelson, December 1987.

676B *HIGH WIRE* 5.12a This route climbs a black seam 30 feet right of *C.S. Special*. FA: Tom Herbert and Alan Nelson, December 1987.

676C *POCKET VETO* 5.10a Just right of *High Wire* follow thin cracks in a faint groove to an alcove, then up a vertical flake/crack in dark rock. FA: Todd Gordon, Mike Schneider and Alan Bartlett, October 1988.

676D *BACON FLAKE* 5.9 This is the obvious crack left of *Flake and Bake*. FA: unknown.

677 *FLAKE AND BAKE* This route is mismarked in the guide; it is slightly right of where shown and is a 2-bolt face climb just right of a prominent crack (*Bacon Flake*).

677A *OUT ON A LIMB* 5.10b Just right of *Flake and Bake* are two wide cracks forming a 'Y'. This is the arete with five bolts just right of these cracks. Start may be more difficult if you're under 5'11" or so. FA: Alfred Randell and Dave Tucker, February 1987.

EAST COVE/ECHO COVE ROCKS

678A *THE REAL MCCOY* 5.12 (TR) Climb the face 25 feet left of *Halfway to Paradise*. FA: John Long and Bob Gaines, November 1986.

EAST COVE – RIGHT SIDE

681A *SOLO DOG* 5.11c This route climbs thin cracks right of *No Mistake or Big Pancake*. FA: John Errin.

681B *THE ROBBINS ROUTE* 5.10+ On the corner/arete right of *Solo Dog* climb a thin crack up and over a small roof. FA: Parrish Robbins.

681C *QUARANTINE* 5.10a Climb a prominent left-facing corner up and left from the "gully". FA: Tim Bluhm and Donald Wise, October 1987.

688 *BROWN OUT* 5.12 (TR) This route has been top-roped free. FFA: Ron Kauk, 1987.

ECHO ROCK

The west face of **Echo Rock,** due to its good rock and moderate angle, is ideally suited to face climbing. Theoretically, face climbs could be done almost anywhere. The following proliferation of new routes clearly demonstrates this point. However, at some point the addition of new bolted climbs only detracts from the existing routes. It is difficult to say whether this point has now been reached. Climbers must draw their own line and conclusions.

692A *TEAM SLUG* 5.10b This is a three-bolt face climb just right of *The Trough*. FA: Alan Nelson and Alfred Randell (TR), December 1985. Todd Gordon, Cliff Pounders and Gabrielle (lead), May 1986.

692B *TOO BOLD TO BOLT* 5.8 Climb loose flakes past one bolt a short distance right of *Team Slug*. The bolt was added after the first ascent. FA: Alan Nelson, December 1985.

692C *PENNY LANE* 5.8 Climb the face between *Too Bold to Bolt* and *Double Dip* with no protection. FA: Bob Gaines and Penny Fogel, February 1987.

693A *BATTLE OF THE BULGE* 5.11a A five-bolt face climb right of *Double Dip*. FA: Bob Gaines, November 1987.

693B *UNZIPPER* 5.10+ This route reportedly climbs the face between *Battle of the Bulge* and *Gone in 60 Seconds* past two hangerless bolts. It may start with the first bolt of *Battle of the Bulge*. FA: Tony Dignam and Jeff Robertson, 1983.

696A *CHERRY BOMB* 5.10c Three-bolt climb a short distance left of *Stichter Quits*. FA: Bob Gaines, Rebecca Foster and Brian Prentice, November 1987.

697A *DAVE'S SOLO* 5.10a This ascends the face between *Stichter Quits* and *Legolas*. FA: Dave Evans, January 1988.

699A *FORBIDDEN PARADISE* 5.10b Climb past four bolts just right of *Stick to What*. FA: Alfred Randell and Dave Tucker.

700A *FALL FROM GRACE* 5.10b/c Just right of *Ten Coversations at Once* is this three-bolt route. FA: Herb Laegar, Vaino Kodas and Bob Kamps, November 1987.

700B *APRIL FOOLS* 5.10c Between *Fall From Grace* and *Quick Draw McGraw* is this runout route with two bolts. FA: Bob Gaines, Yvonne MacPherson and Bill Micklish, April 1988.

703A *LOVE & ROCKETS* 5.10b Climb *Heart and Sole* to its third bolt, then go straight up past three more bolts. FA: Bill Herzog and Rob Mulligan, February 1987.

704A *A DREAM OF WHITE POODLES* 5.8 This is a three-bolt climb just right of *Eff Four*. FA: Bill Herzog and Ernie Ale, February 1987.

705A *CONTROL* 5.10a Left of the *EBGB'S* block is a large boulder on a slab. This ascends a finger and hand crack that turns into a right-facing corner behind the boulder. FA: Tom Davis and Tom Voelkel, January 1987.

705B *CHAOS* 5.11b From the ledge where *Control* ends, this is a crack over a 12-15 foot roof. FA: Davis and Voelkel, January 1987.

705C *JANE'S GETTING SERIOUS* 5.11d This is a six-bolt climb 40 feet left of *EBGB'S*. The first bolt was used for aid on the first ascent. FA: Bob Gaines and Rondo Powell, November 1987; FFA: Tom Herbert, December 1988.

707 *TARZAN* 5.11b A two-bolt arete right of *EBGB'S*. This was erroneously listed as *Corner of Foreigner* in the guide, but it had not been climbed at that time. FA: Gaines and Powell, November 1987.

710A *SUN CITY* 5.11a This is the next dike right of *Sinner's Swing,* with one bolt. FA: Alan Nelson and Alfred Randell, December 1985.

710B *THE TURD* 5.11 Sitting in front of *Sinner's Swing* and *Sun City* is a round boulder. This climbs the south side of the boulder past one bolt. FA: Mike Lechlinski and Ron Carson.

710C *SIN CITY* 5.10c On the backside of the *Sun City* formation (facing the *Pope's Crack* area), this is a slanting dike rising out of the boulders. FA: Alan Nelson, Tom Herbert and Shartel McVoy, January 1987.

714A *RULE BRITANNIA* 5.11c This is a bolted face climb right of *British Airways*. The first bolt is doubled. FA: Jonny Woodward and Rob Raker, December 1985.

ECHO ROCK – EAST FACE

723A *BEADWAGON* 5.10d On the face right of *Second Thoughts* are two left-slanting dikes. This ascends the lower dike past two bolts and a pin. FA: Todd Gordon, Dave Evans and Jim Angione, November 1988.

723B *GUT FULL OF SUDS* 5.9 This route climbs the higher left-slanting dike. FA: Gordon and Evans, May 1988.

723C *THE STINKBUG* 5.10b This climb is located on the smallish tower left of *Closed on Mondays.* Climb a gritty hand crack, then traverse right and go up a thin crack to the top. FA: Evans, Gordon and Brian Sillasen, May 1986.

725A *GUMBY SAVES BAMBI* 5.10d Climb the face right of *Bambi Meets Godzilla* past five bolts. Best done in two pitches. FA: Herb Laegar, Andy Brown and Mike Lindsay, April 1987.

LITTLE HUNK – WEST FACE

729A *PERVERTS IN POWER* 5.9 This is a two-bolt face leading to a corner/arete behind and left from *Abstract Roller Disco.* FA: Alan Nelson and Twilley, November 1986.

LITTLE HUNK – EAST FACE

733A *UNSOLVED MYSTERY* 5.10+ An old bolted line just left of *Energy Crisis.* FA: unknown.

734A *POLICE & THIEVES* 5.11c This is a two-bolt climb right of *Energy Crisis.* FA: Jordy Morgan et al, February 1988.

734B *TVC15* 5.9 Climb the face left of *Team Scumbag.* No bolts. FA: Bob Gaines and Bruce Christle, October 1986.

734C *TEAM SCUMBAG* 5.10b This is a three-bolt climb just left of *ZZZZZ.* FA: Alan Nelson and Bob Van Belle, November 1986.

735A ELECTRIC BLUE 5.11d A five-bolt climb right of **ZZZZZ**. FA: Bob Gaines, March 1988.

736A POWER LICHEN 5.10b Start right of **Power Line** and climb up, then right into a prominent crack leading to the top. FA: Jim Waldron and Bill Waldron, December 1986.

737A POTATO HEAD 5.10c This follows the line marked as **Functional Analysis** in the guide (that route is mismarked – see below). FA: Dave Bruckman, Craig Fry, Mari Gingery and Mike Lechlinski, November 1984.

738 FUNCTIONAL ANALYSIS This route is mismarked in the guide; it climbs the next potential line right, thin seams reached by climbing up and left from the base of the rock.

BIG HUNK

739A WISH YOU WERE HERE 5.10c Start on **Tobin Bias**, then traverse straight right following three discontinuous horizontal cracks, passing one bolt. FA: Scott Fitzgerald and Logan Nelson, January 1985.

739B ELECTRIC EYE 5.11b Climb directly up to the bolt on **Wish You Were Here**, then continue straight up passing two more bolts. FA: Kurt Smith et al, February 1988.

The next two routes are on the west face of the summit block of **Big Hunk,** above and left from the finish of **Tobin Bias.** They can be approached by scrambling up easy rock a few hundred feet left of that route.

739C RAILROAD 5.11a This is a thin crack in a small left-facing, left-leaning book. After the initial crack, a hand traverse along a flake leads to the top. FA: Alan Roberts and Tom Herbert.

739D FINGER FOOD 5.10b This climbs the crack right of **Railroad,** starting in its right branch. The two routes end at the same point. FA: Roberts and John Hayward.

The next four routes are located on the northeast face of **Little Hunk,** several hundred feet left of **Cashews Will Be Eaten.** They are approached by ascending the boulder- filled gully between **Big Hunk** and **Little Hunk** (the same approach as for **Midnight Dreamer**). All four are bolted face climbs.

739E RETURN OF THE CHUCKWALLA 5.10c The farthest left line, with two bolts. FA: Don Wilson and Dave Wonderly, March 1988.

739F SWAIN-BUCKEY 5.10c The next route right, with four bolts. FA: Todd Swain and Peggy Buckey, March 1988.

739G PLAYING HOOKEY 5.10a This three-bolt climb starts off a block. FA: Alan Bartlett and Alan Roberts, February 1988.

739H SHADY GROVE 5.10c The farthest right route, with four bolts. FA: Bartlett, Roberts, Todd Gordon and Don Reid, February 1988.

The next two routes are a few hundred feet left of the previous routes, just left of the descent from those routes and almost directly below the northwest corner of **The Chair.**

739I MOVE TO THE GROOVE 5.10c (TR) Climb directly up to and follow a steep groove. FA: Roberts and John Hayward.

739J GROOVE AVOIDANCE SYSTEM 5.10a (TR) This is a jug problem right of the groove. FA: Roberts and Hayward.

The following route is located on the summit block of the southeast face of **Big Hunk,** above and right from **Midnight Dreamer** and roughly opposite **The Chair.**

740A SUN BOWL 5.13a Climb a steep brown corner past three bolts. FA: Scott Cosgrove, February 1988.

LITTLE HUNK – RIGHT SIDE

746A WHITE LINE FEVER 5.9 Traverse left on exposed face left of the start of **Roofing Company** to a thin crack and follow that to the top. FA: Jack Marshall and M. Golden, 1984.

DWEEB SPIRE

Dweeb Spire is a large white detatched pillar high on the northwest side of **Snickers,** directly across from *Deep Throat.* One route is known.

756A DISOBEDIENCE SCHOOL 5.10c   Climb up and left across the north face with tricky pro, then up a thin crack to an arete finish. One bolt. FA: Todd Gordon and Alan Roberts, February 1988.

LITTLE ROCK CANDY MOUNTAIN

757A SQUIRREL ROAST 5.8   This is a one-bolt face climb right of *Kendall Mint Cake.* FA: Alan Bartlett and Kilian Bäuz, April 1988.

762A LIPS LIKE SUGAR 5.10b   Climb the initial crack of *Chick Flakey,* then move left and go up a brown arete. FA: Dave Evans, Tom Michael, Todd Gordon and Jim Angione, April 1988.

766A McSTUMPY SANDWICH 5.9   Right of *Little Rock Candy Crack,* climb past a bolt into shallow thin cracks. FA: Alan Bartlett, Don Reid, Todd Gordon and Cyndie Bransford, April 1988.

SNICKERS – SOUTH FACE

766B WHEN YOU'RE NOT A JET 5.10b   This is a bolted face on half light/half dark rock across the canyon and about 50 yards left of *Henny Penny.* FA: Vaino Kodas and Matt Olephant, 1983.

767 HENNY PENNY   This route is mismarked in the guide. It actually climbs the next crack right of where it is shown.

767A ROCK SHARK 5.11a   This is the crack/seam left of *Henny Penny.* It is the crack that is shown as being *Henny Penny* in the guide. FA: Alan Nelson, Alfred Randell and Shartel McVoy, December 1987.

768A TOXIC WASTELAND 5.10d   This is a rotten seam with one bolt leading to a hand crack, about 50 yards right of *When You're a Jet.* Very poor rock. FA: Nelson and Randell, December 1987.

768B CAYENNE 5.11c   A short distance right of *Toxic Wasteland* is a large boulder. This climbs the west arete past one bolt. FA: Nelson and Randell, December 1987.

768C SWEET GINGER 5.11a   Right of *Cayenne,* on the south face of the boulder is this six-bolt climb. If under 6'0", the first bolt may be difficult to clip, and the route may be harder than it is rated. FA: Bob Gaines et al, 1987.

HUNK ROCK – EAST FACE

771A HEAT WAVE   5.9   Climb the arete left of *Hunkloads to Hermosa* past one bolt. FA: Bob Gaines and Penny Fogel, February 1988.

773A BREATH OF DEATH   5.11a   This is a left-leaning overhanging 1" crack rising out of the boulders 50 yards right of *Death of a Decade*. FA: Alan Nelson and Bob Van Belle, December 1979.

RICH AND FAMOUS CLIFF

This cliff is about 200 yards west of and facing the *Gunsmoke* traverse.

778A RICH BITCH   5.9+   Climb a small clean brown dihedral on the far left side of the cliff. FA: Brian Sillasen and Todd Gordon, November 1987.

778B FILTHY RICH   5.8   This ascends cracks going over a roof, right of *Rich Bitch*. FA: Gordon and Sillasen, November 1987.

778C RICH AND FAMOUS   5.9   A prominent clean dihedral up high and right of *Filthy Rich*. FA: Sillasen and Gordon, November 1987.

778D FOUR CAR GARAGE   5.9   The farthest right crack, which goes up and right to a steep finish. FA: Gordon and Sillasen, November 1987.

ROCKWORK ROCK

779A ROCKY VS. RAMBO   5.11c   Right of *Rockwork Orange* climb an arete and face past horizontal cracks to a steep hand crack finish. FA: Jack Marshall and R. Mims, 1985.

787A THE PREDATOR   5.11c   Start at *El Blowhole* and climb right past three bolts to a corner leading up to a horizontal crack. Traverse right to finish. FA: Tom Herbert and Dave Hatchett, November 1988.

787B PEPO MOVER   5.10c (TR)   Right of *The Predator* is a corner crack. This route climbs the arete/face right of the crack. FA: Dave Evans and Craig Fry.

The next three routes are on the wall across from **Rockwork Rock.**

787C HOLE IN ONE   5.10b (TR)   This route is directly opposite *Flaming Arrow*. It starts by a hole and hand traverses left to a vertical flake. FA: Alan Roberts and John Hayward.

787D A SCAR IS BORN   5.11c   20 feet right of the preceding route is this finger crack which curves up and right. FA: Tom Herbert, March 1988.

787E WHEN YOU'RE A SANCHO   5.11 (TR)   Right of the previous routes, and across the canyon from *Rockwork Orange,* this climbs a prominent face via a diagonal dike. FA: Scott Cosgrove and Joe Hedge, January 1988.

BED ROCK

790A PEBBLES AND BAM BAM   5.7   This is the easy chimney left of *Barnie Rubble* which has a boulder problem start. FA: Todd Swain, March 1987.

790B EVOLUTIONARY THROWBACK   5.10c   Climb past three bolts on the face left of *Barnie Rubble,* then move left and up an arete past a pin to the top. FA: Todd Swain, Peggy Buckey and John Thackray, March 1987.

790C MEANDERTHAL   5.8 (TR)   Do the boulder start to *Pebbles and Bam Bam,* then climb by the first two bolts of *Evolutioary Throwback* and continue straight up. FA: Thackray and Swain, March 1987.

790D SATIN FINISH   5.9   This is a straight-in crack on the back side of **Bed Rock.** FA: Brian Sillasen, Don Reid and Todd Gordon, March 1988.

ESCAPE ROCK

792A ESCAPE FROM THE PLANET EARTH   5.10a   This route climbs a left-facing dihedral with a bush at its top about 150 feet right of *Psoriasis*. FA: Karen Wilson and Don Wilson, November 1986.

ROCK OF AGES AREA

795A GODZILLA EATS HUMAN SUSHI 5.10d This is a steep hand and finger crack across the canyon fron *Hallow Friction*. FA: Don Wilson and Dave Wonderly, April 1988.

795B BED OF NAILS 5.10d This route is about 100 feet left of *Godzilla Eats Human Sushi*. Climb past a bolt into a crack which doesn't quite reach the top. FA: Jonny Woodward and Dave Bruckman, January 1987.

795C MULLIGAN STEW 5.11b (TR) This is a steep thin crack that starts from a horizontal crack on a north facing wall in the narrow corridor right of *Hallow Friction*. FA: Rob Mulligan, November 1985.

BARKER DAM AREA

796A DENTAL HYGIENE 5.8 Climb a crack and jugs over a small roof 20 feet right of *No Falls*. FA: Jack Marshall and Dave Wonderly, 1983.

LAKESIDE ROCK

797A SHIT SANDWICH 5.9 Carefully climb a rotten seam and detatched flakes between *Fat Man's Misery* and *Thin Man's Nightmare*. FA: Alan Nelson and Bob Van Belle, November 1986.

801A LAURA SCUDDERS 5.10b This is a three-bolt face climb right of *Parental Guidance Suggested*. FA: Vaino Kodas, Mike Dorey and Diana Kodas, October 1987.

801B FATHER FIGURE 5.13a This route is located on the back side of **Lakeside Rock,** reached by walking around right from the preceding route. It is an overhanging face with four bolts. FA: Scott Cosgrove, April 1988.

RAT ROCK

802 RAT LEDGE This route is misdrawn in the guide. It climbs the left-facing corners just right of *Bad Lizards,* and crosses that route where *Bad Lizards* cuts sharply right near the top. It is plainly visible in the photo on page 219, and no route exists where it is shown as being in the photo on page 218.

804A SPRING OR FALL 5.11 Up and left from *Bad Lizards* and right of *The Forsaken Mein-Key,* climb past a bolt to a thin crack and a ledge, then up a dike past another bolt. FA: Herb Laegar, Mike Jaffe and Vaino Kodas, November 1986.

804B DAMM DIKE 5.7 This is a one-bolt face climb on the wall behind *Spring or Fall.* FA: Laegar, Jaffe and Kodas, November 1986.

804C OASIS OF EDEN 5.10d This is a four-bolt climb on the large buttress behind and right from **Rat Rock**. FA: Bob Gaines and Yvonne McPherson, February 1988.

ROOM TO SHROOM AREA

808A MUD DOG 5.10a This is the crack to the right of *Room to Shroom* and leads up to the belay tree where that route finishes. FA: Craig Fry, Jerelyn Taubert, Cathy Boyd and Jim Angione, November 1985.

808B FRANKIE LEE 5.7 This climb is on a east-facing wall opposite *Room to Shroom,* and slightly farther south. It follows a hand crack left of a smooth wall and just right of a wide crack. FA: Todd Gordon and Craig Fry, May 1986.

808C QUEST FOR THE GOLDEN HUBRIS 5.9 This climb is on the east-facing wall behind *Frankie Lee.* It is a thin crack which peters out near the top, and is left of center in a smooth wall in the midst of several wider cracks. FA: Matthew Lamperti, Barb Steffens and Karl Smith, November 1987.

SARGEANT ROCK

811A SCHOOL DAZE 5.10a This follows the line drawn in the guide for **39 Steps,** which is incorrect for that route. FA: Todd Gordon and Cyndie Bransford, November 1988.

811B SUFFERING CATFISH 5.10b Climb the face between **School Daze** and **39 Steps** past two bolts. FA: Todd Gordon, Dave Evans, Jim Angione and Marge Floyd, November 1988.

812 39 STEPS This route is misdrawn in the guide; it is farther right and follows a thin vertical dike with many little steps in it (no pro).

PREVIOUSLY UNRELEASED MATERIAL

813 KNIGHT MARE This route is misdrawn in the guide; it is about 50 feet left of where shown, and just left of the hole in the rock. It climbs straight up, then curves right to reach a ledge below the summit block. The route ends here.

813A ROCKY HORROR 5.7 This route is essentially the second pitch of **Knight Mare.** Climb the diagonal crack on the left side of the summit block, then up an arete to the top. FA: Don Gangware and Zack Smith, January 1979.

The following two routes are on a buttress 300 feet past (north of) the **Bankrupt Wall.**

821A MIGHTY MOUSE 5.9 This route climbs a crack and jugs halfway up the face, then past two bolts to the top. FA: Don Wilson and Karen Wilson, November 1987.

821B MINOR DETOUR 5.10a Ascend a finger crack in a small corner on the block above **Mighty Mouse.** FA: Wilson and Wilson, November 1987.

OB/GYN DOME

This is the formation southeast of **Nomad Dome.** The two known routes are on the northeast face.

828A SPECULUM SCRAPINGS 5.11 Starting atop a pedestal, climb up and right into a left-facing book. From the book's top, go up and left to the summit. FA: Spencer Lennard and Alan North, November 1986.

828B MR. BUNNY'S PETRI DISH 5.9 Right of the preceding route, climb a left-facing book. From its top, unprotected face leads to a left-leaning crack to the top. FA: Lennard and North, November 1986.

DON JUAN BOULDER

829A THE DUKE 5.9 A1 On the northwest corner of the boulder, lasso a horn about 12 feet off the ground, then climb the rope to get on the horn. Continue past two bolts to the top. FA: Tom Grimes and David Katz, November 1986.

SOUTH ASTRO DOME

834A MAMUNIA 5.12c This is a six-bolt climb right of **Strike it Rich,** ending at a rappel station. FA: Troy Mayr, April 1988.

834B STONE IDOL 5.11d Climb the face left of **Bolt Heaven** past six bolts. FA: Jonny Woodward, Darrel Hensel, Maria Cranor and Rob Raker, April 1988.

838A SHOOTING STAR 5.11a Start between **Middle Age Crazy** and **Such a Savage** and climb past two bolts to the third bolt of **Middle Age Crazy.** Go up and left past another bolt to a two-bolt belay. The second pitch goes up and right, then straight up past two bolts. FA: Alan Nelson and Alfred Randell, January 1986.

842A THE BOOGIE WOOGIE BLUES 5.11c This route could be considered the second pitch of **Piggle Pugg.** It is a three-bolt route which climbs up and left of the second pitch of **Breakfast of Champions,** roughly following the band of orange rock. FA: Darrel Hensel and Jonny Woodward, January 1986.

NORTH ASTRO DOME

845 REPO MAN 5.12a This is the former first pitch of **Power Fingers,** which was removed and now replaced on lead with one less bolt. From its top, either rappel or climb up and left (5.8) to join **Zion Train.** FA: Jonny Woodward and Darrel Hensel, January 1986.

848A LIFE'S A PITCH 5.12a This is the left of two bolted lines right of **Lead Us Not Into Temptation.** Eight bolts. FA: Troy Mayr, March 1988.

848B CHUTE TO KILL 5.10c The right bolted line, with six bolts. FA: Troy Mayr, Steve Anderson, Ed Hunsaker and Steve Axthelm, March 1988.

SOUTH ASTRO DOME – WEST FACE

851A MR. LIZARD MEETS FLINTSTONE 5.6 This is a five-bolt climb right of *Bozo Buttress*. FA: Bill Herzog, Rob Mulligan and Laura Rosa, 1987.

851B DIDN'T YOUR MAMA EVER TELL YOU ABOUT A STRANGER'S BOLTS 5.9 Right of the preceding climb, this route has three bolts. FA: Rob Mulligan and Bill Odenthal, November 1985.

851C AIR VOYAGER 5.11b This is the left of two obvious grooves right of the previous routes. There are two bolts at the start. FA: Mulligan and Odenthal, March 1986.

851D IT SEAMS POSSIBLE 5.10c The right groove, with no bolts. FA: Mulligan and Odenthal, December 1985.

852A BOZO'S RAINDANCE 5.11c This is a five-bolt climb (the second bolt is doubled) about 150 feet right of *Aqua Tarkus*. FA: Rob Mulligan, Bill Herzog, Jean-Luc Jezouin et al, 1987.

THE MOONSTONE

854A ANTY MATTER 5.10a Climb the obvious ramp 30 feet left of *Cosmic Debris*, then up the face past two bolts. FA: Todd Swain and John Thackray, March 1987.

854B ONE SMALL STEP 5.6 This is the big crack 10 feet right of *Cosmic Debris*. FA: Thackray and Swain, March 1987.

854C THE MOONWALK 5.6 Climb the short crack 30 feet right of *Cosmic Debris*. FA: Thackray and Swain, March 1987.

PERRY MASONARY

This formation is directly south of **Old A Hotie Rock,** and on the left side of the wash as one approaches **Lenticular Dome** from Wonderland Valley. The routes are all on the northeast face.

854D TROWEL AND ERROR 5.9 This is the obvious curving flake/crack in the left center of the face. FA: Todd Swain and Peggey Buckey, March 1987.

854E SAKRETELIGIOUS 5.8 Climb the left of three cracks right of *Trowel and Error.* FA: Swain and Buckey, March 1987.

854F MORTARFIED 5.10b Climb the right of the three cracks, then continue past three bolts. FA: Swain, Buckey and Bob Hostetter, March 1987.

854G CEMENTARY 5.8 This is the right-facing, right-leaning crack/corner right of *Mortarfied.* It starts behind a tree. FA: Swain, Buckey and Hostetter, March 1987.

854H ANOTHER BRICK IN THE WALL 5.9 (TR) Climb the very thin flake just right of *Cementary,* then up the face. FA: Hostetter, Buckey and Swain, March 1987.

THE SANCTUARY

This is a well-hidden but worthwhile corridor north of **Lenticular Dome.** Follow the approach to that formation and continue past it for about five minutes, then turn back right (northeast) and enter a small wash/gully. The top of the gully is the back of **The Sanctuary.** Walk right to get around the formation and drop down into the corridor. Just before descending into the corridor, look right and you will see a formation peppered with jugs. This is called **The Brain Box.**

858A POP TART 5.8 Climb a hand and fist crack on the left side of **The Sanctuary.** FA: Tom Applegate and Paul, February 1987.

858B HOLY HAND 5.10a This is the next crack right of *Pop Tart.* FA: Eric Gompper and Paul, February 1987.

858C LITURGY 5.11a The next crack right, this is a finger crack. FA: Eric Gompper and Tom Applegate, February 1987.

858D BLACK SLACKS 5.10a This is an offwidth farther right. FA: Eric Gompper and Alfred Randell, February 1987.

858E TOP HAT 5.11+ (TR) This is a crack to face climbing right of *Black Slacks.* FA: Alfred Randell, February 1987.

858G SANCTUARY MUCH 5.11a The farthest crack on the right, this finishes with a left-slanting crack. FA: Dan Parks and Spin Shafer, February 1987.

858H THE BRAIN 5.7 This goes straight up the middle of **The Brain Box,** as viewed from the approach. FA: Eric Gompper and Tom Applegate, February 1987.

OLD A HOTIE ROCK

859A EXISTENTIAL DECAY   5.12a   This route climbs a thin lieback right of **Nihilistic Pillar.** FA: Randy Leavitt.

860A ENDLESS SUMMER   5.9   This route is on the southwest face of the rock, directly opposite the **Perry Masonary** routes. Climb double left-slanting cracks which pass a ledge with a yucca bush on it. FA: Alan Bartlett and Kate Duke, April 1988.

PUNK ROCK

861A BOMBS OVER LIBYA   5.11+   This is a three-bolt climb on the steep right side of the south face of the rock, somewhat above and left from **Scar Wars.** FA: John Yablonski, Mike Lechlinski, Mari Gingery and Tom Gilje, February 1988.

861B SLAVES OF FASHION   5.12b   This is the obvious finger crack left of **Scar Wars,** which starts with face past one bolt. FA: Randy Leavitt and Paul Schweizer, March 1987.

862A COLE-GORDON OFFWIDTH   5.10c   Climb an obvious left-curving chimney to offwidth around the corner to the right of **Scar Wars.**

FREAK BROTHERS DOMES

869A I CAN BELIEVE IT'S A SANDBAG   5.8   On the far right (south) end of the domes, climb a left-leaning ramp to its top, then right past a bolt to the top. FA: Todd Swain and Peggy Buckey, March 1987.

869B WEENIE ROAST   5.11a   This is an overhanging crack to an offwidth finish on the north face of the pinnacle just north of the **Freak Brothers Domes.** FA: Walt Shipley and Roy McClenahan, January 1986.

FAT FREDDIE'S CAT

870A WNW DIHEDRAL   5.5   Climb the left-facing corner 25 feet right of **The North Face** route. FA: Todd Swain, March 1987.

872A TIME AVENGER   5.11b   This is a seven-bolt climb just left of **Early Bird.** FA: Todd Swain and Peggy Buckey. FFA: Bob Gaines, February 1988.

PEA BRAIN

874A SPACELY SPROCKETS   5.8   Climb the face right of **Joan Jetson** past four bolts. FA: Todd Swain, John Thackray and Peggy Buckey, March 1987.

THE RED OBELISK

875 BOOGERS ON A LAMPSHADE   This route is mislocated in the guide. It is actually on the southwest corner, barely visible in the photo on page 250.

DISNEYLAND DOMES

876A INVASION ON MY FANTASY   5.7   This is the crack right of **Thrutcher.** FA: Todd Gordon, December 1983.

877A BRASS MONKEY   5.12a   This is a six-bolt climb between **Tragic Kingdom** and **Walt's Frozen Head.** FA: Tom Herbert, November 1988.

877B WALT'S FROZEN HEAD   5.10b   This is on the right side of the large brown buttress right of **Tragic Kingdom.** The route starts by traversing in from a ledge on the right. Two pitches, some bolts. FA: Bob Gaines and Alfred Randell, February 1988.

877C STEREO IN B FLAT   5.10d (TR)   Climb a thin crack about 100 feet right of **Walt's Frozen Head.** FA: Randy Vogel and Alan Roberts, January 1986.

879A FANTASIA   5.10b   This route starts in the chimney left of **Jungle Cruise.** Climb right out of the chimney in a corner leading to an arete. Go up the arete to a dike and traverse left to a belay with a bolt. Continue left and go up an overhanging crack to the top. Three pitches, one bolt. FA: Roy McClenahan and Walt Shipley, February 1988.

880A AUTOPIA   5.9   This route starts with the first 20 feet of **Mental Bankruptcy** and continues straight up the chimney. The second pitch traverses left out of the chimney before it narrows, and goes up a rotten face to the top of a pillar. The third pitch continues up thin cracks past one bolt. FA: Alan Bartlett and Vicki Pelton, February 1988.

880B THE ROUNDUP   5.11   This is a thin crack leading to face on brown patina plates on a formation east of **Disneyland Domes** and facing **Pea Brain.** FA: Mike Lechlinski, Tom Gilje and Mari Gingery, January 1988.

880C CRACK OF DARK   5.10   This prominent offwidth right of **The Roundup** has a bouldering start. FA: Walt Shipley, Mike Lechlinski and Mari Gingery, February 1988.

PRINGLE ROCK

This is the prominent large rock about 150 yards northwest of the north end of **Duckwaddle Domes.** The one known route is on the southwest face and is best approached via a rocky gully from the west.

> *881A TIGERS ON VASELINE* 5.9 Climb past a horizontal crack and a bolt to a right-facing flake. From the flake's top, continue past two more bolts to the top. FA: Gary Geraths, Deena and Eddy Caparelli, October 1987.

MIND BODY ROCK

This is a large round boulder about 75 yards west of **Pringle Rock.**

> *881B MIND BODY PROBLEM* 5.12c (TR) This ascends the concave east face of the boulder, starting with thin fingers and ending up offwidth. To top-rope the problem, gain the summit via aid off a bolt on the south side of the boulder. FA: Mike Geller, 1987.

> *881C ANECDOTES OF POWER* 5.11c This short, overhanging thin hands crack lies on the east side of a low rock wall about 75 yards north of **Mind Body Rock.** FA: Paul Schweizer (TR), Fall 1986; Tim Wagner and Schweizer (lead), Spring 1987.

DISNEYLAND DOME – NORTH FACE

> *883A WHEEL OF FORTUNE* 5.11b About 70 feet right of **The Weak Force,** climb a left-leaning crack to its end then up past bolts. FA: Paul Schweizer and Randy Vogel, April 1986.

> *883B BRIDGE-IT BARDOT* 5.10d This is a groove/chimney with three bolts around the corner to the right of **Wheel of Fortune.** It is near the northwest end of **Disneyland Dome** and faces into the main approach gully for the north face routes. FA: Charles Cole, Dave Evans and Tom Michael, November 1986.

THE TRAINING GROUND

This formation is 75 yards north of **Disneyland Dome's** north face. The one known route is on the south end of the formation.

> *883C THE UNDERWEAR BANDIT* 5.10a Follow cracks and ramps up and right to a vertical shallow crack leading to the top. FA: Randy Vogel, April 1986.

DUMB DOME

> *884A SOUTH FACE DIRECT* 5.7 Starting from a chimney on the right, face climb into cracks right of **Monument Manor,** and join that route near the top. FA: Rob Mulligan and Bill Odenthal, 1986.

The following two routes are on the west wall of the corridor west of **Boulder Canyon,** due south of the **'B'** in **Dumb Dome** in the map on page 249. Probably best approached from the south, from the vicinity of **Pea Brain.**

> *884B MOTHER BUTLER* 5.10a This is a finger crack near the south end of the corridor. FA: Gary Gunder and Phil Warrender, February 1987.

> *884C THE SECRET OF MOTHER BUTLER* 5.10c A right-leaning finger crack at the north end of the corridor. FA: Gunder, Warrender, Rich Grigsby and Gary Valle, February 1987.

INAUGURON DOME

> *887 THE INAUGURON* 5.11b The first pitch now goes free, and a second pitch has been added going straight up past two bolts. FFA: Jonny Woodward, Maria Cranor and Darrel Hensel, October 1986.

> *887A MORALITY TEST* 5.11b This is a two-pitch climb with four bolts between **The Inauguron** and **Yardy-Hoo and Away.** FA: Woodward, Hensel and Cranor, October 1986.

> *888A BEAFCAKE* 5.10a This route ascends double cracks about 60 feet left of **White Bread Fever.** Start in the right crack, and partway up switch to the left one, which is followed to the top. FA: Kevin Worrell, Randy Vogel and George Meyers.

> *888B WHEAT BERI-BERI* 5.11c Start about 40 feet left of **White Bread Fever.** Climb past a bolt into a left-leaning shallow wide crack. Higher, exit right onto difficult face moves past a bolt. Protection to 5" needed. FA: Jonny Woodward and Darrel Hensel, February 1988.

ELEPHANT ARCHES

893 POM POM DANCER 5.9 This route, formerly called *Under Secretary*, now goes free. FFA: unknown.

893A MILK THE DOG 5.10a Starting from the vicinity of *Pom Pom Dancer*, traverse left along a horizontal crack which cuts across **Elephant Arches** at mid-height. FA: Todd Gordon and Brian Sillasen, April 1986.

DIARRHEA DOME

896 BIG BROWN EYE This route is misdrawn in the guide. It starts in the right crack and traverses to the left (marked) crack at treetop level. About 35 feet above the "eye" traverse left past a bolt and continue up and left to the top.

896A THE MANLY DIKE 5.11a A1 Start about 100 feet left of *Big Brown Eye*. Aid up on bolts to reach a right-ascending dike, and follow this past seven bolts. FA: Charles Cole, Dave Evans, Todd Gordon and Marge Floyd, December 1985.

896B SVAPADA 5.11 This is an eight-bolt climb right of *Big Brown Eye*, ending at a two-bolt stance. FA: Todd Gordon and Tom Atherton, December 1988.

BIGHORN MATING GROTTO

897A EUPHRATES 5.11c/d (TR) Climb improbable thin cracks and face right of *Take Two They're Small*. FA: Craig Fry, 1985.

BIGHORN TERRACE

This area is locted above and northeast of the **Bighorn Mating Grotto.**

901A DOMINATRIX 5.10d This is the left of three west-facing cracks. FA: Alan Nelson, November 1987.

901B WHIPS AND GRAINS 5.9 This is a hand and fist crack on the corner right of *Dominatrix*. FA: Nelson, November 1987.

BIGHORN DOME – NORTH FACE

904A THE LOVE GOAT 5.10a This is the route marked #905 (*Greenhorn Dihedral*) in the photo on page 261. Actually, that route is farther right, as noted below. FA: Craig Fry and Dave Evans, April 1986.

904B ALIENS ATE MY BUICK 5.10b This climb ascends the narrow rib left of *Greenhorn Dihedral* past three bolts and a fixed pin. FA: Don Wilson and Jack Marshall, February 1988.

905 GREENHORN DIHEDRAL This climb is misdrawn in the guide. It lies farther right and climbs a green, right-facing dihedral. In the photo on page 261, it is a line which separates light rock on the left from dark rock on the right, and passes over the left side of a small roof at about ⅔ height.

905A ZORBA 5.11a Right of *Greenhorn Dihedral*, climb a right-leaning pillar and traverse right to a bolt. Angle right to the top with poor pro. FA: Craig Fry and Todd Gordon, April 1986.

905B CUT TO THE BONE 5.10+ Climb stacked blocks right of *Zorba* and continue up face and thin cracks to a roof. Work right under the roof until it is possible to head up to the top. FA: Dave Bruckman and Todd Battey.

905C TIME TO TAKE THE GARBAGE OUT 5.10a On the far right side of the north face, climb a perfect hand crack through a small overhang, then head up and left to the top. FA: Craig Fry, Dave Evans and Marge Floyd, April 1984.

905D HARD ROCK CAFE 5.10d This is a doubly overhanging brown corner on the northwest end of **Bighorn Dome.** FA: Roy McClenahan and Walt Shipley, February 1988.

905E AUTOMATIC TIGER 5.10d Right of *Hard Rock Cafe* climb past a bolt into a thin crack. This climb faces north. FA: Shipley and McClenahan, February 1988.

905F JACK IN THE CRACK 5.10d This ascends the steep arching crack on the east side of the summit block of **Bighorn Dome.** FA: Don Wilson, Karen Wilson and Jack Marshall, November 1987.

905G GET THE BOOT 5.10b This is a three-bolt face climb on a boot-shaped block north of **Bighorn Dome.** FA: Walt Shipley and Roy McClenahan, February 1988.

RED BLUFFS

907A RED RED 5.10d This is the first crack right of **Slip Skrig.** FA: Craig Fry and Bob Roback, April 1986.

DON GENERO CLIFFS

908A WHAT IS THE QUESTION? A2 Left of **Mexican Hat of Josh** is another aid climb. FA: Charles Cole, Craig Fry and Kelly Carignan, January 1984.

THE CORNERSTONE

910A ROPE OPERA 5.11a This route climbs the right side of the **General Hospital** flake with a two-bolt start. FA: Todd Swain and Peggy Buckey, March 1988.

911A ALL MY CHILDREN 5.9 This is a right-arching crack right of **One Move Leads to Another.** FA: Todd Gordon and Kristen Laird, December 1986.

911B TOMATO AMNESIA 5.10 Climb the crack right of **All My Children.** FA: Don Wilson and Ron White, January 1988.

WAVECREST ROCK

This large "block" of rock lies about 75 yards southwest of **Mental Siege Tactics.** Some scrambling is necessary to reach the following three routes, which are on the south face.

915A SOUTH SWELL 5.9 This is an obvious hand crack on the left side of the face. FA: Randy Leavitt and Paul Schweizer, spring 1986.

915B THE SOUND OF WAVES 5.11b (TR) This is the arete right of **South Swell.** FA: Schweizer and Leavitt, spring 1986.

915C WAVECREST 5.12a Climb the left- arching dihedral right of **The Sound of Waves.** Many small nuts needed. FA: Leavitt and Schweizer, spring 1986.

AFRO BLUES WALL

918 BLUE-GRASS 5.10+ This climb was formerly called **My Favorite Things**; it has now been led, with one bolt placed. Jonny Woodward, Darrel Hensel and Rob Raker, September 1986.

918A BLUE RIBBON 5.11a This line is right of **Blue-Grass** and has no bolts. The crux is at the top, face climbing right out of a crack. FA: Woodward, Hensel and Raker, September 1986.

918B FOUNDATION CRACK 5.10b This route is on the wall across from **Afro Blues Wall,** and climbs a corner behind an old cement foundation slab. FA: Alan Roberts and John Hayward.

The following route is located on the west face (the right wall) of the main corridor east-northeast of **Afro Blues Wall.**

918C TRIVIAL PURSUIT 5.7 Climb a face with two bolts. FA: Alan Nelson and Vaino Kodas, December 1984.

THE MILL AREA

919 NAKED REAGAN This climb is mismarked in the guide; it actually lies about 100 feet left of and behind the formation where it is shown on page 268. The description "finger crack in a flare" is applicable.

919A WAYWARD HAYWARD 5.10b This is a right-slanting ramp system right of **Naked Reagan.** FA: Alan Roberts and John Hayward.

919B FLEXIBLE HUEYS 5.10d (TR) This is the route that is shown as **Naked Reagan** in the guide. FA: Robert Carrere, Jack Marshall and Don Wilson, January 1987.

HOOK AND LADDER AREA

923A PINK THING 5.10a This is the crack just left of **City H,** with one bolt near the top. FA: Todd Gordon, Dave Evans, Craig Fry and Jim Angione, November 1985.

IGUANA DOME

This is the large dome east of **Worth Bagly Memorial Dome.** It is on the right (east) as one is approaching the **Hook and Ladder Area.**

926A IGUANA MASTERS   5.10b   Near the south end of the west face of the dome, climb a ramp leading to a face with five bolts. FA: Todd Gordon, Dave Evans, Jim Angione, Craig Fry and Frank Bentwood, November 1985.

926B ANGIONE CRACK   5.6   This is a steep dogleg hand crack on the northwest side of **Iguana Dome.** FA: Todd Gordon and Jim Angione, November 1985.

WEST WORLD

This area is the northeast face of **Iguana Dome.** From the mill, continue northeast along a wash, then north along the east side of the dome. This area can also be approached by walking east from the **Hook and Ladder Area.** The identifying landmark is a striking overhanging, thin, "creatively" pin-scarred crack called **Stingray.** The other routes are all left of this crack.

926C SOUL KITCHEN   5.11a   This is a two-bolt face climb which comes in from the left and ends at a bolted belay. FA: T. Thompson, T. Dorton, D. LeWinter and Mike Paul, March 1988.

The following three routes can be approached by climbing a 5.10 crack left of **Stingray,** or by climbing up easy terrain left of the crack.

926D BOOT HILL   5.10a   A two-bolt climb on the left, ending at a bolt belay. FA: Paul Borne.

926E PALE RIDER   5.11a   Climb the crack right of **Boot Hill.** There is one fixed pin. FA: Mike Paul and Paul Borne, April 1988.

926F FEAR IS NEVER BORING   5.12a   This is a four-bolt climb that slants up and right, ending at the belay bolts atop **Stingray.** FA: Paul Borne, September 1988.

926G STINGRAY   5.13 +   This has been called one of the hardest cracks in the country, maybe *the* hardest. The crack was aided with pitons prior to being freed to both clean and widen sections of the crack. Climb the overhanging thin crack, if you can. Modern protection devices essential (or a top-rope). FA: Mike Paul (TR), May 1988; Hidetaka Suzuki (lead), June 1988.

WAY GONE DOME

927 CRYSTAL VOYAGER   5.11   This route now goes free. FFA: unknown.

927A AIR CRACK   5.6   This route climbs near the left arete of **Way Gone Dome,** as viewed in the photo on page 270. FA: Craig Fry and Kelly Gaynes, April 1988.

LOW MOTIVATION DOME

This is a large formation on the eastern edge of the Wonderland of Rocks, sitting near the hillside that rises up towards the summit of Queen Mountain. It is easily seen from many of the summits in the central Wonderland, as well as from the base of the east faces of the **Astro Domes.** It can be approached by walking up the canyon right (south) of **Nomad Dome,** or from the **Hook and Ladder Area.** It is discernible by several cracks that slant up and left across its large, light-colored west face. One route is known.

927B HEAD, ABDOMEN, THORAX   5.9 A2   This mixed two-pitch route goes up somewhere near the middle of the west face. Look for bolts (there are two of them on the route). FA: Dave Evans and Marge Floyd, February 1986.

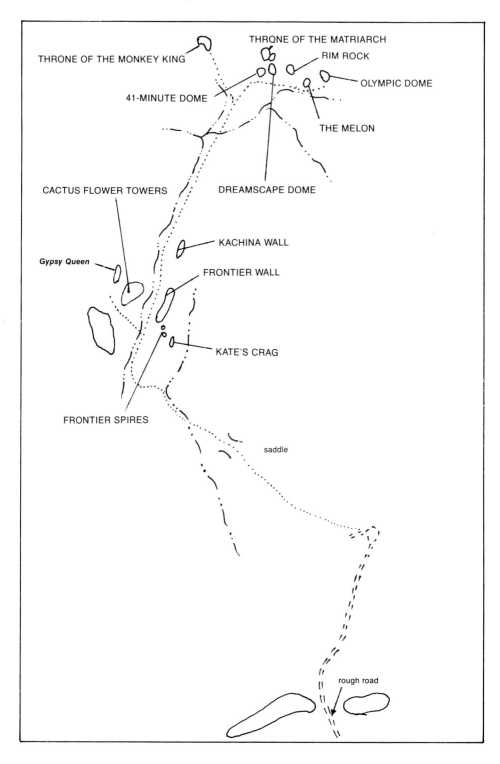

QUEEN MOUNTAIN AREA

This newly-developed area lies about one mile west of the summit of Queen Mountain, and is plainly visible from the Hidden Valley vicinity as a series of dark-colored crags in the saddle down and left from the summit. From Hidden Valley, drive on the Big Horn Pass Road for about ¾ mile past the Wonderland Valley (Uncle Willie's) turnoff to a three-way fork. Take the left fork and follow it for about two miles as it curves around to the north and heads straight for Queen Mountain. The road continues up and over a saddle between some small hills. This part is rough and rocky and good vehicle clearance is desirable, though 4-wheel drive is not really necessary. Park about ½ mile past the saddle, at the base of Queen Mountain. See map, page 54.

THE HAPPY HUNTING GROUND

Walk west-northwest from the parking area up a hillside and over an obvious saddle to reach a wash which curves to the right (north). Follow the wash for a short distance, then head up the rocky hillside to the left and enter a broad north-south running valley. Continue north about ¼ mile to reach the first of the formations. The routes are generally listed from right to left throughout this section, the manner in which they are approached. Map, supplement page 54.

KATE'S CRAG

This is a brown west-facing crag with two prominent cracks. Map, supplement page 54.

927C QUEEN FOR A DAY 5.7 Climb the buttress right of the cracks, starting off a boulder. FA: Alan Bartlett and Kate Duke, May 1988.

927D LADY IN WAITING 5.5 The right crack. FA: Kate Duke and Alan Bartlett, May 1988.

927E TAR FACE 5.10b (TR) The face just left of **Lady in Waiting.** FA: Rob Stahl, Dave Stahl and Craig Fry, April 1988.

927F IT'S NEVER ROBOT CITY 5.10d (TR) Arete left of **Tar Face.** FA: Rob Stahl, Dave Stahl and Craig Fry, April 1988.

927G QUEEN BEE 5.6 The left crack. FA: Kate Duke and Alan Bartlett. May 1988.

FRONTIER SPIRES

These are two pointed formations about 100 yards northwest of Kate's Crag.

927H ROCKET MAN 5.5 This climbs a crack on the backside of the smaller, lower spire. FA: Todd Battey, Dave Evans, Rob Stahl, Dave Stahl, Paul Binding, Jim Angione and Tom Burke, April 1988.

927I HOMO ERECTUS 5.6 Climb the upper spire from the notch. FA: Todd Battey and Dave Stahl, June 1988.

FRONTIER WALL

This long, northwest-facing wall is just north of the Frontier Spires. The routes are generally of high quality. Map, supplement page 54.

927J PROM QUEEN 5.9 A right-facing book containing a wide crack on the far right side of the wall. FA: Alan Bartlett and Kate Duke, May 1988.

927K THE CONUNDRUM 5.11c Left of **Prom Queen,** this is a left-slanting crack system with a difficult start. FA: Todd Battey and Todd Gordon, August 1988.

927L JUST DRIVE, SHE SAID 5.10b Around and left from the previous routes, this is a deceptively easy-looking offwidth/chimney in a large left-facing book. FA: Dave Evans and Dave Stahl, May 1988.

927M METTLE DETECTOR 5.11a This starts from a tree left of **Just Drive, She Said** and climbs into a small dihedral, then moves up and left to join **Forbidden Zone** near the top. FA: Todd Battey and Todd Gordon, August 1988.

927N FORBIDDEN ZONE 5.11b Just left of the preceding route, this climbs past a pin and fixed nut before moving right, then back left to the top. FA: Dave Evans, Rob Stahl and Todd Battey, May 1988.

927O MEATLOCKER 5.11b The next route left, this starts in a V-slot leading to a thin crack. FA: Dave Stahl and Dave Evans, May 1988.

927W 927V 927U

927R 927Q 927O 927N 927L 927K

Photo: Todd Battey

927P SNAKE BITE   5.11c   Just left of **Meatlocker,** this crack starts thin and goes through varying sizes before passing a roof near the top. FA: Todd Battey and Dave Stahl, June 1988.

927Q RITES OF PASSAGE   5.11a   This is a long left-facing dihedral with several fixed pins, left of the previous route. FA: Todd Battey and Dave Stahl, April 1988.

927R DELUSIONS   5.10c   A wide crack left of **Rites Of Passage.** FA: Dave Evans and Dave Stahl, May 1988.

927S GORDOBA   5.10d   About 150 feet left of **Delusions,** this is a right-slanting overhanging hand crack. FA: Todd Gordon, Alan Bartlett and Pat Brennan, May 1988.

927T KISS ME WHERE I PEE   5.9   Left of **Gordoba,** face climbing leads to a ramp and a corner. FA: Pat Brennan, Todd Gordon, Jim Angione, Dave Evans and Alan Bartlett, May 1988.

927U GNATTY DREAD   5.9   Left of the preceding route, this climbs a left-facing book and goes left around a flake/roof. FA: Alan Bartlett, Pat Brennan, Jim Angione and Todd Gordon, May 1988.

927V LAND OF WONDER   5.10c   Start behind a yucca bush left of the previous routes and climb an overhanging thin crack leading to a slab. FA: Todd Gordon, Dave Evans, Pat Brennan, Jim Angione and Alan Bartlett, May 1988.

927W QUEEN MOTHER'S ROUTE   5.2   This is an obvious right-slanting break in the wall left of **Land Of Wonder.** It is somewhat loose. FA: Alan Bartlett and Kate Duke, May 1988.

927X MAN FROM GLAD   5.10d   This is a three-bolt variation start to **Glad Hander.** FA: Dave Evans et al, May 1988.

927Y GLAD HANDER   5.9   The dogleg hand crack on the very left end of the wall. FA: Dave Evans, Tom Burke and Todd Battey, May 1988.

Dave Stahl and the Cactus Flower Towers

Photo: Todd Battey

CACTUS FLOWER TOWERS

These are two large formations west of and across the valley from the Frontier Wall. The existing routes are all on the steep west sides of the towers. Map, supplement page 54.

927Z THE ORGAN GRINDER 5.10b This and the following route are on the larger, southwest tower. This route climbs a wildly overhanging crack system. FA: Todd Battey and Dave Stahl, April 1988.

927AA THE PILGRIM 5.11a Left of **The Organ Grinder,** climb a prominent overhanging dihedral. FA: Rob Stahl, Dave Stahl, Karl Doerstling, Jim Angione, Todd Battey, Dave Evans and Craig Fry, April 1988.

927BB THE FLANGE 5.11a (TR) This is a steep face on the northwest tower, finishing left of a crack. FA: Dave Stahl, Rob Stahl, Dave Evans, Todd Battey and Jim Angione, April 1988.

927CC GYPSY QUEEN 5.9 This route lies on a small west-facing wall to the northwest of the **Cactus Flower Towers.** Climb a zig-zag crack leading up into a right-facing book. FA: Alan Bartlett and Kate Duke, May 1988.

Photo: Todd Battey

KACHINA WALL
Continue walking north past the Frontier Wall for several hundred yards to reach this west-facing light-colored slabby face. Map, supplement page 54.

927DD THE RIGHT STUFF   5.10c   On a brown wall up and right (south) from the main Kachina Wall, this is a straight-in crack left of a curving, left-facing corner. FA: Todd Battey and Dave Stahl, June 1988.

927EE STEPPIN' OUT   5.10a   Cracks on the right side of the Kachina Wall. FA: Dave Stahl and Todd Battey, June 1988.

927FF KACHINA   5.10a   Cracks in the center of the wall which diagonal sharply left near the top. FA: Dave Stahl and Rob Stahl, May 1988.

THRONE OF THE MATRIARCH

DREAMSCAPE DOME

41-MINUTE DOME

927JJ

927II

927HH

Photo: Todd Battey

NORTH RIDGE OF QUEEN MOUNTAIN AREA

The remaining routes in this section are on crags on the southwest side of the ridge running northwest fron the summit area of Queen Mountain, approached by continuing past the Frontier Wall for about ¾ mile. It should take about 20 minutes to reach **41-Minute Dome,** the closest of the formations. The formations and routes are listed from left to right throughout this section. Map, supplement page 54.

THRONE OF THE MONKEY KING

This is the farthest northwest (left) of the crags, reached by turning left from the main approach valley a short distance before reaching **41-Minute Dome.** Map, supplement page 54.

   927GG MONKEY KING   5.10a   Ascend the left branch of the jam crack to the right of the prominent corner on the south face of the crag. FA: Dave Stahl and Todd Battey, June 1988.

THRONE OF THE MATRIARCH

This is the northmost of several closely-spaced crags, plainly visible on the approach. Map, page 54.

   927HH RED SONJA   5.10c   On the southeast face, a finger and hand crack leads to a ledge. Continue up thin cracks and face on an arete. FA: Todd Battey, Dave Evans, Craig Fry, Dave Stahl and Jim Angione, August 1988.

41-MINUTE DOME

This is the western and smaller of two crags southeast of **Throne Of The Matriarch.** Map, page 54.

927II RAVING SKINHEAD 5.10c Face climb up to the crack on the south arete of the formation. FA: Dave Evans, Jim Angione, Rob Stahl, Craig Fry, Dave Stahl, Todd Battey and Paul Binding, August 1988.

DREAMSCAPE DOME

The larger, eastern of the two previously mentioned crags. Map, supplement page 54.

927JJ SPIRITWORLD 5.10c Climb a finger crack just left of the south arete, and continue up a left-slanting hand crack. FA: Dave Stahl and Todd Battey, June 1988.

RIM ROCK

This crag is east of **Dreamscape Dome,** and is hidden for most of the approach. Map, page 999.

927KK BROKEN CHINA 5.10b A 140-foot jam crack on the west face. FA: Craig Fry, Dave Stahl, Todd Battey, Rob Stahl, Dave Evans, Tom Burke and Jim Angione, August 1988.

THE MELON

Southeast of **Rim Rock,** and low on the hillside, this is a round dome with several vertical cracks. Map, supplement page 54.

927LL FRUITS OF LABOR 5.11+ (TR) On the south face, overhanging thin cracks lead to a right-slanting hand crack. FA: Todd Battey, August 1988.

927MM FRUIT FLY 5.10A On the southeast face, a tree start leads to a hand crack. FA: Todd Battey and Bob Roback, August 1988.

OLYMPIC DOME

East of The Melon, this is a large formation with a left-slanting crack on its west face. Map, supplement page 54.

927NN MATT BIONDI CHIMNEY 5.5 An obvious parallel-sided chimney right of the left-slanting crack. FA: Todd Gordon, September 1988.

927OO BODY SHAVING FOR COMPETITION 5.9 Right of **Matt Biondi Chimney** is this crack line with loose rock at the start. FA: Todd Gordon, Jim Angione, Dave Evans, Craig Fry and Tom Burke, September 1988.

927PP ICON 5.10c This is a beautiful hand crack right of the previous routes, on the south side of the formation. FA: Dave Evans, Todd Gordon, Todd Battey, Tom Burke, Jim Angione and Craig Fry, September 1988.

THE DAKOTA DOMES

These two small rocks sit in the desert west of the **Herman Rocks.** The **Herman Rocks** are misdescribed in the guide, and actually sit against the hillside north of the **Comic Book Area,** east of the trail leading to the **Comic Book Area,** if one is coming from the Bighorn Pass Road. Some climbers have stumbled upon the **Dakota Domes,** thinking they were the **Herman Rocks.** The *north* rock is **South Dakota Dome** and the *south* rock is **North Dakota Dome,** to add to the confusion.

SOUTH DAKOTA DOME

929A NOT WORTH YOUR WHILE   5.5   On the south face, this is a dogleg crack containing a bush. FA: David Estey and Gene West, December 1986.

NORTH DAKOTA DOME

929B NORTH DAKOTA BIG WALL PROBLEM   5.10   This is the right of two cracks on the north face. FA: West and Estey, December 1986.

929C MAYBE BABY   5.5   Climb the center crack on the south face. FA: West, Estey and Sherry Chandler, December 1986.

929D SOUTH END OF A NORTHBOUND POODLE   5.8   This climb is to the right of *Maybe Baby.* FA: West and Estey, December 1986.

COMIC BOOK AREA

939A COMBINATION LOCKS   5.11b   Climb the thin crack just left of *Alice in Wonder-jam.* There is one bolt at the start. FA: Jonny Woodward and Darrel Hensel, November 1986.

941A EDCHADA   5.7   This is a thin crack just left of *Urine Trouble.* FA: Bob Gaines and Mark Bowling, February 1988.

946A BRAIN DAMAGE   5.12a   This is a crack and face climb to the right of *Brain Death,* with one bolt. FA: Jonny Woodward and Darrel Hensel, January 1987.

WATERGATE ROCK

950A PARDON ME   5.9   Climb the face left of *White Collar Crime* past one bolt. FA: Todd Swain, Allen Steck, Steve Roper and John Thackray, December 1988.

953A POLITICAL ASYLUM   5.7   This route climbs the outer face of the boulder right of *H.R. Hardman. Fifteen Minute Gap* chimneys behind this boulder. Starting off a block, climb past one bolt to the top. FA: Todd Gordon and Cyndie Bransford, September 1988.

953B T-N-T   5.10c   Right of *Political Asylum,* on the right side of the boulder is this four-bolt face climb. FA: Gordon, Bransford, Jim Angione, Tom Beck and Tom Atherton, September 1988.

954 DIRTY TRICKS   This route has had a valid lead. Jonny Woodward and Darrel Hensel, November 1986.

The next three routes are on the north side of the *Deja Vu* pinnacle, around and left of that route.

954A PARANETIEUM   5.8   Climb the disjointed cracks on the left side. FA: Todd Swain, Allen Steck, Steve Roper and John Thackray, December 1988.

954B SHIRLEY MaCLAINE MEETS EDLINGER   5.9   Just right of the previous route, climb past a bolt to a short, varnished dihedral. FA: Swain, Steck, Roper and Thackray, December 1988.

954C DAZE OF WHO   5.10a   Down and right from the preceding route, climb to a bolt 25 feet up. Move right over a bulge, then back up left to the top. FA: Swain, Steck, Roper and Thackray, December 1988.

ASTEROID BELT

Left of *Asteroid Crack* are three short cracks.

956A KILOBYTE   5.11a   The left crack, steep fingers. FA: Alan Nelson and Tom Herbert, December 1986.

956B MEGABYTE   5.11a (TR)   The center crack, also steep fingers. FA: Nelson and Herbert, December 1986.

956C COSMIC BOOK   5.10c   The right crack, an overhanging corner. FA: Nelson and Herbert, December 1986.

CAP ROCK AREA

958A BEAVER BOULDER FREE ROUTE 5.10+ This is a one-bolt climb to the right of *Lost Lid,* starting with a step-across from an adjoining boulder. FA: Mike Lechlinski, Mari Gingery, John Long, Todd Gordon, Cyndie Bransford et al.

960A RETIREMENT 5.10a Climb thin cracks to a face with two bolts just left of *Nutcracker.* FA: Todd Gordon and Dan Hugglestein, September 1987.

962A BUSH EVICTION 5.9 This is the crack on the arete just left of *False Layback.* FA: Tom Michael and Michael Harrington, December 1986.

963A FALSE PROPHET 5.9+ Start right of *False Layback* and undercling a flake up and left until one can make a difficult step left to meet *False Layback* near the top. FA: unknown.

963B BLACK ICE 5.10b Start at the same place as *False Prophet* and climb straight up past one bolt. Runout. FA: Bob Gaines and Brian Prentice, October 1985.

964A HORROR-ZONTAL TERROR-VERSE 5.10b This follows the horizontal crack which crosses *The Ayatollah* from left to right. There is one bolt. The route joins the last moves of *Circus, Circus.* FA: Herb Laegar, Vaino Kodas and Andy Brown, October 1986.

964B CIRCUS, CIRCUS 5.9 Climb the ramp 20 feet left of *Circus,* finishing with a few steep mives. FA: Bob Gaines and Rebecca Foster, October 1985.

967A SLIMMER PICKINS 5.10d This climb is just right of *Slim Pickins* and passes four bolts. FA: Herb Laegar and Eve Laegar, December 1986.

967B NOSE TO THE GRINDSTONE 5.11a Climb easy rock right of *Slimmer Pickens* to a very thin crack with one or two fixed pins. Take RP's or equivalent. FA: Mark Spencer and Shirley Spencer (TR), 1986. Dave Evans, Todd Gordon and Fred Ziel (lead), January 1988.

967C THE TERMINATOR 5.9 Third class up the chimney right of *Nose to the Grindstone,* then follow five bolts leading almost straight right, then up. FA: Herb Laegar and Jan McCollum, November 1984.

967D ROBOCOP 5.7+ Climb to the first bolt on *The Terminator,* then go straight up past three more bolts. FA: Jeff Rhoades and Kate Ridgeway, April 1988.

967E DUNCE CAP 5.13a This is an overhanging bolted climb below and right of *The Terminator.* FA: Kurt Smith, March 1988.

967F HEY TAXI 5.11a Climb the right-spiralling crack right of *Dunce Cap.* FA: Charles Cole, Todd Gordon and Herb Laegar, December 1985.

969A CATCH A FALLING CAR 5.10c This is a direct start to the upper section of *Catch a Falling Star,* with one bolt. FA: Andy Brown and Lotus Steele, April 1987.

969B TUMBLING DICE 5.10a Climb the face right of *Catch a Falling Car* with one bolt. FA: Dave Kozak and Linda Pritchett, May 1987.

South of **Cap Rock,** the nature trail passes between rock formations.

969C METEORITE CRACK 5.10c This is a striking thin hands crack on the left formation FA: John Yablonski, 1980.

969D TWEENERS OUT FOR GLORY 5.6 Right of the *Meteorite Crack* are two cracks. This is the right one. FA: David Kozak and Linda Pritchett, May 1987.

THE RABBIT WARREN

The following routes are on two boulders south off the nature trail past the previous two routes.

969E HEARTBREAK RIDGE 5.8 Climb past two bolts on the north side of the larger boulder. FA: Ben Chapman, Sue Ann Murray and Warren Mellinger, January 1986.

969F 24 CARROT 5.8 This is a finger crack just right of the preceding route. FA: Todd Gordon, Kathy Boyd and Brian Sillasen, June 1986.

969G MR. BUNNY MEETS THE EXPANDO FLAKE 5.10b (TR) On the back of this formation is a lieback up an expanding flake. FA: Todd Swain, March 1988.

969H LITTLE BUNNY FU-FU 5.7 Climb past two bolts on the southeast arete of the smaller, eastern boulder. FA: Todd Swain, Peggy Buckey, Sara Batelle and Bunny Ingalls, March 1988.

969I MR. BUNNY GOES ROLLERSKATING 5.9 (TR) This is the face right of *Little Bunny Fu-Fu,* starting with a hard mantel move. FA: Swain and Buckey, March 1988.

THE MOLAR
This is the formation containing the route *Up 40.*
    970A TOOTH DECAY   5.11   Climb the northeast arete of the boulder past one bolt. FA: Mike Lechlinski, Mari Gingery, Tom Gilje and John Yablonski, January 1988.

WALLY WORLD
This crag is approached by driving towards Keys View from **Cap Rock.** Park at the first large turnout on the left, about one mile from the **Cap Rock** intersection. **Wally World** is the leftmost of several crags on the hillside about ¼ mi. left (east) of the road. Four routes have been reported.
    970B LARGE MARGE   5.7   This is a straight-in crack on the left of the formation, facing the road. FA: Marge Floyd and Todd Gordon, January 1988.
    970C FACE   5.11a (TR)   Climb the very short face above *Large Marge.* FA: Todd Gordon and Dave Evans, January 1988.
    970D DEVIL INSIDE   5.10c   Around the corner to the right of *Large Marge* is this two-bolt route up an overhanging knobby face. FA: Evans, Gordon and Jim Angione (TR). Evans and Craig Fry (lead), January 1988.
    970E WALLY GEORGE   5.9+   This climbs a large dihedral on the right side of the formation. The route cuts left at the very top. FA: Evans, Gordon and Angione, January 1988.

HEADSTONE ROCK
    980A HEADMASTER   5.12b (TR)   This climbs the north face of **Headstone Rock,** crossing the old bolt ladder from left to right. FA: Jonny Woodward, November 1987.
    980B HEADBANGERS' BALL   5.12   This is a four-bolt climb on the west face of **Headstone Rock.** It starts with a roof and finishes on the northwest corner. FA: Terry Ayers et al, 1988.

HALFWAY ROCKS
    984A BETTER YOU THAN ME   5.10b   This is a two-bolt face climb on orange rock up and right from *Ancient Future.* FA: Mark Uphus and Bill Cramer, March 1988.

SADDLE ROCKS AREA
    988A BRUSH YOUR TEETH WITH JESUS   5.10c   Left of the **Theoretical Boulder** is another boulder containing two routes. This is the right route and climbs thin cracks to a bolt. Above it, move left to a ramp/crack leading to the top. FA: Todd Gordon and Tom Beck, September 1988.
    988B BLIND MAN'S BLUFF   5.11c   Left of the previous route is this four-bolt climb. FA: Dave Griffith et al, December 1988.
    991A RAGING BULL DIKE   5.11d   Down and right from the start of *The Narwhal,* this climbs up an overhanging dike with four bolts, then continues up a finger and hand crack to end at the finish of *The Narwhal.* FA: Tom Herbert, Chris Snyder and Tracy Dorton, November 1988.
    991B KNOT AGAIN   5.9   This route is reported as starting 125 feet uphill from *R & R* in a left-leaning ramp system. It must go for at least two pitches, staying right of *Raging Bull Dike,* and end at the point where *The Narwhal* meets *Orange Flake.* FA: Hamilton Collins and Paul Kaplan, 1986.
    992A KID CALINGULA   5.10a   From the first bolt on *Orange Flake,* climb straight up past bolts to a belay in an undercling. The second pitch follows a thin crack up and right, then moves left to a bolt, then up to the upper ramp of *R & R.* FA: Parrish Robbins and Tom Beck, April 1988.
    994A BOSCH JOB   5.11d   This is a bolted two-pitch climb between *Right On* and *High Cost of Living.* FA: Jonny Woodward, Darrel Hensel and Maria Cranor, September 1988.

The following three routes are on the detatched slab right of **Walk on the Wild Side.**

999A THE KID   5.9   Climb the left side of the slab past bolts. FA: Kurt Smith and Dave Hatchett.

999B THE LANDLORD   5.10d   This route up the center of the slab has many bolts. FA: Scott Cosgrove, March 1988.

999C THE RENTER   5.9   Climb the crack right of **The Landlord** and join that route for its last four bolts. FA: Cosgrove and Kevin Bell, April 1988.

1000 MONEY FOR NOTHING   5.12a   This route, formerly known as **A2**, now goes free. FFA: Scott Cosgrove (TR), June 1986. Tom Herbert (lead), April 1988.

1000A CHICKS FOR FREE   5.12b   This climbs the left arete of the small brown blocky formation left of **Money For Nothing** past three bolts. FA: Skip Guerin (TR), May 1986. Kurt Smith (lead), April 1988.

1000B WALK ON THE STEEP SIDE   5.10   To the right of **Money for Nothing** is this steep, 50-foot route with three bolts. FA: Herb Laegar and Andy Wall, October 1987.

COWBOY CRAGS

1007A THE UNBEARABLE LIGHTNESS OF BEING   5.9   Climb a J-shaped crack on the buttress 100 feet left of **Cling Peaches.** FA: Bob Gaines and Bruce Christle, March 1988.

1008 BABY FAE   This route should be rated 5.11a.

HALL OF HORRORS

1013A CACTUS FLOWER   5.11+   This is a three-bolt climb just right of **Lazy Day,** leading to the upper crack of **Perhaps.** FA: Troy Mayr and Charles Cole, February 1988.

1013B MY SENIOR PROJECT   5.9+   Up and right from **Cactus Flower** is this two-bolt route, starting out of the wide crack on the right. FA: Todd Gordon and Deanne Gray, May 1987.

1013C FLASH GORDON   5.7   Right of **My Senior Project,** climb a crack, then continue up to the top of the summit block. FA: Todd Gordon, et al.

1017 GLUMPIES   This route is misdrawn in the guide. It is around the corner to the right, much closer to **Grit Roof,** and not really visible in either of the photos on page 297. It climbs a dihedral with a wide crack narrowing to hands.

1017A UNGAWAA   5.11b   Climb the arete with two bolts right of where **Glumpies** is shown (wrongly) in the guide. FA: Troy Mayr and Curt Lyons, April 1988.

1019A GUARDIAN ANGELS   5.10a   This route is located in a small alcove 100 feet southeast of **Zardoz** and climbs past four bolts on a steep face. FA: Larry Kuechlin Jr. and Cory Zinngrabe, October 1988.

1020A BUNNIES   5.12 (TR)   This is the face between **Zardoz** and **Lickety Splits.** FA: Troy Mayr, April 1988.

1023 DOUBLE JEOPARDY   This route is misdrawn in the guide. It is left of where shown, and starts by clipping a bolt, then traversing left along a ramp/ledge. From the ramp's end, climb up past two more bolts. This route has a potentially bad fall for the follower as well as the leader.

1030A LOVE GODDESS   5.12c   This is a four-bolt climb on the north side of the block between **What** and **Aero Space.** FA: Troy Mayr and Rob Mulligan, November 1988.

1030B LA CHOLLA   5.13a   On the west side of the block is this eight-bolt climb. FA: Mayr, November 1988.

1035A SEARCH FOR KLINGONS   5.7   Climb the face left of **Hemroidic Terror** past two bolts. FA: unknown.

1036A RINGS AROUND URANUS   5.7   Climb a curving hand crack to a face with one bolt right of **Hemroidic Terror.** FA: Todd Swain, Peggy Buckey and Tad Welch, March 1986.

1036B HUECO WALL   5.5   This is the pocketed face 40 feet right of the preceding route. FA: Swain, March 1986.

1037A SHAKING HANDS WITH THE UNEMPLOYED   5.10b   This climb is a short distance left of **Jessica's Crack,** and has two bolts. FA: Andy Brown and Jeff Rhodes, April 1987.

REAL HALL OF HORRORS

This is the narrow corridor behind *Jessica's Crack*, best entered through a narrow opening at the south end of the formation, about 200 feet left of *Jessica's Crack*. There are four reported routes, two on each side of the corridor.

1039 FIRST ELEVEN This route is mislocated in the guide; it is approached from the left of *Jessica's Crack*. Walking into the **Real Hall of Horrors,** it is the most obvious crack on the right wall, about 100 feet inside the corridor.

1039A GOOD INVESTMENT 5.12 (TR) Right of *First Eleven*, climb a steep face to two overhanging cracks. Variations exist. FA: Vaino Kodas and Larry Siebold, November 1987.

1039B NO OPTIONS 5.11b Across the corridor from *Good Investment* is this three-bolt route, whose difficulty is belittled by the fact that one can chimney/bridge off the back wall during the crux. Done this way, the route warrants a 5.8/9 rating. FA: Vaino Kodas, Herb Laegar and Bob Kamps, November 1987.

1039C ROUTE RIGHT OF THE DUMBEST CLIMB IN THE MONUMENT 5.10+ Right of *No Options* and across from *First Eleven,* is this steep thin crack. FA: Todd Gordon and Parrish Robbins, April 1988.

HALL OF HORRORS – WEST WALL (West Face)

1043 PULLUPS TO PASADENA This route is misdrawn in the guide; it is about 20 feet right of where shown, and passes by the right end of the lower horizontal crack.

KING DOME

1047A MAGIC KINGDOM 5.8 This is a one-bolt face climb about 50 feet right of *Trashman Roof.* FA: Todd Swain, Peggy Buckey and Tad Welch, March 1986.

CAVE CORRIDOR

1047B WAIT UNTIL DARK 5.10b This route is on the formation *very* near the road at the east exit of the **Cave Corridor** parking lot. Climb a left-facing corner past two bolts. FA: Todd Gordon and Reggie Thomson, October 1988.

1056A SHIFTING SANDS 5.11b This is a two-bolt climb on the east face of a boulder facing the route *Chocolate Chips.* There is no belay on top; downclimb the back side and belay from a tree on the ground. FA: Jonny Woodward, Darrel Hensel, Rob Raker and Dave Bruckman, January 1988.

1057A OMAHA BEACH 5.8 This is an old two-bolt climb about 50 feet left of *Caramel Crunch.* FA: unknown.

1057B PEANUT BRITTLE 5.8 (TR) Start 20 feet left of *Omaha Beach* and climb a flake, then up face to the top. FA: Todd Swain and Peggy Buckey, November 1987.

1059A POX ON YOU 5.11d Climb the face between *Rocky Road* and *Whipped Topping* (Route #1060). There are three bolts. FA: Jonny Woodward and Darrel Hensel, November 1986.

SHEEP PASS CAMPGROUND

WAILING SAX WALL

This wall is the back side (west face) of the **Timeless Void Clump.** It is approached by scrambling up the gully behind campsite #2. Going up this gully, one passes *Sanctify Yourself* (route 1068A) on your right and *Ripples in Time* (route 1068) on your left. The **Wailing Sax Wall** is just over the notch at the top of the gully, on one's left. The guide listed two routes here, *Holy Cross* (route1066) and *Tipples in Rime* (route 1067). They were listed from right to left; this guide will list the routes from left to right, which is why the numbers decrease.

1067 TIPPLES IN RIME The guide gave erroneous information about this route; it should have read "Thirty feet left of *Holy Cross*". This is a top-rope problem on the extreme left end of the **Wailing Sax Wall.** It is just left of a route with a bolt.

1067A WAILING SAX 5.9 Ten feet right of *Tipples in Rime* climb discontinuous cracks over a roof and past one bolt. FA: Dimitri, January 1988.

1067B JO MAMA 5.8 This is the crack just right of *Wailing Sax.* FA: Bruce Morris, January 1988.

1066 HOLY CROSS   5.10b   The next crack right of *Jo Mama,* very thin over a tricky roof.

1066A THE MORNING AFTER   5.8   The next crack right, going over the same roof as *Holy Cross.* It is also thin and zigzags. FA: Michael Harrington, January 1988.

1066B TAKE FIVE   5.8   This is the main system on the wall, thin to double cracks through a bulge. FA: Dimitri, January 1988.

1066C IN A SILENT WAY   5.11c   This climb is right of *Take Five,* and passes five bolts. FA: David Rubine and Russell Revenaugh, January 1988.

1066D MAIDEN VOYAGE   5.10a   Down and right from *In a Silent Way,* climb past four bolts into a crack. FA: David Rubine and Rich McDonald, January 1988.

1066E CAROLA'S HIP   5.7   This is a wide crack just right of *Maiden Voyage.* FA: Bill Goyette, January 1988.

1066F MISHA'S MADNESS   5.9+ (TR)   Climb the shallow crack immediately right of *Carola's Hip.* FA: Michael Bostick, Januery 1988.

1066G FLAKEY PUFFS FROM HELL   5.10 (TR)   A short, steep corner leads to face climbing just right of *Misha's Madness.* FA: Bill Goyette, Januery 1988.

1066H BIRDLAND   5.10c   This is a roof crack forty feet right of *Flakey Puff from Hell.* FA: David Rubine and Rich McDonald, Januery 1988.

1066I SATCHMO   5.8   This climb ascends cracks on the face right of the corner next to *Birdland.* FA: Bruce Morris and Michael Harrington, Januery 1988.

To the right of the **Wailing Sax Wall** is a small tower with two top-rope routes.

1066J SMALL TOWN TASTE   5.10c (TR)   This route follows a left-facing corner to a crack. FA: Harrington and Morris, January 1988.

1066K ONE STORY TOWN   5.10 (TR)   Climb the face/arete right of the preceding route. FA: Harrington and Morris, January 1988.

Across from the **Wailing Sax Wall** are three cracks.

1066L AULD LANG SYNE   5.8   This is a crack around the corner to the left of *New Year's Quickie.* FA: Harrington and Morris, January 1988.

1066M NEW YEAR'S QUICKIE   5.7   This is an obvious hand crack. FA: Phil Kline, January 1988.

1066N SKIN DEEP TOWN   5.6   This is a crack system on a pinnacle to the right of *New Year's Quickie.* FA: Rich Turner, January 1988.

1068A SANCTIFY YOURSELF   5.9   This is a two-bolt face climb on the right side of the approach gully to the **Wailing Sax Wall,** about ⅔ of the way up the gully. FA: David Rubine and Rich McDonald, January 1988.

1071A EVENING WARM-DOWN   5.2   This is a crack left of *Hob Nob.* FA: Roger Linfield and Steve Unwin, April 1987.

1072A SMALL WORLD   5.8   Across the road from the entrance to Sheep Pass Campground is a small, black, east-facing buttress. This route climbs a finger to hand crack on the buttress. FA: Brian Sillasen, February 1988.

GEOLOGY TOUR ROAD

ROCKY MARCIANO

1073A DIGITIZER 5.11b This is a clean, overhanging fingertip dihedral in the boulders at the southeast corner of the **Rocky Marciano** clump. FA: Alan Nelson and Tom Herbert, December 1986.

ISLAND IN THE STREAM

This formation is about ½ mile due west of **Rocky Marciano.** The routes are on the north face.

1073B MESSAGE IN A BOTTLE 5.10c The leftmost line, this route has three bolts. FA: Troy Mayr, Ed Hunsaker and Steve Anderson, February 1988.

1073C MIDDLE OF SOMEWHERE 5.12a This is the direct (left) finish to *Message in a Bottle.* FA: Mayr, February 1988.

1073D ADRIFT 5.11b The next bolted line right, with four bolts. It joins *Message in a Bottle* for its regular finish. FA: Mayr, Anderson and Amy Sharpless, February 1988.

1073E SHARKS IN THE WATER 5.10c This is a two-bolt climb right of *Adrift.* FA: Mayr, Hunsaker and Anderson, February 1988.

1073F WHISPER WHEN YOU SCREAM 5.9 The farthest route right, this climb has three bolts. FA: Mayr, et al, February 1988.

The next seven routes are found on several formations just west of the road about ¼ mile north of the parking area for **Rocky Marciano.**

CROWS' NEST

This is the northmost crag, closest to the road.

1073G TRENCH CONNECTION 5.6 This is the left of two obvious cracks on the formation, and leads into a chimney. FA: Ed Hunsaker, Troy Mayr, Steve Anderson, Amy Sharpless, Posey and Doque, February 1988.

1073H NO STRINGS ATTACHED 5.6 This is the right obvious crack. FA: Mayr, February 1988.

REEF ROCK

This formation is west of the **Crows' Nest.**

1073I TRAIL OF TIERS 5.10a On the northeast side of the rock is this obvious tiered face. FA: Mayr, February 1988.

LAVA DOME

This crag is south and slightly west of **Reef Rock.**

1073J NOTHING TO FEAR 5.6 This is the left most crack on the west face. FA: Mayr, Anderson, Sharpless and Hunsaker, February 1988.

1073K BUT FEAR ITSELF 5.8 Climb the crack right of the previous route. FA: Mayr, Anderson, Sharpless and Hunsaker, February 1988.

1073L HOT FLASHES 5.11c Right of the two previous cracks, this climb has two bolts. FA: Mayr, February 1988.

1073M STANDING OVATION 5.9+ Right of the previous routes, this climb is on the south face of **Lava Dome.** FA: Mayr, Sharpless, Anderson and Hunsaker, February 1988.

SKYSCRAPER ROCK

This formation is 100 feet northeast of **Jerry's Quarry.**

1073N CROSS FIRE 5.12a This is a three-bolt climb leading to a rap anchor. FA: Troy Mayr and Charles Cole, January 1988.

1073O THE RUSTLER 5.11+ Right of *Cross Fire,* an undercling leads to face climbing. FA: Tom Gilje, Mike Lechlinski and Mari Gingery, January 1988.

JERRY'S QUARRY

1074A TO HOLD AND TO HAVE 5.12+ (TR) Around the corner to the right of **Ali Shuffle** is a chimney. To the right of this is a short buttress with a thin crack on its right edge which doesn't quite reach the top. This is the route. FA: John Reyher and Kevin Thaw, March 1988.

1074B ZEN AND THE ART OF PLACEMENT 5.11c This climbs the next crack right of the previous route. FA: Thaw and Reyher, March 1988.

1074C SPANK THE MONKEY 5.10b This is a slab and overhang climb right of the preceding route, finishing up the left edge above the overhang. FA: Thaw and Reyher, March 1988.

1074D IGOR'S FAILED ROAD TRIP 5.11a Climb the blunt arete and slab right of **Spank the Monkey.** FA: Thaw and Reyher, March 1988.

1074E TOFFIED EAR WAX 5.9 This climbs a slab left of the **Equinox** formation. FA: Thaw and Reyher, March 1988.

1074F ELEPHANT WALK 5.11+ Climb the arete 40 feet left of **Equinox** past five bolts. FA: Mari Gingery, Tom Gilje, John Yablonski and Mike Lechlinski, January 1988.

1075A HUEVOS RANCHEROS 5.10 On the first small group of rocks southeast of **Equinox,** this is a hand traversing face climb going up and right. FA: John Yablonski, February 1988.

VIRGIN ISLANDS AREA

1077A WOODWARD CRACK 5.12a Climb the obvious crack just left of the **Lechlinski Cracks** and continue up the face past a bolt. FA: Jonny Woodward, November 1987.

1079A VOGEL CRACK 5.8 This is a crack right of and around the corner from **Waugh Crack.** The top of the crack can be seen in the top photo on page 312 just left of where **S Crack** (route #1079) is shown. FA: Randy Vogel, November 1987.

THE VOLCANO AREA

1084A FRAT BOYS IN THE GYM 5.11b (TR) This climbs the overhanging south face of the formation containing **Krakatoa** (route #1084). FA: Paul Schweizer and Tim Wagner.

1087A NO NUTS, NO HUEVOS 5.9 This is located on the south side of the formation on the west side of the pass that splits **The Volcano** clump. It is a five-bolt face leading to a rappel bolt. FA: Mark Wilson, Suzanne Wilson, Cory Zinngrabe and Larry Kuechlin, November 1988.

1087B THE GO-GO'S ON QUAALUDES 5.10c This route is directly north of **No Nuts, No Huevos.** It has five bolts and moves across an offwidth crack from left to right. FA: Mike Humphrey, Larry Kuechlin and Cory Zinngrabe, December 1988.

1087C SHARP DESIRE 5.8 Another five-bolt route on an east-facing wall on the southwest side of the pass that splits **The Volcano.** FA: Kuechlin, Zinngrabe and Brian Talbert, December 1988.

1088A DEFENDERS OF THE FARCE 5.10a Climb the northwest face of the **Human Sacrifice** boulder past one bolt. FA: Tim Wagner and Gerry Morgan, March 1987.

1088B DICTATORS OF ANARCHY 5.12c This route is located on the south arete of the **Human Sacrifice** boulder. FA: Tim Wagner and Paul Schweizer.

1091A THE CAT IN THE HAT 5.10a This is a steep three-bolt climb on a pillar 150 feet left of **Raker's Blaring Hat Rack.** FA: Brad Singer, Dave Evans, Craig Fry, Marge Floyd and Jim Angione, January 1988.

1091B CHOLLA CRACK 5.10b This is a short crack on the tier below **The Cat in the Hat.** FA: Fry, Singer and Evans, January 1988.

PERPETUAL MOTION AREA

1101A GEORGIA O'KEEFE 5.10b About 60 feet right of **Hoser** is a pillar lying against the face. This climbs the outer face of the pillar past three bolts. FA: Brandt Allen and Larry Cote, November 1987.

1102 LEFT ARCHIMEDES' CRACK This route should be rated 5.11a.

STAR WARS ROCK

1107A THE LEMMING 5.10d This climbs the arete across from **Apollo** via a steep layback and finishing with a mantel. FA: unknown, February 1988.

1109A TWO BLIND MICE 5.10 On the northeast face of the rock, this route ascends a flared bombay chimney leading to a hand crack. FA: Alan Roberts and Mark Dubé.

DIAMOND CLUMP

1114A JUST FOR THE THRILL OF IT 5.11a (TR) This climbs the face left of **Clearasil**. FA: David Larson, December 1987.

1116A RING OF FIRE 5.11b This route climbs a dike on a formation below **Centurion**. There are three bolts. FA: Troy Mayr.

EAST VIRGIN ISLANDS

HONE DOME

1119A KLEPTOMANIA 5.10a (TR) This climbs the right arete right of **No Holds Barred**. FA: Todd Gordon and Bryn Palmer, February 1987.

ORIENT ROCK

This formation is above and to the south of **Pac Man Rock.**

1138A GIVEN UP FOR DEAD 5.10d This is the slanting, overhanging crack on the north face of the rock. FA: Vaino Kodas and Greg Vernon, 1985.

1138B MISSING IN ACTION 5.10+ (TR) This is the crack splitting the east face. FA: Kodas and Vernon, 1985.

DESERT ISLAND

1143A RUMBLERS BELOW THE FOOF 5.3 This climbs an easy crack left of **Fumblers Below the Roof.** FA: Todd Gordon, Peggy Buckey, Cyndie Bransford and Dan Phillips, September 1987.

SQUAW TANK

Squaw Tank is located approximately 1¼ mile south of the **Virgin Islands** on the east side of the Geology Tour Road. A small parking area is located here.

1145A PICKPOCKET 5.6 On the left side looking east from the Squaw Tank parking area, is a wall of giant solution pockets. Climb this, with no protection. FA: Alan Nelson and Mike Beck, 1982.

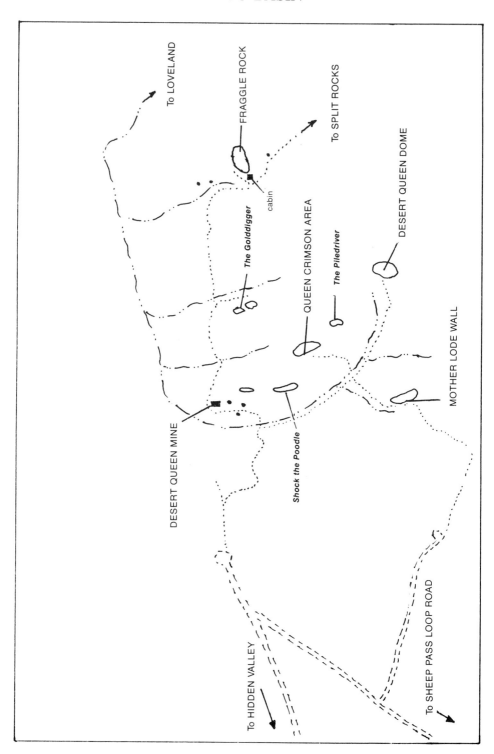

To LOVELAND

FRAGGLE ROCK

To SPLIT ROCKS

cabin

DESERT QUEEN DOME

The Golddigger

QUEEN CRIMSON AREA

The Piledriver

MOTHER LODE WALL

DESERT QUEEN MINE

Shock the Poodle

To HIDDEN VALLEY

To SHEEP PASS LOOP ROAD

DESERT QUEEN MINE AREA

The information given in the guide about this area was erroneous and has led to much confusion. The problem is that the six routes listed are not on one formation, but on two separate crags about ½ mile apart. Hopefully, this will help explain this complicated area which will undoubtedly see much more development in the future. Map, supplement page 70.

MOTHER LODE WALL

This wall is reached by following the approach driving descriptions given in the guide. From the car, continue up the road past a locked gate for about ¼ mile until this wall is seen off to the left, across a small valley.

1146 THIN IS IN 5.9 Climb a vertical thin crack on a slab left of the main west face.

1146A MY HUBBY IS CHUBBY 5.8+ Climb the slab 100 feet left of *Thin is In* past a bolt into a corner. FA: Todd Swain, Randy Schenkel amd Andy Schenkel, December 1988.

1146B LEAN AND SCREAM 5.10d (TR) This is a vertical series of dikes on the left side of a large corridor 50 feet left of *Thin is In*. FA: Eric Charlton, Don Wilson and Karen Wilson, November 1987.

1146C FAT IS WHERE IT'S AT 5.8 Climb the crack just right of the chimney right of *Thin is In*. FA: Todd Swain, Kip Knapp and Peggy Buckey, November 1987.

1147 MOTHER LODE 5.10b Right of the previous routes, climb a right-slanting dike to a bolt, then up a steep crack.

1147A AN UNRULY CAMEL 5.10/11 This is the face right of *Mother Lode* with four bolts. The move by the first bolt has not yet been freed; traversing in from the right to the second bolt avoids this A1 start. FA: Dave Evans, Marge Floyd and Brian Sillasen, October 1986.

DESERT QUEEN DOME

This is the large formation about ½ mile east of the **Mother Lode Wall.** It is one of the highest summits in the area, and is the location of guidebook routes #1148-#1151; their descriptions are applicable. It can be approached from the **Mother Lode Wall,** or from the Desert Queen Mine parking area. See map, supplement page 70.

DESERT QUEEN MINE AREA

The remaining routes in this section are best approached from the Desert Queen Mine parking area. This is best reached from Hidden Valley Campground by driving the Bighorn Pass Road past the Wonderland turnoff to a three-way fork and taking the middle fork to its end. It also can be reached by continuing on the dirt road past the **Mother Lode Wall** turnoff. See map. page 70.

1151A FREE FOR A FEE 5.10c This is a short thin crack somewhere above and to the right of the mine shafts. FA: Tim Wagner and Kevin Fosburg.

1151B SHOCK THE POODLE 5.9 In the wash 200 yards south of the first hole of the Desert Queen Mine is a large black face with several overhangs. This route follows a large dike slanting up and right. FA: Reggie Thomson and Mike Brown, winter 1985.

QUEEN CRIMSON AREA

The next five routes are on a cliff band on the hillside southeast of the previous climbs. Map, supplement page 70.

1151C NERVE STORM 5.11c On the steep left-most formation, a thin lieback leads to a left-facing corner and finishes with friction past one bolt. FA: Walt Shipley and Kevin Fosburg, March 1987.

1151D WALT'S SOLO 5.8 This is a fingercrack on the south face of a small dome above **Nerve Storm**. FA: Walt Shipley, March 1987.

1151E DIG ME 5.11b (TR) Climb the face right of **Walt's Solo** leading into small dihedrals. FA: Jordy Morgan and Kenim Fosburg, March 1987.

1151F SOFTWARE SLUTS 5.10c This is on a smooth face 150 feet right of **Nerve Storm** and climbs past a pin and two bolts. FA: Dave Bruckman, Don Wilson, Karen Wilson, Dave Evans and Jim Angione, December 1987.

1151G MANWICH QUEEN 5.8 Climb the face right of **Software Sluts** past three bolts. FA: Don Wilson and Karen Wilson, December 1987.

1151H QUEEN CRIMSON 5.10b This is a nice thin crack in brown rock about 200 feet right of the two previous routes. FA: Jordy Morgan, Kevin Fosburg, Walt Shipley and Karl Withak, March 1987.

The following route is located in a boulder pile about ¼ mile south of the **Queen Crimson Area.**

1151I THE PILEDRIVER 5.11+ This is an east-facing overhanging thin crack hidden in a corridor amidst the boulder pile. FA: Mike Paul.

The following routes in this section are all best approached by walking east (left and behind) from the Desert Queen Mine. Map, supplement page 70.

1151J SILVERADO 5.11b Turn right into the second wash east of the mine. This is a lieback on the north face of several small formations on the west side of the wash. FA: Mike Paul, 1987.

1151K THE GOLDDIGGER 5.10c This is a hand crack left of **Silverado,** on the east face of the formation. FA: Mike Paul, Dave Tucker, Chuck Tucker and D. Durban, 1987.

FRAGGLE ROCK

This is a large formation on a hillside about ½ mile east of the Desert Queen Mine. It has a slightly overhanging north face and there are some mine shafts and a miners' cabin below its west side. It could perhaps be approached as easily from the **Split Rocks** area. See map, page 70.

1151L THE STILL 5.10c This route is on the left side of the east face, and climbs a seam to a face with three bolts. FA: Vaino Kodas and Diana Leach, 1985.

1151M POPPIN' AND BREAKIN' 5.10a This is a bolted line on the right side of the east face. FA: Kodas and Leach, 1985.

1151N GIGANTOR 5.11b On the northeast side of the rock, ascend double thin cracks in an overhanging dihedral. FA: Mike Paul and Dave Tucker, 1987.

1151O PETRODYNAMICS 5.10d On the left side of the north face, this is an overhanging thin crack in a corner. FA: Kodas and Leach, 1985.

1151P TIERS FOR FEARS 5.10d 100 feet right of **Petrodynamics** is this three-tiered hand crack. FA: Kodas and Leach, 1985.

1151Q WUTHERING HEIGHTS 5.9 On the west side of the formation is this three-bolt route. FA: Kodas and Leach, 1985.

1151P SCATTERED REMAINS 5.11b Right of **Wuthering Heights,** this is a left-slanting crack. It is reportedly strenuous to protect. FA: Rob Robinson et al, fall 1988.

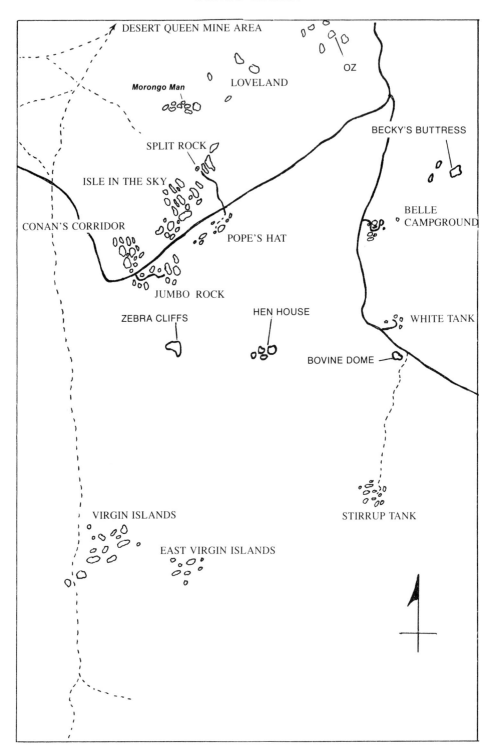

JUMBO ROCKS CAMPGROUND
SKY KING ROCK
This formation is almost directly east from the end of the campground loop.

1152A CHANCE MEETING 5.6 A3 This mostly-aid route climbs discontinous thin cracks on the right side of the west face of the rock, plainly visible form the end of the loop. There is a tension-traverse left at about ⅔ heught. Pitons necessary. FA: Robert Nichols and Ed Lahatt, March 1986.

1152B FLASHPOINT 5.11d This is a difficult thin crack left of **Chance Meeting.** FA: Jonny Woodward and Rob Raker, Januery 1987.

1152C THE FIRÉ GLOVE 5.10a Climb a flare 15 feet left of **Flashpoint.** FA: Charles Cole, Randy Vogel, Todd Gordon and Scott Gordon, March 1986.

NEW SAGE ROCK
This is the large formation 100 yards northeast of **Sky King Rock.** *Not a Hogan* (route #1152) is on the west face of this rock.

1152D AGAINST ALL TODDS 5.10c This is on the south face, around and right from **Not a Hogan.** Climb a crack above a bucketed face. FA: Todd Gordon, Charles Cole, Randy Vogel, Scott Gordon and Frank Bentwood, March 1986.

THE FRUIT CAKE
This is the wall/formation just east of **New Sage Rock.**

1152E GRAINY TRAIN 5.10c On the west side of the rock (the right side of the canyon between **New Sage Rock** and **The Fruit Cake**) is an obvious left-slanting crack leading to a roof. Surmout the roof via a hand crack. FA: Cole, Bentwood, Vogel, T. Gordon, Dave Evans and Marge Floyd, March 1986.

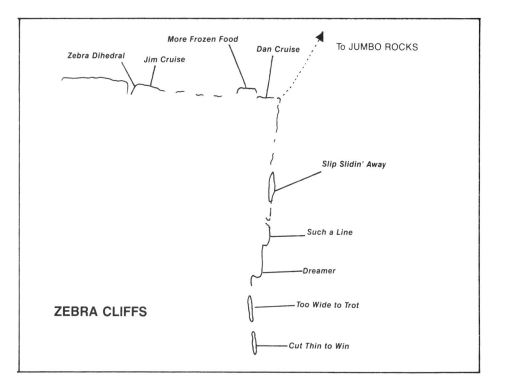

ZEBRA CLIFFS

HEN HOUSE

11700

Looking south from the summit of the Pope's Hat

ZEBRA CLIFFS

The **Zebra Cliffs** are a series of east- and north-facing cliffs about ½ mile southeast from Jumbo Rocks Campground. Walk southeast from the end of the campground, staying left of a hill. The cliffs will soon be seen on a hillside to the south as a band of dark rock with distinctive horizontal streaks. Approaching the cliffs, you should come in at the northeast corner of the formation. Half the routes are left, on east-facing cliffs, and half are to the right, on smaller north-facing cliffs. Maps, supplement pages 74, 75.

1156A CUT THIN TO WIN   5.10c   This is the farthest left (south) route, on a formation left of the main cliff. It is a distinct, right-slanting thin crack leading to a horizontal crack. FA: Mike Waugh and Will Chen, November 1986.

1156B TOO WIDE TO TROT   5.10c   Right of the preceding route, on a separate wall, is this crack with a wide start. FA: Waugh, November 1986.

1156C DREAMER   5.10d   Farther right, near the left side of the largest section of the cliff band, is this striking right-leaning crack. FA: Waugh and Chen, November 1986.

1156D UP AND DOWN   5.10a   This is a three-bolt climb down and right from *Dreamer.* FA: Waugh and Jim Mathews, November 1986.

1156E SUCH A LINE   5.10d   Right of *Up and Down* is this difficult-looking crack which splits and rejoins about halfway up. FA: Waugh and Mathews, November 1986.

1156F AROUND THE WORLD   5.8   This climb starts high in the gully right of *Such a Line,* and is best approached from above. Traverse left around a corner in a horizontal crack which curves upward after about 30 feet. FA: Waugh and Mathews, November 1986.

1156G SLIP SLIDIN' AWAY   5.10a   About 50 yards down and right from the previous routes is this four-bolt face climb that starts in very steep buckets. FA: Waugh and Mathews, December 1986.

The following six routes are on a short wall just right of the northeast corner of the formation, facing north.

    1156H CORNER N' CRACK   5.10a   Start on the left edge of the wall. Climb up, then right to reach a thin crack. FA: Waugh, Mathews and Dan Hershman, January 1987.

    1156I SHORT CRACK   5.10a   Start in the obvious central crack, then traverse left on a dike to reach a thin crack just right of the upper crack of **Corner n' Crack**. FA: Waugh, Mathews and Hershman, January 1987.

    1156J DAN CRUISE   5.7   Climb the obvious central crack/corner. FA: Dan Hershman, January 1987.

    1156K MRS. PAUL'S   5.9   Right of **Dan Cruise,** face climb up to a hand crack. FA: Waugh, Mathews and Hershman, January 1987.

    1156L FROZEN FISH FINGERS   5.9   This is another hand crack right of **Mrs. Paul's.** FA: Waugh, Mathews and Hershman, January 1987.

    1156M MORE FROZEN FOOD   5.9   Down and right from the previous routes, on the outer face of a block, climb a face to a crack. FA: Waugh, Mathews and Hershman, January 1987.

The next three routes are about 200 yards right of **More Frozen Food.**

    1156N JIM CRUISE   5.8   This route climbs a bucketed wall to a crack. FA: Mathews, Waugh and Chen, December 1986.

    1156O SHORT AND CRANK   5.10b'   Just rught of **Jim Cruise,** climb a crack and continue up a face using a tied-off knob for protection. FA: Waugh and Mathews, December 1986.

    1156P ZEBRA DIHEDRAL   5.9+   Around and right from the previous routes is this large left-facing, curving dihedral. FA: Waugh and Mathews, December 1986.

Todd Battey on Zebra Dihedral

Photo: Steve Van Horn

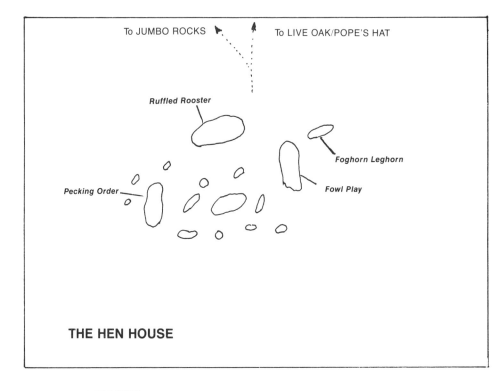

To JUMBO ROCKS

To LIVE OAK/POPE'S HAT

Ruffled Rooster

Foghorn Leghorn

Pecking Order

Fowl Play

THE HEN HOUSE

THE HEN HOUSE

The Hen House is a cluster of giant boulders about ¾ mile east-northeast of the **Zebra Cliffs**. They can be approached from Jumbo Rocks Campground or from the Live Oak Picnic Area (**Pope's Hat**). It is about a mile, whichever way you go. Maps, supplement pages 74, 80.

1156Q OUEF'S UP 5.10a This and the following four routes are on an east-facing wall near the northeast corner of the clump of boulders. This is an unprotected face (solo or top-rope) near the left side of the wall. FA: Jonny Woodward, February 1988.

1156R FOWL PLAY 5.11a Right of *Ouef's Up* climb past a bolt into a thin crack. FA: Jonny Woodward, Darrel Hensel, Kevin Powell and Greg Epperson, October 1987.

1156S TAR 5.10d Right of *Fowl Play,* this is a two-bolt face climb. From the second bolt, go left to the top. FA: Hensel and Woodward, November 1987.

1156T FEATHERS 5.11b From the second bolt of *Tar,* go straight up into a thin crack. FA: Woodward, Hensel and Rob Raker, February 1988.

1156U TALON SHOW 5.12b (TR) Climb the arete right of *Tar* and *Feathers.* FA: Woodward, February 1988.

1156V FOGHORN LEGHORN 5.7 This route is on the south face of a large boulder northeast of the previous routes. Climb an unprotected face right of a right-facing book. FA: Greg Epperson, October 1987.

1156W RUFFLED ROOSTER 5.9 This climb is on the northwest corner of a large boulder on the north side of **The Hen House.** Climb past two bolts to a prominent horizontal crack. Continue up easier unprotected face. FA: Woodward and Hensel, February 1988.

1156X PECKING ORDER 5.10c This and the following route are on a large west-facing boulder/pinnacle on the west side of **The Hen House.** This is the left route, with four bolts. FA: Woodward, Hensel, Powell and Epperson, October 1987.

1156Y CHICKEN RUN 5.11d The right route, with two bolts. FA: Woodward and Hensel, November 1987.

CONAN'S CORRIDOR AREA

CORRIDOR FACE

1157A FOOL'S GOLD   5.8   This is the farthest left route on the **Corridor Face,** and follows a prominent trough. FA: Tom Davis, January 1987.

1157B SONG OF THE SIREN   5.10c   Start off a boulder right of *Fool's Gold.* Climb past a bolt to a horizontal crack, then up into a bottoming offwidth to the top. FA: Tom Davis and Tom Voelkel, January 1987.

NUCLEAR REACTOR ROCK

1162A CUNNING LINGUIST   5.8   This climbs a hand crack to a face with one bolt left of *We'll Get Them Little P's.* FA: unknown.

1163A STAN AND OLLIE   5.7   This climbs a dike right of *We'll Get Them Little P's.* Starting the route directly is 5.9. FA: Mike Brown and Rick McKay, April 1984.

PATHETIC DOME

This formation is south of **Nuclear Reactor Rock,** the closest climbable formation to the road.

1164A PATHETIC DIKE   5.8   Climb a dike on the right side, with one bolt. FA: unknown.

1164B PATHETIC CRACK   5.6   Ten feet left of the dike is an obvious hand crack. FA: unknown.

1164C PATHETIC FACE   5.8   Ten feet left of the crack is this unprotected face. FA: unknown.

1164D RYE NOT?   5.9   On the east face of the formation west of **Pathetic Dome** is a dike with one bolt. FA: Todd Swain and Peggy Buckey, December 1987.

THE WEDGE AREA

1167A LITTLE CEASAR   5.8   This is a three-bolt climb on a gritty low-angle slab facing the road somewhere across from **Skull Rock.** FA: Dave Evans and Marge Floyd, 1986.

1167B WHEN LIGHTNING STRIKES   5.10c   About 200 yards east (right) of **The Wedge** is a rounded formation with two big horizontal cracks. This is a four-bolt climb on the north face (away from the road). FA: Geoff Archer and Dave Stoner, November 1987.

1167C CUNNING ROUTE   5.10a   Across the canyon and a short distance right of the previous route (facing the road) is this incipient crack with four bolts. FA: Keith Cunning et al.

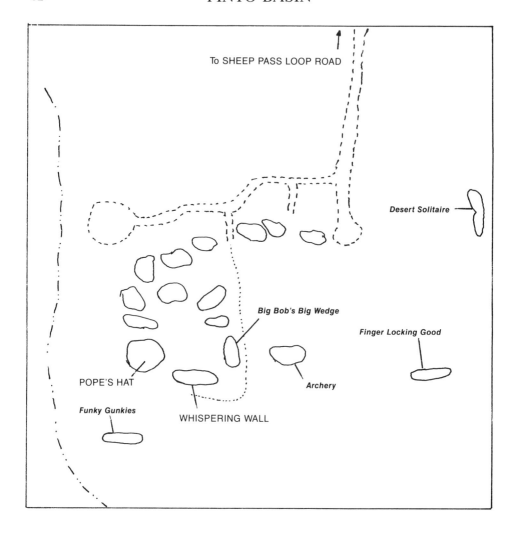

LIVE OAK PICNIC AREA
This area has seen a bit of development. See map above.

POPE'S HAT

1168A POPE AND CIRCUMSTANCE   5.9   Climb the south face of the **Pope's Hat** past three bolts. The second bolt is doubled and needs tie-offs or keyhole hangers. FA: Todd Swain and Peggy Buckey, November 1987.

1168B IS THE POPE CATHOLIC?   5.6 (TR)   Climb the rappel line along the arete on the **Pope's Hat.** FA: Swain and Buckey, November 1987.

1168C OH GOD!   5.2   This is the south-facing slab on the large boulder 50 feet south of the **Pope's Hat.** It is in front of the rappel line, and there is a rappel bolt on top. FA: Swain and Buckey.

1169 TODD SQUAD   This route is not on the **Pope's Hat.** It will appear below as route #1170G and is called *Hobo Chang Ba.*

The remaining routes in this section are scattered throughout the Live Oak area, mostly east of the **Pope's Hat.** Map, supplement page 82.

1170A DESERT SOLITAIRE 5.7 This route is located on the west face of a formation 100 yards southeast of the entrance road to Live Oak. It climbs a partially hidden finger and hand crack in a right-facing corner. FA: Todd Swain, May 1984.

The next two routes are on a north-facing rock about 200 yards southeast of ***Desert Solitaire.*** There are two obvious cracks. Map, supplement page 82.

1170B LEARNING TO CRAWL 5.6 The left crack, an offwidth. FA: Swain, May 1984.

1170C FINGER LOCKING GOOD 5.7 The right crack, leaning fingers. FA: Swain, May 1984.

1170D ARCHERY 5.4 Behind the rock west of the **Pope's Hat** is a small natural arch. Climb a crack on its left side, traverse right across the arch, and finish up a hand crack. FA: Swain, May 1984.

1170E WASHOE CRACK 5.11a This is a diagonal thin crack above and right from ***Big Bob's Big Wedge.*** It slants from left to right and faces east. FA: Todd Gordon and Dave Evans, February 1986.

1170F BEAM ABOARD 5.9+ Northwest of, and facing ***Big Bob's Big Wedge,*** this is a three-bolt climb on a large boulder/face. Rap slings are visible below the summit. This route is somewhat left of ***Washoe Crack.*** FA: Jim Kominski and Ann Kominski.

1170G HOBO CHANG BA 5.9 This climb was listed as ***Todd Squad*** (route #1169) in the guide. It is not on the **Pope's Hat,** but at the top of the gully west of ***Big Bob's Big Wedge*** on the right, about 200 feet up and left from ***Beam Aboard.*** Climb an RP crack to a horizontal, go left and then up past two bolts. FA: Todd Gordon and Brian Smith, January 1985.

THE WHISPERING WALL

This is a large, south facing wall east of the **Pope's Hat**. It is best approached up the canyon southwest of *Big Bob's Big Wedge*. This is the canyon left of the one containing routes 1170F and 1170G. It can be approached from the base of the **Pope's Hat** by heading east over several small summits to reach rap anchors on the top left side of the wall, above *Jeepers Leepers* (two ropes needed). Six routes have been reported here. Map, supplement page 82.

1170H STEMSKI   5.6   Climb double cracks starting in an open book on the left side of the wall. FA: Jim Kominski and Ann Kominski.

1170I JEEPERS LEEPERS   5.9   This is a two-bolt face climb right of *Stemski.* FA: The Kominskis.

1170J MY 3 FRIENDS   5.7   Climb the first crack right of *Jeepers Leepers.* FA: The Kominskis.

1170K INDIAN GARDEN   5.6   The second crack right of *Jeepers Leepers,* with many bushes. FA: The Kominskis.

1170L MORE CRAZY THAN LAZY   5.10   Immediately right of *Indian Garden,* climb a thin crack, then go past two bolts to a ledge. several variations from here lead to the true summit of the wall. FA: The Kominskis.

1170M MOTHER BOARD BREAKDOWN   5.10c   Climb the face right of *More Crazy Than Lazy* past nine bolts. FA: Richard Jensen et al, 1987.

The next two routes are on a large, low-angle, north-facing rock due south of the **Pope's Hat**. Map, supplement page 82.

1170N WESTWARD HO!   5.2   This is a wide crack 10 feet left of a right-slanting dike. FA: Todd Swain and Thom Scheuer, April 1984.

1170O FUNKY GUNKIES   5.4   Climb the aforementioned dike with no pro. FA: Swain and Scheuer, April 1984.

SPLIT ROCKS AREA

1171A L 'CHAIM 5.10b (TR) Climb the face just right of *Split Rocks Layback*. FA: Mark Spencer and Shirley Spencer, April 1986.

1171B DOUBLE OR NOTHING 5.9 This ascends right-slanting wide cracks right of *L 'Chaim*, plainly visible in the photo on page 338. FA: Mark Spencer, April 1986.

1171C CAPTAIN SAFE 5.10a This the left of two bolted routes on the boulder just northeast of **Split Rock**. It has two bolts. FA: Mark Spencer and Jim Cunningham, April 1986.

1171D BOULEVARD OF DREAMS 5.10c The right route, with three bolts. FA: Spencer and Cunningham, April 1986.

The next two routes are located directly across the road from the outhouse (which may or may not still be there). They are on the right, as one is driving into the **Split Rocks Area.**

1174A THE NIPPLE 5.10b Climb a left-curving crack, then go up the face past a black chickenhead. FA: Herb Laegar and Eve Uiga, February 1979.

1174B CLEAVAGE 5.10c Lieback an overhanging corner left of *The Nipple*, and meet that route at the end of its left-curving crack. FA: Laegar and Uiga, February 1979.

1175A THE POPSICLE 5.11 This route climbs the southwest corner/arete of a very large boulder a short ways north of *Cleared for Takeoff* past two bolts. FA: Tony Yaniro, 1982.

1175B BLACK PANTHER 5.11c East of *The Popsicle*, on the first tier above the corridor is a west-facing black crack rendered challenging by a large roof six feet off the ground. FA: Tony Yaniro and Vaino Kodas, 1982.

1176A DIKE FLIGHT 5.10+ This is a two-bolt face climb on a large boulder about halfway between **Split Rocks Parking Area** and **Future Games Rock**. It follows a dike slanting up and left. FA: Jim and Ann Kominski.

FRIGID TOWER

1177A THE SPUR OF THE MOMENT 5.12a To the right of *Puss Wuss*, this is a four-bolt climb leading to a two-bolt anchor. FA: Jonny Woodward and Darrel Hensel, March 1988.

FUTURE GAMES ROCK

1178A ORNO-NECRO 5.11c This is the first crack left of *Therapeutic Tyranny* FA: Mike Lechlinski and Eric Ericksson, March 1986.

1178B THE BENDIX CLAWS 5.11a Just right of *Therapeutic Tyranny*, climb a crack to a bolt, then move right into a crack leading to the top. FA: Lechlinski et al, March 1986.

1179A INVISIBLE TOUCH 5.10b Climb *Invisibility Lessons* about halfway, then move left and follow thin cracks to the top. FA: Herb Laegar and Andy Brown, October 1986.

1180A DISAPPEARING ACT 5.10c Ten feet right of *Invisibility Lessons* a lieback corner leads to a face with four bolts. FA: Laegar, Brown and Vaino Kodas, November 1986.

The next two routes are on the rock about 100 feet right of **Future Games Rock.**

1182 CASUAL AFFAIR 5.10d This route is mentioned in the guide, but no information is given. It ascends the left edge of the rock.

1182A SAFETY PIN 5.11c Just right of *Casual Affair*, this route goes over a roof and passes a fixed pin. FA: Vaino Kodas, 1984.

The next four routes are on the steep wall to the left and on the same formation as *Grand Canyon Donkey Trail*.

1183A ELECTRIC BIRTHDAY PARTY 5.12 This is the farthest left line, with three bolts. FA: Jonny Woodward, September 1987.

1183B MIDNIGHT LUMBER 5.10d Just right of the preceding route is a left-facing dihedral that peters out into face climbing past a bolt. FA: John Long et al.

1183C EVERY WHICH WAY BUT UP 5.12a Climb *Midnight Lumber* to mid-height, then traverse right on a dike past four bolts to hit the upper section of *The Woodshed*. FA: Jonny Woodward, September 1987.

1183D THE WOODSHED 5.11d This is the most obvious crack on the wall, about forty feet left of ***Grand Canyon Donkey Trail.*** FA: Mike Paul and Todd Gordon, 1970's. FFA: (TR) Unknown. FFA: Jonny Woodward (lead), September 1987.

1183E SENDERO LUMINOSO 5.9 This route is directly opposite ***Grand Canyon Donkey Trail*** and climbs the west-southwest corner of a crag, passing three horizontal dikes and finishing with a hand crack. Two prominent chickenheads mark the route. FA: David Kozak and Linda Pritchett, May 1987.

1184A FOR PETER 5.11c Directly across from ***Rubicon,*** this climbs up to and traverses a large dike. FA: Vaino Kodas, Herb Laegar and Eve Laegar, October 1987.

1184B TOTAL GENERIC PACKAGE 5.11c (TR) This climbs the face left of ***Rubicon.*** FA: Roger Whitehead and Chris French.

1184C SEIZURE 5.12 This route climbs the initial (right) start of ***Rubicon,*** then continues straight up past five bolts. FA: Kris Solem and Charles Crist, October 1988.

ISLES IN THE SKY

1188A YOUNG GUNS 5.11d This is a free version of the old bolt ladder left of ***Bird of Fire.*** It was first freed using the old bolts, and finished by traversing right into ***Bird of Fire*** below the final headwall (5.10b). It has since been rebolted with new ⅜" bolts and finishes directly up the final headwall. FFA: Jordy Morgan and Chris Snyder, February 1988. FA: (direct finish) Snyder, Tom Herbert and Tracy Dorton, November 1988.

1189A WINGS OF STEEL 5.11c This is a free version of the old bolt ladder right of ***Bird of Fire.*** Hangers may not be in place. FA: Morgan and Snyder, February 1988.

The next two routes are on a wall down and right from **Isles in the Sky.** The wall is characterized by large black flakes.

1190A SAVE THE LAST STANCE FOR ME 5.9 Start right of a juniper tree and climb past four bolts. FA: Herb Laegar, Vaino Kodas and Kurt Shannon, May 1986.

1190B SLAM DANCE 5.10c Right of the previous route, this climb has three bolts and passes a low-angle roof. FA: Kodas and Laegar, May 1986.

ISLES CORRIDOR

1195A METTLE DETECTOR 5.12b This is a two-bolt climb between ***Crack #5*** and ***Crack #6.*** FA: Jonny Woodward, Septenber 1988.

The next two routes are on the formation northwest of ***Angular Momentum,*** obvious in the map on page 337. Approach as for that route, and notice that the trail splits just before it ends on the map. The two routes are above the two ends of the trail.

1204A BEAUTIFUL SCREAMER 5.12a This is the left route and climbs a crack past a bolt and three pins. FA: Vaino Kodas and Herb Laegar, February 1987.

1204B UNNAMED 5.9 The right route. FA: Jonny Woodward and Maria Cranor, 1988.

The next two routes are in the narrow corridor around and to the left of ***Angular Momentum,*** facing northwest.

1204C CLING OR FLING 5.11 − This is a steep bolted face on the right side of the corridor. FA: Herb Laegar, Eve Laegar and Bob Kamps, September 1987.

1204D GREEN MANSIONS 5.8 Climb the crack just right of ***Cling or Fling.*** FA: Laegar, Laegar and Kamps, September 1987.

The next four routes are on the wall opposite ***Brits in Drag.***

1205A LEADBELLY 5.10b The farthest left route, this is a steep, widening crack. FA: Jonny Woodward and Alan Roberts, December 1988.

1205B BATTERING RAM 5.12b The next route right, this climbs past a bolt into a thin crack. FA: Woodward, December 1988.

1205C THE ACUPUNCTURIST 5.10b This and the previous route are the ones that are most directly opposite ***Brits in Drag.*** Climb a steep face (no bolts) into a crack. FA: Woodward and Alfred Randell, November 1988.

1205D TWITTISH EMPIRE 5.11b The farthest right route, this has one bolt and climbs face leading into a crack. FA: Woodward, November 1988.

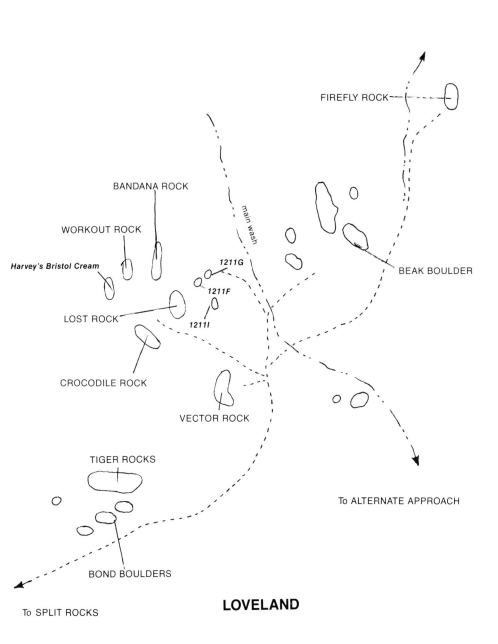

FIREFLY ROCK

BANDANA ROCK

WORKOUT ROCK

main wash

Harvey's Bristol Cream

1211G

1211F

LOST ROCK

1211I

BEAK BOULDER

CROCODILE ROCK

VECTOR ROCK

TIGER ROCKS

To ALTERNATE APPROACH

BOND BOULDERS

To SPLIT ROCKS

LOVELAND

LOVELAND
TIGER ROCKS

Tiger Rocks are the obvious south-facing rocks near the bottom of the hillside to the southwest of **Vector Rock.** One walks below them and the **Bond Boulders** (see below) when approaching **Loveland** from **Split Rocks.** They can be seen in the photo on page 345 where the arrow below the words "over crest" is pointing. Map, supplement page 87.

1206A KON-TIKI 5.11c (TR) This is located on the west side of the **Kon-Tiki Boulder,** a large boulder about 100 feet west of the **Tiger Rocks.** It is almost exactly midway between the two arrows in the photo on page 345. FA: Alan Nelson, Mike Guardino and Bill Leventhal, December 1986.

1206B QUASAR 5.12 Climb the amazing dihedral at the left (west) end of **Tiger Rocks.** FA: Tony Yaniro and Vaino Kodas, 1982.

1206C ONE ARM GIANT 5.10+ This is the bottomless, bombay chimney just right of *Quasar.* FA: Yaniro and Kodas, 1982.

1206D FLY AWAY 5.10+ Ascend the overhanging, widening crack to a chimney right of *One Arm Giant.* FA: Kodas and Yaniro, 1982.

BOND BOULDERS

Below Tiger Rocks are two large boulders; these are the Bond Boulders.

1206E RCA 5.11a This route climbs the south face of the northern boulder past three bolts. FA: Ron Carson, Brett Maurer and Tony Yaniro, 1983.

1206F MOONRAKER 5.10 This route is on the north face of the south boulder. Mantle, then climb past one bolt. FA: Carson, Maurer and Yaniro, 1983.

1206G DIAMONDS ARE FOREVER 5.10d Ascend the steep dike past two bolts on the right side of the south face of the south boulder. FA: Carson, Maurer and Yaniro, 1983.

1206H LIVE AND LET DIE 5.11a This is a three-bolt route left of *Diamonds Are Forever,* in the middle of the south face. FA: Carson, Maurer and Yaniro, 1983.

1206I DEEP, SHALLOW AND TWISTED 5.10c Below and left (west) of the South Bond Boulder is a short, steep buttress of rock. Climb past three bolts on the left side of the south face. FA: Bill Odenthal, Bill Herzog and Rob Mulligan, 1987.

CROCODILE ROCK

1207A I GET BY WITH A LITTLE HELP FROM MY FRIENDS 5.10a This is the wide hand and fist crack to the left of *B-Movie.* FA: Roger Linfield and Dennis Yates, November 1986.

1209A HARVEY'S BRISTOL CREAM 5.10a About 50 yards northwest of **Crocodile Rock** is this double crack on the east face of a 50-foot rock. FA: Vaino Kodas and Diana Leach, 1983.

1209B SKETCHES OF STRAIN 5.10d A short distance right of *Harvey's Bristol Cream,* and on a separate formation, this ascends a finger crack in a dihedral via stemming. FA: Alan Roberts and Eric Gompper.

WORKOUT ROCK

This rock is about 30 yards northeast of *Harvey's Bristol Cream,* and about 70 yards north-northwest of **Crocodile Rock.** Map, supplement page 87.

1209C SPREAD & BUTTER 5.10b This is the obvious right-facing dihedral which lies on the east face of **Workout Rock.** FA: unknown.

1209D LET'S GET PHYSICAL 5.10b This is an offwidth/fist crack which starts 15 feet right of *Spread & Butter.* FA: Roger Linfield and Dennis Yates, Novem,ber 1986.

1211A ALMOST LIKE REAL CLIMBING 5.7 This lies between **Vector Rock** and the main Loveland wash and faces southeast. Climb an obvious finger to hand crack on a large boulder. FA: Yates and Linfield, November 1986.

1211B FISTING IN LOVELAND 5.9 This is a fist crack on a small buttress somewhere between **Vector Rock** and **Bandana Rock.** It faces northeast. FA: Yates and Linfield, November 1986.

LOST ROCK

This is a large boulder/formation about 50 yards northeast of **Crocodile Rock.** Three routes ascend its northeast face. Map, supplement page 87.

1211C MISSING PERSONS 5.11c This is the left of two bolted routes. There are seven bolts. FA: Tony Yaniro and Brett Maurer, 1982.

1211D DESTINATION UNKNOWN 5.11d The right route, with four bolts. FA: Yaniro and Maurer, 1982.

1211E PEBBLE BEACH 5.7 Start right of *Destination Unknown* and climb up and right past a "hole" and a flake to the top (no pro). FA: Jonny Woodward, March 1988.

The next three routes are on large boulders east of **Lost Rock.** Map, supplement page 87.

1211F SHARP ARETE 5.10c This is the southeast arete of the westmost of the two boulders and has three bolts. FA: Vaino Kodas and Tony Yaniro.

1211G SON OF OBSIDIAN 5.11c This is a two-bolt climb in the middle of the south face of the eastern boulder. FA: Jonny Woodward and Darrel Hensel, March 1988.

1211H FORGOTTEN VENTURE 5.10b Right of *Son of Obsidian,* on the southeast corner of the boulder is this short, two-bolt route. FA Vaino Kodas and Larry Seibold.

1211I TRICKY MOVE 5.10a This is a bolted route on the west face of another large boulder south of the previous three routes. FA: Herb Laegar and Vaino Kodas, February 1986.

1213A DARK AGES 5.10a Walk up the main Loveland wash between **Vector Rock** and the **Beak Boulders,** then go left up the hillside past a large "Don Juan-type" boulder. Another 70 yards west past this is a formation called **Midieval Highlands** with a crack splitting it. This route climbs past three bolts on the face left of the crack. FA: Bill Herzog and Rob Mulligan, 1987.

THE BEAK BOULDER ROCKS

The next two routes are on a west-facing wall about 150 yards west of *Goin' Down the Road Feelin' Bad.*

1215A I'M PREGNANT WITH SATAN'S BABY 5.11a This is a face with four bolts left of an obvious arching finger crack. FA: Jack Marshall, Don Wilson, Karen Wilson and Robert Carrere, September 1988.

1215B STATUE OF ELVIS ON MARS 5.10b This is the obvious arching finger crack. FA: Marshall, Carrere, Wilson and Wilson, September 1988.

The following three routes are on a boulder with sharp aretes directly in front of the **Beak Boulder.**

1216A SLEEK BEAK 5.10/11 This is on the east face, and passes three bolts. FA: Dave Evans, Rob Stahl and Todd Gordon, May 1987.

1216B SUPER BEAK OF THE DESERT 5.9 Climb the poorly-protected north arete of the boulder. FA: Gordon, Evans and Jim Angione, May 1987.

1216C BEAK OF THE WEEK 5.7 This is the knife-edged south arete. FA: Gordon, Stahl, Evans, Angione and Tom Burke, May 1987.

1220A THROBBING GRISTLE 5.12a (TR) This is the leftmost of the three offwidth cracks on the backside of the **Beak Boulder Rocks.** FA: Alan Nelson, 1983.

The next seven routes are found by continuing up the main Loveland wash past all the previous routes. The point where the wash makes a distinct turn to the left (west) will be used as an identifying landmark.

1123A FOOL FOR A PRETTY FACE 5.10c This is on the west face of a large boulder a few hundred yards northwest of the **Beak Boulders,** several hundred yards before the wash turns west. It is a three-bolt face climb just right of the northwest arete. FA: Dennis Yates and Roger Linfield, March 1987.

1223B HEARTLESS 5.7 This is a prominent 40-foot long south-facing dihedral which lies about 500 feet southeast of where the wash turns left (this is still well to the northwest of the **Beak Boulder Rocks**). FA: Yates and Linfield, February 1987.

1223C CRACK ADDICTION 5.10b On the north side of the formation with *Heartless*, this is a right-slanting finger and hand crack. FA: Linfield and Yates.

1223D HEART TRANSPLANT 5.10a This is located 100 yards north of where the main wash turns west. It is a hand crack right of a large roof on a southwest facing formation. FA: Linfield and Yates, February 1987.

1223E REFLECTOR OVEN 5.10a This is a thin face with two bolts on a formation about ½ mile north of the **Beak Boulders.** It faces southwest. FA: Yates and Linfield, March 1987.

1223F FIVE TWO-ISH 5.2 A crack and left-leaning lieback just right of *Reflector Oven*. FA: Yates, March 1987.

1223G YUPPIES DON'T DO OFFWIDTHS 5.9 Up the hillside to the west of *Reflector Oven* is an overhanging crack splitting the smooth east face of a large boulder. Around right and 100 feet up from this is a clean offwidth, which is the route. FA: Linfield and Yates, March 1987.

The next two routes are found on the alternate (not from **Split Rocks**) approach to Loveland, described on page 343 of the guide.

1223H WACKO PLACKO 5.10d This route is on a formation just west of the road and parking area. On its west side, climb up and left to a crack leading around a corner, then face climb past two bolts to the top. FA: Vaino Kodas and Alan Placko, December 1982.

1223I TIDBIT 5.10a About halfway along the mining road on this alternate approach, a small formation will be seen on the hillside to the left. On its southeast face climb a fingercrack which lies on the right wall of a small dihedral. FA: Alan Nelson, 1982.

BELLE CAMPGROUND AREA
CASTLE ROCK

1235A LOVE AT FIRST BITE 5.8 Climb the unprotected face ten feet right of *Diagnostics*. FA: Dave Wonderly and Jack Marshall, 1982.

1235B DIABETICS 5.4 This is the obvious crack right of *Love at First Bite*. FA: unknown.

1236A BELL-E-UP 5.11+ This route starts right of *Belly Dancer* and goes up and left around the corner passing three bolts to join *Belly Dancer* at its last bolt. FA: Herb Laegar and Vaino Kodas, December 1985.

1236B BONNY'S BOO-BOO 5.9 This is the left of three bolted routes on the east face of **Castle Rock.** It goes up where *Bonnie Brae* is drawn in in the picture on page 349. FA: Bill Herzog et al.

1237 BONNIE BRAE 5.7 This route is misdrawn in the guide; it is the middle of the three bolted routes and climbs where *Bubba's Tourist Trap* is shown.

1238 BUBBA'S TOURIST TRAP 5.9 The right bolted route, it climbs the face right of where it is marked in the guide.

1238A DRILL DUST 5.9 About 100 feet right of *Bubba's Tourist Trap* is this three-bolt route starting from ledges 30 feet up. FA: unknown, October 1988.

1240A ASHES TO ASHES 5.10b This is a steep three-bolt climb on the large formation behind and right from *Short Cake*. There are other bolted routes in this vicinity about which no information is presently known. FA: Geoff Archer and Dave Stoner, November 1987.

Looking east from near the base of Route #1240F

BECKY'S BUTTRESS AREA

This is the group of rocks about ½ mile northeast of Belle Campground. They can be approached from the campground, but a slightly closer approach may be from a point midway along the road between the campground and the intersection of the Sheep Pass Loop Road with the Pinto Basin Road. **Becky's Buttress** is the largest formation, a west-facing rib leaning against a hillside. See map, supplement page 74.

1240B BECKY'S BUTTRESS 5.9 Climb the outer face of the buttress past four bolts. FA: Geoff Archer, Dave Stoner and John Stone, December 1987.

1240C ROAD DOGS 5.7 Left of the previous route, this climbs a dihedral and overhanging thin crack on the right side of the steep north face of **Becky's Buttress.** FA: Archer and Stoner, November 1987.

1240D GRAVITY PIRATES 5.10 (TR) 25 feet left of *Road Dogs,* climb overhanging buckets to reach a crack. FA: Archer, Stoner and Stone, December 1987.

1240E GORBY GOES TO WASHINGTON 5.8 This is a two-bolt climb on the north face of the clump of rocks 100 yards northeast of **Becky's Buttress.** FA: Archer and Stoner, November 1987.

1240F BOB 5.10a This route ascends the dark east face of a rock 300 yards west of **Becky's Buttress** past three bolts. FA: Stoner and Archer, January 1988.

WHITE TANK CAMPGROUND

1242A QUAKING HAS-BEENS   5.9   This climbs the south face of the ***Desiderious Delight*** pinnacle. It has three bolts, but take some other pro along. FA: Herb Laegar and Rich Perch, November 1988.

1242B DOUBLE TROUBLE   5.11b (TR)   Southwest of ***Desiderious Delight,*** climb double cracks on the north face of a formation. An old bolt will be found on top. FA: Craig Fry, January 1986.

The next route lies on a large west-facing formation (perhaps the largest in White Tank Campground) that has dark rock on its left side and contains several right-diagonalling cracks. This formation is called **Tierra Incognito.**

1242C TRICK OF THE TAIL   5.10a   Climb the most prominent right-diagonalling crack on **Tierra Incognito.** FA: Todd Gordon, Mike Brown, Shari Brown and Reggie Thomson, February 1979. FFA: Gordon and Craig Fry, January 1986.

1242D JODY   5.10b   This steep finger crack is located on the south face of a small boulder north of ***Trick of the Tail.*** FA: Todd Gordon and Craig Fry, January 1986.

BOVINE DOME

This small formation is located at the intersection of the Pinto Basin Road and the Stirrup Tank turnoff, ⅓ mile past White Tank Campground. There is a paved parking area here. Map, page 74.

1242E FOOTLOOSE   5.9   This is a short right-curving crack just right of the descent route on the face facing the main road (northeast face). It is 90 feet left of ***Where Two Deserts Meet.*** FA: Mark Spencer and Dwight Simpson, March 1986.

1242F FLAKEY FLIX   5.7   Climb obvious rotten cracks and flakes 30 feet left of ***Where Two Deserts Meet.*** FA: Mark Spencer, Shirley Spencer and Dwight Simpson, March 1986.

1242G WHERE TWO DESERTS MEET   5.8   This is a right-curving thin crack on the north corner of the formation. FA: Spencer, Spencer and Simpson, March 1986.

1242H LOS TRES BOVINES   5.10c   Just right of ***Where Two Deserts Meet*** is this three-bolt climb. It starts by traversing right from the start of that route. FA: Alan Bartlett, Randy Vogel and Todd Gordon, October 1988.

1242I WAITING FOR ALAN   5.4   On the southwest corner, climb a crack right of a block, follow it right until it fades, then face climb to the top. FA: Randy Vogel, October 1988.

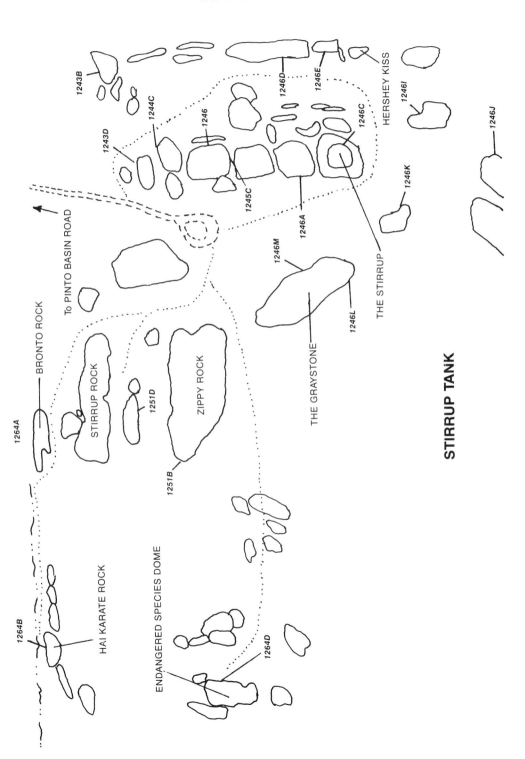

STIRRUP TANK

1243B

1244C

1243D

1246D

1246E

1246

1246C

HERSHEY KISS

1246I

1246J

1245C

1246A

THE STIRRUP

1246K

To PINTO BASIN ROAD

1246M

1246L

THE GRAYSTONE

BRONTO ROCK

STIRRUP ROCK

1251D

ZIPPY ROCK

1264A

1251B

HAI KARATE ROCK

1264B

ENDANGERED SPECIES DOME

1264D

STIRRUP TANK AREA

This area has seen some development. Map, supplement page 93.

1243A POTLATCH 5.8 This is a straight-in finger crack on the northwest face of a large boulder about 150 yards northeast of **Wooly Spider.** It is easily seen on the drive in. FA: Mark and Shirley Spencer, March 1986.

1243B ACCELERATOR 5.10b This and the following route are on another large boulder right (southeast) of the previous route. This climbs the center of the north face past one bolt. FA: Geoff Archer and Doug Aagesen, 1986.

1243C RUDY VALENTINE DAY 5.8 This is a poorly-protected climb 15 feet right of **Accelerator.** FA: Todd Swain and Peggy Buckey, February 1987.

1243D ARACHNIDS 5.5 Climb the face left of **Tarantula** past one bolt. FA: Todd Swain, Kip Knapp and Patty Furbush, March 1986.

1244A NOT KING COLE 5.8 Climb the chimney right of **Wooly Spider.** FA: Charles Cole.

1244B BLACK WIDOW 5.10c Around the corner to the right of **Not King Cole** is this two-bolt face climb. FA: Geoff Archer and Doug Aagesen, November 1986.

1244C TRAP DOOR 5.6 This is a short left-facing book formed by a white pillar leaning against a brown face, on the north end of the rocks around and left (southeast) from **Wooly Spider.** FA: Archer and Aagesen, 1986.

1245A ROLLERSKATING WITH ALIENS 5.8 Climb the face left of **Beam Me Up Scottie** past two bolts. FA: Todd Swain, Peggy Buckey, Dave Saball, Marie Saball and Dana Bartlett, March 1988.

1245B THE ENTERPRISE 5.9 (TR) This is the face and arete just right of **Beam Me Up Scottie.** FA: Swain and Buckey, March 1988.

1245C I SLEPT WITH L.K. 5.10a This climb is located where **Hand Grenade** is indicated in the guide. It follows a thin crack which passes a horizontal crack midway up. FA: Todd Gordon, Lori Graff, Tom Michael, Brian Povolny, Jeff Hamlin and Steve Strong, March 1986.

1246 HAND GRENADE This climb is mislocated in the guide. It is in a narrow corridor on the east side of the formation, best approached from the north.

1246A FILET OF COLE 5.10b This is on the west face of the next block south of **Beam Me Up Scottie** and just north of **The Stirrup** (see below). Climb a discontinuous crack that ends at a brown patch of rock, and continue past two bolts to the top. FA: Charles Cole and Russ Walling, fall 1985.

THE STIRRUP

This is the prominent perched tower at the southern end of the main Stirrup Tank formation. It is the formation for which the entire Stirrup Tank area is named. Two routes are known. Map, page 93.

1246B NOTCH ROUTE 5.6 Climb a hand crack out of the notch, on the north side of the tower. FA: unknown.

1246C EAST FACE 5.10a Climb the steep, plated east face. No bolts. FA: Geoff Archer and Dave Stoner, March 1987.

The next two routes are on the west-facing row of rocks east of the main Stirrup Tank formation.

1246D STOP THE PRESSES 5.10 This is a three-bolt climb on a short face. FA: unknown, October 1988.

1246E WAR BABY 5.10a (TR) Climb a very short smooth face 50 feet right of *Stop the Presses*. FA: Geoff Archer et al.

The next three routes are on a small pointed formation known as the **Hershey Kiss,** about 50 feet right of *War Baby*. There are two curving dikes on the north side. Map, supplement page 93.

1246F HERSHEY HIGHWAY 5.9 (TR) This is the left dike. FA: Geoff Archer and Doug Aagesen, 1986.

1246G SPINAL TAP 5.9 The right dike, with one bolt. FA: Archer and Aagesen, 1986.

1246H TRIAL BY FIRE 5.7 On the east face of **Hershey Kiss,** this climbs a thin vertical dike. FA: Archer, 1987.

1246I PRIMAL URGE 5.9 This climb ascends a brown open book on the east side of a small formation 100 yards southwest of **Hershey Kiss.** FA: Archer et al.

1246J LESS THAN MEETS THE EYE 5.8 This route is on the east face of a large formation about 75 yards south-southwest of *Primal Urge*. It ascends a right-slanting system of discontinuous cracks to a large ledge. FA: Randy Vogel and Marjorie Shovlin, October 1988.

1246K CRACKUP 5.7 West of *Primal Urge* and north of *Less Than Meets the Eye* is a small formation. This route climbs a short vertical crack on its southeast corner. FA: Miguel Carmona and Alois Smrz, April 1988.

THE GRAYSTONE

This is the large rock southeast of **Zippy Rock** and opposite *Filet of Cole*. It has four known routes. Map, supplement page 93.

1246L COWS IN THE SHADE   5.9   Start in a short right-slanting crack on the southeast side of the rock. Traverse left and go past two bolts to a bolt anchor on top. FA: Miguel Carmona and Alois Smrz, May 1988.

1246M CONVERGENCE CRACKS: Left, 5.9; Center, 5.8; Right, 5.10 (TRs)   On the left side of the northeast face are these three prominent converging cracks. They have been reported as top-ropes, but look very leadable. FA: Carmona and Smrz, April 1988.

1246N THE MICRO MILLENIUM   5.11d   A short distance right of the *Convergence Cracks,* climb a face up and right, staying above an overhang until a very thin RP crack is reached. Continue up the crack with so-so protection. A later party, believing the climb to be undone, added several bolts and finished to the right of the crack (easier). These bolts have been removed. FA: Jonny Woodward, Darrel Hensel and Maria Cranor, November 1986.

1246O THE EDGE   5.10b   This two-bolt route lies on the left edge of the north side of a flake of rock 50 feet right of *The Micro Millenium.* FA: Miguel Carmona and Alois Smrz, April 1988.

ZIPPY ROCK

1247A CANALIZO   5.10c   This is a four-bolt climb just left of *Gargoyle.* FA: Mike Stewart and Miguel Carmona, April 1987.

1250A SHONGO PAVI   5.10c   This climb is ten feet left of *Hans Solo* and passes one bolt. FA: David Kozak and Linda Pritchett, May 1987.

1251A J.B. GOES TO J.T.   5.8+ (TR)   Start just right of *Hans Solo* and after 15 feet angle up and right across the face. FA: Kozak and Pritchett, May 1987.

1251B WILD DREAM   5.10+   On the northwest side of **Zippy Rock,** start at the left margin and diagonal right to two bolts on the skyline. FA: Miguel Carmona and Alois Smrz, May 1988.

The next two routes are on the south face of a small rock between **Zippy Rock** and **Stirrup Rock.** Map, supplement page 93.

1251C CAT PAWS   5.10b   The left route, with three bolts. FA: Carmona and Smrz, April 1988.

1251D BLUE MOON   5.10b   The right climb, with two bolts. FA: Carmona and Smrz, May 1988.

STIRRUP ROCK

1253 *PETER EATER PUMPKIN EATER* This climb should be rated 5.10+.

1254 *OVERPOWERED BY FUNK* This has been led with one bolt, and should probably be rated 5.12a. Kurt Smith, 1987.

1257 *FRECKLE FACE* This climb has been led, with three bolts. The bolted line starts a little right of the line shown in the guide. Jonny Woodward, 1987.

BRONTO ROCK

1264A *BUCKEYE* 5.4 On the north face of the rock, climb an obvious dike left of center. FA: J.A. Morris and Chris Scheck, March 1987.

HAI KARATE ROCK

Walk west in a wash from **Bronto Rock** for 250-300 yards. This is a short brown wall up and left, facing north. Map, supplement page 93.

1264B *FULL CONTACT KARATE* 5.9 Climb an overhanging crack in a dark brown dihedral. FA: Mike Stewart and Gary Hinton, April 1987.

1264C *ZEN GOBLINS* 5.10a This is the steep brown face with two bolts right of *Full Contact Karate*. FA: Stewart and Hinton, April 1987.

ENDANGERED SPECIES DOME

This dome is located about ⅓ mile west of the Stirrup Tank parking area. Walk west, passing along the south side of **Zippy Rock**. Continue up slabs and enter a hidden valley. This is the large east-facing rock at the end of the valley. There are two routes, both with bolts. Map, page 93.

1264D *REVENGE OF THE HERDS* 5.8 The left bolted route. FA: Steve McAllister, Mary McAllister, Lauri Sheridan and Mike Stewart, April 1987.

1264E *THE RIGHT TO ARM BEARS* 5.11b The right bolted route. FA: Mike Stewart, Miguel Carmona and Malcolm Ball, April 1987.

OZ

This is the vast group of rocks about one mile northeast of **Loveland.** More routes have been done than are listed here, but information is lacking. This area will undoubtedly see much more development. The following six routes are best approached from a dirt pullout on the east side of the road about 1.2 miles north of the Sheep Pass Loop Road/Pinto Basin Road intersection. **Oz** will be seen as a cluster of dark rocks in a canyon to the southwest. Map, supplement page 74.

1264F *NOT IN KANSAS ANYMORE* 5.9+ This route is located in the first canyon entered after crossing the initial ridge on the approach. The canyon narrows to the north. This route climbs an 80-foot torpedo-shaped buttress past three bolts. FA: Dave Stoner and Geoff Archer, January 1988.

1264G *WALKING THE DOG* 5.8/9 This climbs a roof and arete atop a large jumbled formation about 250 yards south of *Not in Kansas Anymore.* Start on jugs leading to a bolt, then traverse left and follow the arete past two more. FA: Archer and Stoner, February 1988.

The next four routes are reached by continuing west from the canyon containing the two previous routes. Go over the next ridge and drop down into a wash. The wash winds its way northwest to a large cluster of crags on a hillside. These routes might well be approached directly from the Sheep Pass Loop Road/Pinto Basin Road intersection.

1264H *ROBOCOP MEETS THE MUNCHKINS* 5.9/10 This route ascends the southwest corner of the first large crag, starting with an overhang with a fixed pin and continuing past three bolts and moving left at the top. FA: Geoff Archer, Dave Stoner, Jeff Kasten and Bill Freeman, February 1988.

1264I *OVER THE RAINBOW* 5.10+ This route is ten feet right of the preceding route and climbs a dike and waterstreak past three bolts. FA: Archer and Kasten, February 1988.

1264J IF I ONLY HAD A BRAIN   5.10a   This climb is located in a hidden canyon behind (north of) the crag with the two previous routes. It is the left of two obvious flake systems on a beautiful brown wall and has two bolts. (The right system has apparently also been climbed and has three bolts). FA: Archer and Kasten, January 1988.

1264K DOROTHY DOES THE WIZARD   5.10b   This route is located on the east side of the deep canyon 300 yards west of *If I Only Had a Brain*. It starts as a thin crack, widening all the way to the top. FA: Archer, Stoner, Kasten and Fernando Corona.

MAGIC MOUNTAIN AREA

This is the small group of rocks on the west side of the road and just inside the Monument from the 29 Palms Entrance Station. The first two routes are on a small dark tower 100 yards southwest of a parking area with a Park Information exhibit.

1264L OATMEAL EATING AARDVARKS   5.7   Climb the north face of the tower above a bowl. FA: Todd Swain, Peggy Buckey and Dan Wirth, April 1986.

1264M FLAKEY FRIENDS   5.7 (TR)   Climb the face 15 feet right of *Oatmeal Eating Aardvarks*. FA: Swain, Buckey and Wirth, April 1986.

The following five routes are on the rocky hillside northwest of the dark tower.

1264N ROARING RAPIDS   5.5   On the left side of the hillside is a boulder with a large flake/crack. This climbs the face left of the flake/crack. FA: Swain and Buckey, April 1986.

1264O COLOSSUS   5.8   This climbs the aforementiond flake/crack. FA: Swain and Buckey, April 1986.

1264P DISPOSABLE HEROES   5.8   This is a two-bolt face climb about 150 feet right of the two previous routes. FA: Geoff Archer, Dave Stoner and John Stone, January 1988.

The next two routes are on the largest face on the right side of the hillside.

1264Q FREE FALL   5.10a (TR)   Climb the left side of the face. FA: Todd Swain and Peggy Buckey, April 1986.

1264R JET STREAM   5.8   Climb the right side of the face past two bolts. FA: Swain and Buckey, April 1986.

INDIAN HEAD

1265A OH GOD!   5.10c   This two-pitch climb starts in a seam about 30 feet left of *Rude Awakening*. FA: Charles Cole, Bob Bolton and Darryl Nakahira, 1985.

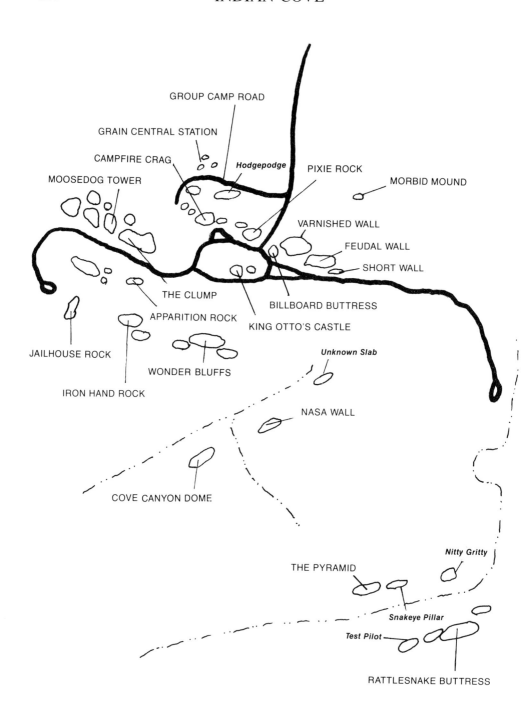

GROUP CAMP ROAD

GRAIN CENTRAL STATION

CAMPFIRE CRAG

Hodgepodge

PIXIE ROCK

MORBID MOUND

MOOSEDOG TOWER

VARNISHED WALL

FEUDAL WALL

SHORT WALL

THE CLUMP

BILLBOARD BUTTRESS

APPARITION ROCK

KING OTTO'S CASTLE

JAILHOUSE ROCK

Unknown Slab

WONDER BLUFFS

IRON HAND ROCK

NASA WALL

COVE CANYON DOME

Nitty Gritty

THE PYRAMID

Snakeye Pillar

Test Pilot

RATTLESNAKE BUTTRESS

INDIAN COVE CAMPGROUND
GROUP CAMP ROAD

The following fifteen routes are found on cliffs behind the various group campsites. These are reached by turning right on a paved road 200 yards before the billboard in Indian Cove Campground. No routes were reported here in the guide, but some of these are obviously old routes. Map, supplement page 100.

1267A JAIME'S BIG SHOW 5.7 In the box canyon behind GC1 is this bottoming hand/fist crack with an overhang at the bottom. FA: Jaime Lara, Warren Mellinger and Ben Chapman, April 1986.

The next nine routes are on a crag between GC4 and GC5. It has an easy-appearing bucketed face very close to the road.

1267B MY WIFE IS AN ALIEN 5.9 A1 Up and left from the bucketed face is this five-bolt route. The move by the last bolt hasn't gone free yet. FA: Todd Swain and Peggy Buckey, September 1988.

1267C HODGEPODGE 5.2 Climb the aforementioned easy bucketed face. FA: unknown.

1267D MORNING STAR 5.8/9 Climb the face right of *Hodgepodge* past one bolt. FA: Bill Todd and Laurent Mounoud, January 1987.

1267E TUMBLEWEED 5.6 This, and the following five routes are around right of *Hodgepodge*, on the west face of the rock. This is the central crack, which diagonals right at the top. FA: unknown.

1267F BAKERSFIELD BOMB 5.8 Right of *Tumbleweed*, this is a two-bolt face climb. An old TR. First lead; Bill Todd and Laurent Mounoud, January 1987.

1267G BRIAR RABBIT 5.7 Climb groove cracks right of *Bakersfield Bomb*. FA: unknown.

1267H SHORT CRACK 5.4 Right of *Briar Rabbit* is this 35-foot crack in a right-facing corner. FA: unknown.

1267I BITTERSWEET 5.9 This is a two-bolt face right of *Short Crack*. FA: Bill Todd and John Nye, January 1987.

1267J SEMISWEET 5.9 Climb the unprotected face right of *Bittersweet*. FA: Alan Nelson, November 1987.

The next three routes are located behind GC7.

1267K PORTAL 5.9 This is an obvious steep crack directly behind the campsite. FA: Bill Todd.

1267L THE FAR SIDE 5.4 Left of *Portal,* climb up and right on varnished knobs to a right-leaning fingercrack. FA: Todd Swain, October 1988.

1267M MILK RUN 5.9 Start about 70 feet right of *Portal* and climb past a bolt and over a roof to the top. FA: unknown.

1267N FLAKE ROUTE 5.5 Approach this route through a gap behind GC12. It ascends a continuous 150-foot flake system. FA: unknown.

The following route is on the northwest face of a large formation 300 yards north of the road's end and 100 yards east of a huge arroyo.

1267O B.M.T.C. LEADER 5.7 This ascends the right side of a large detached flake then up face to the top. FA: Warren Mellinger, Dan Newman and Ben Chapman, April 1986.

GROUP CAMP SHORT WALL

This is the flat 40-foot face 100 yards north of the road's end. Two thin cracks are both 5.10 + . There are also two nice 5.7 hand cracks.

GRAIN CENTRAL STATION

This is a group of crags 100 yards north of and across the road from GC7. Map, page 100.

1267P THE GREAT GRAIN ROBBERY 5.6 On the farthest east face, climb a finger crack to a grainy face leading up and right to a notch. Unprotected climbing leads to the top. The arete left of the grainy face has been top-roped. FA: Todd Swain, Peggy Buckey, Randy Schenkel and Andy Schenkel, December 1988.

1267Q MY GRAIN 5.11/12 40 feet left of the previous route, this is a bolted route leading to a flake and then an arete. FA: Swain, December 1988.

1267R ZINGING IN THE GRAIN 5.8 This is a south-facing slab with one bolt, 100 feet left of the previous routes. FA: Swain, Buckey, R. Schenkel and A. Schenkel, December 1988.

CAMPFIRE CRAG

1280A UNNAMED 5.11+ From the start of *Prejudicial Viewpoint* climb an RP seam straight up. FFA: Mike Lechlinski, Terry Ayers, Tom Gilje, Mike Paul and Danno, January 1988.

CIRCLE CRAG

1283A SCOTCH WITH A TWIST 5.8 Climb overhanging face and a bottoming crack left of *Scotch*, joining that route near the top. FA: Warren Mellinger, Ben Chapman and Jaime Lara, April 1986.

1283B GIN FIZZ 5.7 Between *Scotch* and *Whiskey*, climb an incipient crack to several mantel moves and the top. FA: Chapman, Mellinger, Lara and Dick Seward, February 1985.

1284A AA 5.7 Climb cracks stacked on top of each other 100 feet right of *Whiskey*. FA: Todd Swain and Stan Frome, December 1983.

1284B JUGGURNOT 5.6 100 feet right of *AA* (toward the entrance road) climb a south face on desert varnish. FA: Swain and Frome, December 1983.

The next six routes are found on the southwest face of **Campfire Crag**, starting about 70 feet left of *Picnic*. They are listed from right to left.

1284C LUNCH 5.6 Climb the groove crack 70 feet left of *Picnic*. FA: unknown.

1284D HEART SLAB 5.8 70 feet left of and up from *Lunch* is this heart-shaped slab with four bolts. FA: Bill Todd et al, October 1986.

1284E SPUD OVERHANG 5.9 Below and left from *Heart Slab* (behind campsite #55) is a wall with several cracks. This is the right crack, starting in an overhang. FA: unknown.

1284F GENUINE COWHIDE 5.10a The center crack, which slants right and starts in an overhang. FA: unknown.

1284G ALPENTINE 5.9+ This is the left crack. FA: unknown.

1284H ILLEGAL CAMPFIRE 5.7 Above and left from the previous routes, this is a prominent left-slanting crack in brown rock. FA: unknown.

THE CLUMP

1287 MOMMA SPIDER This route is mislocated in the guide; it is farther west (left) than indicated, and climbs an easy ramp to a roof, then up left into a thin lieback crack.

1287A SPIDER'S WEB 5.8 Left of *Momma Spider* is this right-slanting crack which passes through an apex of cracks. FA: unknown.

1287B PALMREADER 5.8 This is a short perfect hand crack seen above the turnout road just west of **The Clump**. FA: unknown.

DOS EQUIS WALL

1287C SOUTH BUTTRESS 5.7 A two-pitch climb up the broken buttress facing the road. FA: unknown.

1290B ROADRUNNER 5.11a Climb the face left of *Air Play* past four bolts. FA: unknown.

APPARITION ROCK
This rock is almost directly across the road from **Dos Equis Wall.** The three routes are on the north face, visible from the road. Map, supplement page 100.

    1290B APPARITION   5.9   Climb a prominent right-leaning crack, starting with a hand traverse from the left. FA: Herb Laegar, Eve Uiga, John Lonne and R. Saum, February 1979.

    1290C COSMOSIS   5.9/10   Start on the mosaic wall right of *Apparition,* then follow a thin left-slanting crack to join *Apparition* below the top. FA: unknown.

    1290D MOSAIC WALL   5.7   Go straight up the wall right of *Apparition.* FA: unknown.

IRON HAND ROCK

This is a brown formation about 200 yards behind **Apparition Rock.**

1290E DOGLEG RIGHT 5.10c Climb a dogleg crack on the left side of the face. FA: Bill Todd and Laurent Mounoud, November 1987.

1290F IRON HAND 5.9 This is the next line right of *Dogleg Right.* FA: Todd and Mounoud, November 1987.

1290G BROWN CAVE 5.0 An easy chimney on the right side of the wall. FA: Todd and Mounoud, November 1987.

THE TOOTH

This is a prominent spire in the towers between **Dos Equis Wall** and **Moosedog Tower.** There are rappel bolts on top.

1290H MOUNTAINEERS' ROUTE Class 4 or 5 Climb **The Tooth** from the notch. FA: unknown.

1290I WEST FACE 5.7 or 5.9 Start in a left-leaning crack (5.9) or just right (5.7). Higher, follow a crack around right onto the south face. FA: unknown.

1290J HANDCRACKER 5.8 About 150' left of **The Tooth** is this nice jam crack on an arete facing the campground. FA: unknown.

MOOSEDOG TOWER

1291A LUCKY CHARMS 5.7 Start about 100 feet left and uphill from *Third Time's a Charm* and climb a corner up and right to intersect that route. Continue up and right to the ridge to join *Traquility,* etc. FA: Todd Swain, March 1988.

1291B BITCH IN HEAT 5.9 This is a two-pitch climb between *Third Time's a Charm* and *Wandering Winnebago.* The second pitch follows an arete past a bolt. FA: Alan Nelson and Andrea Conner, November 1987.

1295A ROADSIDE SLAB 5.9+ 150 feet along the road past **Moosedog Tower** (behind campsite #92) is this slab with an obvious crack. Hard to protect, easily top-roped. FA: unknown.

JAILHOUSE ROCK

This rock was somewhat mislocated in the guide. Map, supplement page 100.

1297A A SNITCH IN TIME 5.8 Climb the crack through the overhang 15 feet left of *Jailbreak.* FA: Todd Swain, Peggy Buckey and Andy Schenkel, March 1987.

KING OTTO'S CASTLE

1297B DON GENERO CRACK 5.10a This is an obvious slanting crack on a separate formation 200 feet left of *Sweat Band.* FA: unknown.

1297C THE BRIDGE 5.11 This is the leftmost of three bolted routes left of *Sweat Band.* It is around the corner, on the west face of **King Otto's Castle.** FA: unknown.

1297D GOODBYE MR. BOND 5.10c The middle bolted route, this lies near the southwest corner of the rock. FA: Jay Smith, Robert Finley and Rondo Powell, December 1988.

1297E QUIVERING SAVAGES 5.11 The right bolted route. It is about 30 feet left of *Sweat Band.* FA: Dave Caunt et al, December 1986.

1297F PANAMA RED 5.11c (TR) Climb the face 15 feet left of *Sweat Band,* following a thin seam near the top. FA: Alan Nelson, March 1987.

1300A DATE QUEEN 5.7 Climb the offwidth crack right of *Plain but Good Hearted.* FA: unknown.

1300B DATE QUEEN CORRIDOR CRACK 5.11b In a corridor right of the preceding route is this radically overhanging crack. FA: unknown.

1301 THE CONDOR This route is mismarked in the guide; it is actually about 50 yards to the right (west) of where it is indicated in the photo on page 364.

WONDER BLUFFS

1302A GYPSY 5.10a Climb the thin crack 25 feet left of **Slam Dunk**. FA: Bill Todd and Laurent Mounoud, January 1987.

1308A BLOODY BUDDY 5.9 High on the ridge southwest of the **Wonder Bluffs** is a large roof with a chimney splitting it. This is a two-pitch route leading up to it, starting on a dike with two bolts. Descend to the south. FA: Frank Bentwood and Bill Todd, November 1987.

COVE CANYON

This is the first wash/canyon south of **Indian Cove,** behind the ridge containing the **Wonder Bluffs.** It is best approached from the **Short Wall** area by walking due south to the start of the wash, which runs southwest. Map, supplement page 100.

1308B UNKNOWN SLAB 5.6 This is a five-bolt route on a slab on the left at the start of the wash; it is directly across from the **Short Wall.** FA: unknown.

NASA WALL

This wall is ¼ mile up the wash from **Unknown Slab** on the left. It is a squarish 100-foot wall.

1308C NASA CRACK 5.9 On the left, a bolt protects a traverse into this thin crack. FA: unknown.

1308D X-15 5.7 This is the corner right of **NASA Crack.** FA: unknown.

1308E EL CAP 5.9 This is a smooth, overhanging offwidth 100 feet right of **X-15**. Pro to 5". FA: Bill Todd and John Nye, January 1987.

COVE CANYON DOME

Continue walking past the **NASA Wall** and a tributary wash to reach this large formation on the left.

1308F UNDER THE HILL 5.9 This is the left obvious line on the dome and starts in a groove/trough. 3 pitches. FA: unknown.

1308G THE FLAKES 5.9 The right route starts in a steep left-facing book leading to a thin flake system. 3 pitches. FA: unknown.

RATTLESNAKE CANYON

This beautiful canyon is approached from the picnic area east of Indian Cove Campground. In ascending the canyon, some class 2-3 slabs are encountered. After about ½ mile, the canyon levels off and turns west. The following ten routes are reported, but more climbing has certainly been done than that. Map, supplement page 100.

1308H NITTY GRITTY　5.9　Just after the wash levels out and turns west, look right (north) to this light-colored, east-facing wall. The route is a thin right-slanting crack that leads past two small bushes. FA: Alan Bartlett, Mike Schneider and Katie Wilkinson, October 1988.

1308I AROUND THE CORNER　5.8　A short distance up the wash past *Nitty Gritty,* there are some large boulders on the left (south). This ascends the north arete/fin of a boulder past two bolts. FA: Todd Swain, Randy Schenkel and Andy Schenkel, December 1988.

1308J RATTLESNAKE BUTTRESS　5.7 or 5.9　High on the south side of the canyon is this clean, smooth formation with twin curving cracks. A 5.9 pitch goes up a crack which slants left, then back right to a huge ledge at the base of the upper twin cracks. This crux pitch can be avoided by walking around to the right. Above, start in the right crack and switch to the left thin crack partway up. A slightly harder variation stays in the right one to its end. FA: unknown.

To the right of **Rattlesnake Buttress** is a smooth dome known as **The Dune.** There are two partially completed face climbs here. No more information is known.

1308K TEST PILOT   5.10b   On the wall right of **The Dune** is this obvious right-slanting offwidth which leads to a hand traverse exit. Pro to 5". FA: Bill Todd, November 1987.

1308L GREAT COMMISSION   5.11a   Somewhere on the hillside west of **Test Pilot** is this 50-foot low-angle thin crack in a west-facing formation. FA: Doug Englekirk and Randy Leavitt, February 1987.

1308M LOVE COMES IN SPURTS   5.10d   This route is located on a large boulder right in the wash, about ¼ mile after it has leveled off and turned west. Climb past three bolts on the boulder's north side. FA: Todd Gordon, Cyndie Bransford and Jim Angione, May 1988.

1308N SNAKEYE PILLAR   5.7   This and the following two routes are on the north side of **Rattlesnake Canyon,** facing south. Continue past the **Love Comes in Spurts** boulder for about 200 yards. This is a five-bolt route on a pillar/slab with a roof scar about halfway up. This feature is right of a larger face. FA: Bill Todd and John Nye, 1987.

THE PYRAMID
This is the large face left (west) of **Snakeye Pillar.**

1308O PYRAMID POWER   5.9   Climb cracks near the left edge of the face. FA: unknown.

1308P SHAKE, RATTLE AND ROLL   5.11c   This is a two-pitch bolted route up the center of the formation. Rappel the route with two 80-foot rappels. FA: Todd Swain, Peggy Buckey and Karl Pearson, January 1989.

1308Q CHEOPS   5.10a   Follow thin cracks right of the center of the face. FA: unknown.

BILLBOARD BUTTRESS

1311A BILBO 5.8 This is the steep crack above the initial crack of **Squat Rockets**. FA: unknown.

1314A RED BECKEY 5.10a This climbs the corner and crack to the right of **The Reverend**. FA: unknown.

VARNISHED WALL

1316A EAST MEETS WEST 5.7 Climb the face left of **With Malice and Forethought** past a bulge and a roof with a bolt. FA: Todd Swain and Bob Elsinger, April 1984.

1316B ABSENCE OF MALICE 5.11 (TR) Climb the face and seam left of **Double Crux**. FA: John Thackray and Todd Swain, March 1987.

WILLIT PILLAR

1320 UNKNOWN HIGHWAY A1 This is still an old ladder and has not been freed.

1320A HOLLYWOOD AND VAINO 5.10c This is a free version on an old bolt ladder right of **Unknown Highway**. FFA: Vaino Kodas, Herb Laegar and Mike Jaffe, November 1980.

1320B CALL OF THE WEST 5.9 This climbs zig-zag cracks right of the previous route and left of route #1321. FA: Ken Black, 1983.

INDIAN PALISADES CORRIDOR,

1321A WILLIT SLAB 5.7 Climb the face behind **Willit Pillar** past five bolts. FA: unknown.

1321B TOE THE LINE 5.9 Left of **Willit Slab**, climb up and right on a bolt-scarred seam, then left to a finishing crack. FA: unknown.

1321C BITTER BREW 5.8 Climb thin cracks and corners 20 feet right of **Willit Slab**. FA: Alan Nelson, March 1987.

1321D EYES OF AMBER 5.8 This route ascends the brown face 25 feet left of **Water Moccasin**. FA: Nelson, March 1987.

THE FEUDAL WALL

1328A THE BLOCK 5.10a (TR) This climbs the 35-foot block right of **Swishbah**. There ia a fixed pin on top. FA: unknown.

1328B THE CHESSBOARD 5.8 Climb the face left of and around the corner from **La Reina**. FA: Todd Swain and Stan Frome, November 1983.

1335A COCO-LOCO 5.9 This is the thin crack just right of **Marchesa**. FA: Bill Todd and Rosie, November 1986.

1335B NOT JUST ANOTHER PRETTY FACE 5.10b Right of **Coco-Loco** is this climb with one bolt. FA: Bill (from Colorado), Todd Trautner and Robert Alexander, November 1986.

1335C CROWN JEWELS 5.7 Start just left of **Dum Roodle** and climb up and left past a bolt to the large ledges. Continue up past three more bolts. FA: unknown.

1336A CASTLES BURNING 5.12a This is a five-bolt climb just right of **Dum Roodle**. FA: Bob Gaines, January 1988.

1341A TRAUTNER-FRY 5.10c Right of **Minion/El Rey,** climb past a bolt into a thin crack. FA: Trautner and Fry.

1342A PANTHER CRACK 5.10d This is an overhanging crack on the east end of the **Feudal Wall.** It doesn't quite reach the ground. FA: Jon Lonne and Herb Laegar, January 1976.

SHORT WALL

1343A DOUBLE TROUBLE 5.10a (TR) This is a line right of **Step 'n Out.** The original bolts, placed on lead, have been chopped. FA: Herb Laegar and Eve Laegar, March 1981.

1344A RIFF RAFF ROOF 5.10a Start 15 feet left of **Bombay,** and climb a corner up and over a roof to a belay. Continue up a crack past a bush. FA: Alan Nelson and John Cartwright, March 1987.

1348A FACE TO FACE 5.11c (TR) Climb the face between **Right V Crack** and **Linda's Face.** FA: Bob Gaines, April 1986.

1358A AFTERNOON SHAKEDOWN 5.10a This is the face right of **Morning Warm-Up.** FA: unknown.

MORBID MOUND

1367A DEADHEADS 5.4 Start on **Brimstone Stairway,** then climb the face to the right. FA: Todd Swain, Patty Furbush, Kip Knapp, Colette Bein and Jim Schlinkman, March 1986.

1369A DOA 5.8 Climb the face left of **Bouncer** to a ledge, then past a bolt to the top. FA: Swain, Schlinkman, Knapp and Furbush, March 1986.

1373A UNNAMED 5.11a (TR) Start in a thin crack 40 feet right of **Be Wary,** then go left on the face and exit out the left of two roofs. FA: Andy Puhvel and Ian Walker.

1373B 'TIL DEATH DO US FART 5.10a This route is right of the preceding route and left of **A Last Cigarette Señor?.** Climb a vertical crack then go over a roof at a double crack. FA: Swain, Knapp and Schlinkman, March 1986

ROUTES BY RATING

4th

- [ ] Chockstone Chimney
- [ ] Mountaineers' Route

5.0

- [ ] Brown Cave
- [ ] Chimney Sweep
- [ ] Trough, The
- [ ] Trough, The (Echo Rock)

5.1

- [ ] Ambulance Driver
- [ ] B-1
- [ ] Bozo Buttress
- [ ] Brimstone Stairway
- [ ] Eye, The
- [ ] Eyesore
- [ ] Fissure of Men
- [ ] Simpatico
- [ ] Two Point Crack

5.2

- [ ] Be Wary
- [ ] Beginner's Two
- [ ] Button Soup
- [ ] Chute Up
- [ ] Circus
- [ ] Decent Buckets
- [ ] Descent Crack
- [ ] Evening Warm-Down
- [ ] Five Two-ish
- [ ] Helix
- [ ] Hodgepodge
- [ ] Junction Chimney
- [ ] Linda's Crack
- [ ] Marchesa
- [ ] Mastering 5.2
- [ ] North Face (Fat Freddie's Cat)
- [ ] Northwest Chimney
- [ ] Nutcracker
- [ ] Oh God!
- [ ] Queen Mother's Route
- [ ] Route 1326
- [ ] Rusty Pipes
- [ ] Scaramouch
- [ ] Tarantula
- [ ] Through the Hole and Up the Wall
- [ ] Westward Ho!
- [ ] Wooly Spider

5.3

- [ ] B-2
- [ ] B-3
- [ ] Beginner's One
- [ ] Beginner's Three
- [ ] Cary Granite
- [ ] Double Crack
- [ ] Flake Hickey
- [ ] For Sure
- [ ] Half Crack
- [ ] Jailbreak
- [ ] Knaug and Hyde
- [ ] Rumblers Below the Foof
- [ ] Shardik
- [ ] Ski Track, Upper Right
- [ ] Southeast Corner
- [ ] Toe Jam Express
- [ ] Turtle Soup
- [ ] Walkway
- [ ] Wandering Tortoise

5.4

- [ ] 39 Steps
- [ ] Archery
- [ ] Belly Scraper
- [ ] Bisk
- [ ] Bivvy at Gordon's
- [ ] Blue Bayou
- [ ] Bong, The
- [ ] Buckeye
- [ ] Carolyn's Rump
- [ ] Chicken Bones
- [ ] Cornered
- [ ] Crack' n' Up
- [ ] Deadheads
- [ ] Desiderious Delight
- [ ] Diabetics
- [ ] Dos Dedos
- [ ] Duchess Left
- [ ] Easy Day
- [ ] Eschar
- [ ] False Layback
- [ ] Far Side, The
- [ ] Final Act
- [ ] Finally
- [ ] Fright Night
- [ ] Funky Gunkies
- [ ] Gotcha Bush
- [ ] Hillside Strangler
- [ ] Holds to Hollywood
- [ ] Hoopharkz
- [ ] Mad Race
- [ ] Minion
- [ ] Myrmecocystus Ewarti
- [ ] Nectar
- [ ] Northwest Chimney (Outhouse)
- [ ] Ohm on the Range
- [ ] Once in a Blue Moon
- [ ] One Point Crack
- [ ] Outhouse Flake
- [ ] Papal Pleaser
- [ ] Penelope's Walk
- [ ] Pokie's Big Chance
- [ ] Route 66
- [ ] Short Crack
- [ ] Skinny Pin
- [ ] Squat Rockets
- [ ] Tubers in Space
- [ ] Waiting For Alan
- [ ] Wall of 10,000 Holds
- [ ] Water Moccasin
- [ ] Wedge

5.5

- [ ] Adams' Happy Acres
- [ ] Arachnids
- [ ] Bat Crack
- [ ] Blistering
- [ ] Blue Sky, Black Death
- [ ] Boom Boom O'Hara
- [ ] Card Chimney
- [ ] Cellbound
- [ ] Chapter 7
- [ ] Chief, The
- [ ] Dial-a-Pile
- [ ] Dilly Bar
- [ ] Donna T's Route
- [ ] Filch
- [ ] Heffalump
- [ ] Hueco Wall
- [ ] Jump Back Loretta
- [ ] Kodiak
- [ ] Lady in Waiting
- [ ] Lizard Taylor
- [ ] Matt Biondi Chimney
- [ ] Maybe Baby
- [ ] Men With Cow's Heads
- [ ] Mr. Bunny's Tax Shelter
- [ ] Not Worth Your While
- [ ] Ricochet
- [ ] Right On
- [ ] Roaring Rapids
- [ ] Roboranger
- [ ] Rocket Man
- [ ] Secovar
- [ ] Tang
- [ ] Too Silly to Climb
- [ ] Wilson Regular Route
- [ ] WNW Dihedral

5.6

- [ ] Air Crack
- [ ] Angione Crack
- [ ] Ashtray, The
- [ ] Awful Loose
- [ ] Black & Blue
- [ ] Calcutta
- [ ] Chance Meeting
- [ ] Chili Dog
- [ ] Circe
- [ ] Cow Pie Corner

5.6 *(cont.)*

- [ ] Crack #2
- [ ] Creditor's Claim
- [ ] Curtain Call
- [ ] D.E. Chimney, The
- [ ] Damn Jam
- [ ] Date Shake
- [ ] Deflowered
- [ ] Diagnostics
- [ ] Diagonal Chimney
- [ ] Double Decker
- [ ] Double Dip
- [ ] Dover Sole
- [ ] Duchess
- [ ] Dum Roodle
- [ ] Easy Looker
- [ ] Easy Off
- [ ] Eff Four
- [ ] Fat Man's Misery
- [ ] Fields of Laughter
- [ ] Fifteen Minute Gap
- [ ] Fool's Ruby
- [ ] Fote Hog
- [ ] Foul Fowl
- [ ] Gargoyle
- [ ] Gaz Giz
- [ ] Great Grain Robbery, The
- [ ] Gut Reaction
- [ ] Hhecht
- [ ] Holy Roller
- [ ] Homo Erectus
- [ ] Hoser
- [ ] Hush Puppies
- [ ] Indian Garden
- [ ] Is the Pope Catholic?
- [ ] Jaws
- [ ] Jessica's Crack
- [ ] Juggurnot
- [ ] Junkie Thrill
- [ ] Karpkwitz
- [ ] Kendal Mint Cake
- [ ] Klingon Pizza
- [ ] Last Angry Arab
- [ ] Last Minute Additions
- [ ] Leaping Leaner
- [ ] Learning to Crawl
- [ ] Linda's Face
- [ ] Lunch
- [ ] Mikado, The
- [ ] Mike's Books
- [ ] Moment's Notice
- [ ] Moonwalk, The
- [ ] Mr. Lizard Meets Flintstone
- [ ] New Toy
- [ ] Notch Route
- [ ] Nothing to Fear
- [ ] Nuts and Cherries
- [ ] Omega
- [ ] One Small Step
- [ ] Outer Limit
- [ ] Pathetic Crack
- [ ] Pickpocket
- [ ] Picnic
- [ ] Plain but Good Hearted
- [ ] Poodlesby
- [ ] Queen Bee
- [ ] Ranger J.B.
- [ ] Ranger J.D.
- [ ] Rejuvenation
- [ ] Rip Off
- [ ] Ripples in Time
- [ ] Roach Roof
- [ ] Robaxol
- [ ] Roy's Solo
- [ ] Scotch
- [ ] Self Abuse
- [ ] Short Flake
- [ ] Skin Deep Town
- [ ] Solar Technology
- [ ] Split
- [ ] Split Mitten
- [ ] Splotch
- [ ] Stemski
- [ ] Suzie's Cream Squeeze
- [ ] Swain in the Breeze
- [ ] Swiss Cheese
- [ ] SW Corner (Headstone Rock)
- [ ] Talus Phallus
- [ ] Tanning Salon
- [ ] This Puppy
- [ ] Thumb, The
- [ ] Tobin Bias
- [ ] Tranquility
- [ ] Trap Door
- [ ] Trench Connection
- [ ] Tulip
- [ ] Tumbleweed
- [ ] Tweeners Out For Glory
- [ ] Unknown Slab
- [ ] Upevil
- [ ] Wasting Assets
- [ ] West Chimney
- [ ] Whiskey
- [ ] Who's First
- [ ] Zap #4

5.7

- [ ] *13 Year Old Death Trap*
- [ ] *AA*
- [ ] *Able Was I Ere I Saw Ellsmere*
- [ ] *Acuity*
- [ ] *Almost Like Real Climbing*
- [ ] *Almost Vertical*
- [ ] *Andromeda Strain*
- [ ] *As the Crags Turn*
- [ ] *As the Wind Blows*
- [ ] *Aztec Twostep*
- [ ] *Baby Banana*
- [ ] *Baby Face*
- [ ] *Ballbury*
- [ ] *Barely Crankin'*
- [ ] *Beak of the Week*
- [ ] *Beck's Bear*
- [ ] *Betty Gravel*
- [ ] *Bighorn Hand Crack*
- [ ] *Bitch, Bitch*
- [ ] *Bleed Proof*
- [ ] *Bleed Proof*
- [ ] *Bonnie Brae*
- [ ] *Bonzo Dog Band*
- [ ] *Boomerang*
- [ ] *Boulder Face*
- [ ] *Brain, The*
- [ ] *Briar Rabbit*
- [ ] *Bucket Brigade*
- [ ] *Buissonier*
- [ ] *Bushcrack*
- [ ] *Captain Kronos*
- [ ] *Carola's Hip*
- [ ] *Chips Ahoy*
- [ ] *Chocolate Decadence*
- [ ] *Classic Corner*
- [ ] *Clearasil*
- [ ] *Commander Cody*
- [ ] *Court Jester*
- [ ] *Crackup*
- [ ] *Cranny*
- [ ] *Crown Jewels*
- [ ] *Damm Dike*
- [ ] *Dan Cruise*
- [ ] *Dan's Paperbacks*
- [ ] *Date Queen*
- [ ] *Deceptive Corner*
- [ ] *Desert Solitaire*
- [ ] *Die-hedral*
- [ ] *Dimorphism*
- [ ] *Disappearing Belayer*
- [ ] *Dolphin*
- [ ] *Double Crux*
- [ ] *Double Delight*
- [ ] *Double Dogleg*
- [ ] *Double Start*
- [ ] *Dr. Seuss Vogel*
- [ ] *Drawstring*
- [ ] *Dreams of Red Rocks*
- [ ] *Dry Rain*
- [ ] *Duchess Right*
- [ ] *Dung Fu*
- [ ] *East Meets West*
- [ ] *Easy as Pi*
- [ ] *Edchada*
- [ ] *Elusive Butterfly*
- [ ] *False Smooth as Silk*
- [ ] *Finger Locking Good*
- [ ] *Flake Route*
- [ ] *Flakey Flix*
- [ ] *Flakey Friends*
- [ ] *Flash Gordon*
- [ ] *Flies on the Wound*
- [ ] *Foghorn Leghorn*
- [ ] *Frankenwood*
- [ ] *Frankie Lee*
- [ ] *Free As Can Be*
- [ ] *Freeway*
- [ ] *Frosty Cone*
- [ ] *Gin Fizz*
- [ ] *Goldilocks*
- [ ] *Gorgasaurus*
- [ ] *Grand Theft Avocado*
- [ ] *Granny Goose*
- [ ] *Heart Slab*
- [ ] *Heartless*
- [ ] *Hemroidic Terror*
- [ ] *Hex*
- [ ] *Hex Marks the Poot*
- [ ] *Hoblett*
- [ ] *Howard's Horror*
- [ ] *I'm So Embarrassed For You*
- [ ] *Illegal Campfire*
- [ ] *Illusion*
- [ ] *Insider Information*
- [ ] *Invasion on my Fantasy*
- [ ] *It Satisfies*
- [ ] *Jaime's Big Show*
- [ ] *Jim Cruise*
- [ ] *Jumping Jehosaphat*
- [ ] *Jungle*
- [ ] *Knight Mare*
- [ ] *Large Marge*
- [ ] *Last Ticket to Obscuritiville*
- [ ] *Lazy Day*
- [ ] *Leap Year Flake*
- [ ] *Lickety Splits*

5.7 (cont.)

- [ ] Little Bunny Fu-Fu
- [ ] Little Rock Candy Crack
- [ ] Lizard's Landing
- [ ] Look Mom No Hands
- [ ] Lost and Found
- [ ] Lucky Charms
- [ ] Lumping Fat Jennie
- [ ] M.F. Dirty Rat
- [ ] Middle Finger
- [ ] Minotaur
- [ ] Mosaic Wall
- [ ] Mr. Misty Kiss
- [ ] My 3 Friends
- [ ] Nereltne
- [ ] New Year's Quickie
- [ ] Nickel Slots
- [ ] Oatmeal Eating Aardvarks
- [ ] One Way Up
- [ ] Ostrich Skin
- [ ] Other Voices
- [ ] Out of Step
- [ ] Ovehang Bypass
- [ ] Paint Me Gigi
- [ ] Palm-u-Granite
- [ ] Pebble Beach
- [ ] Pebbles and Bam Bam
- [ ] Pile, The
- [ ] Pinnacle Stand
- [ ] Polar Bears in Bondage
- [ ] Political Asylum
- [ ] Power Line
- [ ] Presto in C Sharp
- [ ] Princess
- [ ] Queen for a Day
- [ ] Quien Sabe
- [ ] Rattlesnake Buttress
- [ ] Resurrection
- [ ] Rings Around Uranus
- [ ] Ripples
- [ ] Road Dogs
- [ ] Roast Leg of Chair
- [ ] Rock-a-Lot
- [ ] Rocky Horror
- [ ] S Crack, Left
- [ ] Sabretooth
- [ ] Sandblast
- [ ] Scrumdillishus
- [ ] Search for Klingons
- [ ] She's So Unusual
- [ ] Skinny Dip
- [ ] Slanta Claus, Left
- [ ] Slippery When Wet
- [ ] Smooth as Silk
- [ ] Snakeye Pillar
- [ ] South Buttress
- [ ] South Face Direct
- [ ] Spaghetti & Chili
- [ ] Spinner
- [ ] Spud Patrol
- [ ] Stan and Ollie
- [ ] Steady Breeze
- [ ] Stichter Quits
- [ ] Suzanna's Bandana
- [ ] Swift, The
- [ ] Swishbah
- [ ] Thrutcher
- [ ] Tight Shoes
- [ ] Tiptoe
- [ ] Toe Jam
- [ ] Tom Bombadil
- [ ] Trial by Fire
- [ ] Trivial Pursuit
- [ ] Unwed Mudders
- [ ] Vagmarken Buttress
- [ ] Vaino's Lost in Pot
- [ ] Velveeta Rabbit
- [ ] We Dive at Dawn
- [ ] West Face Overhang
- [ ] West Face, The Tooth
- [ ] Wheat Chex
- [ ] Where Janitors Dare
- [ ] White Lightning
- [ ] White Powder
- [ ] Willard
- [ ] Willit Slab
- [ ] Wisest Crack
- [ ] With Malice and Forethought
- [ ] Worthwhile Pile
- [ ] X-15
- [ ] Zigzag

5.7+

- [ ] Big Bird
- [ ] Crack A
- [ ] Double Cross
- [ ] Mental Physics
- [ ] Robocop
- [ ] Walk on the Wild Side

5.8

- [ ] 24 Carrot
- [ ] 3rd Class It
- [ ] A Bolt, a Bashie and a Bold Mantle
- [ ] A Dream of White Poodles
- [ ] A Snitch in Time
- [ ] Acupuncture
- [ ] All-Reet Arete
- [ ] Altitude Sickness
- [ ] An Officer and a Poodle
- [ ] Annoited Seagull
- [ ] Aquino
- [ ] Are We Ourselves
- [ ] Around the Corner
- [ ] Around the World
- [ ] Arturo's Special
- [ ] Auld Lang Syne
- [ ] Baby Roof
- [ ] Baby-Point-Five
- [ ] Bakersfield Bomb
- [ ] Beck's Bet
- [ ] Berkeley Dyke
- [ ] Big Step
- [ ] Bilbo
- [ ] Bitter Brew
- [ ] Bivo Sham
- [ ] Blue Nun
- [ ] Bombay
- [ ] Boulder Crack
- [ ] Bouncer
- [ ] Bryant Gumbel
- [ ] Buckets to Burbank
- [ ] Bullocks Fashion Center
- [ ] But Fear Itself
- [ ] C.F.M.F.
- [ ] Cashews Will be Eaten
- [ ] Catch a Falling Star
- [ ] Cementary
- [ ] Cerro Torre, SW Face
- [ ] Chaffe n' Up
- [ ] Chessboard, The
- [ ] City H
- [ ] Climb of the Cockroaches
- [ ] Colossus
- [ ] Conservative Policies
- [ ] Convergenge Crack, Center
- [ ] Crank Queenie
- [ ] Cryptic
- [ ] Cuban Connection
- [ ] Cunning Linguist
- [ ] Dancin' Daze
- [ ] Dappled Mare
- [ ] Deliver Us From Evil
- [ ] Dental Hygiene
- [ ] Desert Queen
- [ ] Dinkey Doinks
- [ ] Disposable Heroes
- [ ] DOA
- [ ] Dogleg
- [ ] Edge of the Knife
- [ ] Eff Eight
- [ ] Eyes of Amber
- [ ] Fabulous T. Gordex Cracks, The
- [ ] False Tumbling Rainbow
- [ ] Fat Freddie's Escape
- [ ] Fat Is Where It's At
- [ ] Fat Man's Folly
- [ ] Fatal Flaw
- [ ] Feltonian Physics
- [ ] Filthy Rich
- [ ] Fingertip Traverse of Josh
- [ ] First Steps
- [ ] Five-Four-Plus
- [ ] Flake and Bake
- [ ] Flake, The
- [ ] Flared Bear
- [ ] Flat Tire
- [ ] Flue, The
- [ ] Fool's Gold
- [ ] Friend Eater
- [ ] Fun Stuff
- [ ] Funky Dung
- [ ] Funny Bone
- [ ] Gem
- [ ] Generic Route
- [ ] Go 'Gane
- [ ] Go for Broke
- [ ] Goof Proof Roof
- [ ] Gorby Goes to Washington
- [ ] Grain Surplus
- [ ] Green Mansions
- [ ] Gumby Goes to Washington
- [ ] H.R. Hardman
- [ ] Ham Sandwich
- [ ] Handcracker
- [ ] Hands Off
- [ ] Hang Ten
- [ ] Hard Science
- [ ] Heartbreak Ridge
- [ ] Hit It Ethel
- [ ] I Am Not a Crook
- [ ] I Can Believe it's a Sandbag
- [ ] Isotope
- [ ] Jack the Ripper
- [ ] Jam Crack
- [ ] Jane Pauley
- [ ] Jet Stream

5.8 *(cont.)*

- [ ] *Jo Mama*
- [ ] *Jugular Vein*
- [ ] *Kate's Bush*
- [ ] *Kickoff*
- [ ] *Laid Back*
- [ ] *Leader's Fright*
- [ ] *Less Than Meets the Eye*
- [ ] *Little Ceasar*
- [ ] *Lost in Space*
- [ ] *Love at First Bite*
- [ ] *Lucky Lady*
- [ ] *Luminous Breast*
- [ ] *Lurch*
- [ ] *Lurleen Quits*
- [ ] *Lusting CLH*
- [ ] *Magic Kingdom*
- [ ] *Manwich Queen*
- [ ] *Meanderthal*
- [ ] *Monkey Business*
- [ ] *Monument Manor*
- [ ] *More Hustle Than Muscle*
- [ ] *Morning After, The*
- [ ] *Mosiac*
- [ ] *Mr. Bunny vrs. Six Unknown Agents*
- [ ] *Mr. Michael Goes to Washington*
- [ ] *Music Box*
- [ ] *Not King Cole*
- [ ] *Nurn's Romp*
- [ ] *Old Man and the Poodle, The*
- [ ] *Omaha Beach*
- [ ] *On the Air*
- [ ] *Outward Bound Slab Route*
- [ ] *Owatafooliam*
- [ ] *Palmreader*
- [ ] *Paranetieum*
- [ ] *Parental Guidance Suggested*
- [ ] *Pathetic Dike*
- [ ] *Pathetic Face*
- [ ] *Peanut Brittle*
- [ ] *Penny Lane*
- [ ] *Perhaps The Surgeon General*
- [ ] *Peyote Crack, Right*
- [ ] *Poodle in Shining Armor*
- [ ] *Pop Tart*
- [ ] *Pops Goes Hawaiian*
- [ ] *Potlatch*
- [ ] *Pumpkin Pie*
- [ ] *Quivering Lips*
- [ ] *R & R*
- [ ] *R.M.L.*
- [ ] *Raindance*
- [ ] *Raker Mobile*
- [ ] *Ranger Danger*
- [ ] *Rat Ledge*
- [ ] *Red Eye*
- [ ] *Revenge of the Herds*
- [ ] *Reverend, The*
- [ ] *Rhythm of the Heart*
- [ ] *Right n Up*
- [ ] *Roan Way*
- [ ] *Robotics*
- [ ] *Rollerskating with Aliens*
- [ ] *Rudy Valentine Day*
- [ ] *S Crack, Right*
- [ ] *Safe Muffins*
- [ ] *Sail Away*
- [ ] *Sakretiligious*
- [ ] *Satchmo*
- [ ] *Savwafare ist Everywhere*
- [ ] *Sawdust Crack, Right*
- [ ] *Scientific Americans*
- [ ] *Scotch with a Twist*
- [ ] *Season Opener*
- [ ] *Sentinel Beach*
- [ ] *Sharp Desire*
- [ ] *Sheet Bends*
- [ ] *Sheltered*
- [ ] *Slam Dunk*
- [ ] *Slanta Claus, Right*
- [ ] *Small But Short*
- [ ] *Small World*
- [ ] *Snnfchtt*
- [ ] *Solar Wind*
- [ ] *Solo*
- [ ] *Soma*
- [ ] *Sound of One Shoe Tapping, The*
- [ ] *South End of a Northbound Poodle*
- [ ] *Southwest Passage*
- [ ] *Space Walk*
- [ ] *Spacely Sprockets*
- [ ] *Span-nish Fly*
- [ ] *Sparkle*
- [ ] *Spider*
- [ ] *Spider's Web*
- [ ] *Split Rocks*
- [ ] *Squirrel Roast*
- [ ] *Straight Flush*
- [ ] *Supercollider*
- [ ] *Tabby Litter*
- [ ] *Take Five*
- [ ] *Tennis Shoe Crack*
- [ ] *Thomson Roof*
- [ ] *Ticket to Nowhere*
- [ ] *Tige*
- [ ] *Too Bold to Bolt*
- [ ] *Totally Tubular*

5.8 (cont.)

- [ ] Tragic Kingdom
- [ ] Treadmark Left
- [ ] Treadmark Right
- [ ] Tri-step
- [ ] Troglodyte Crack
- [ ] Tucson Bound
- [ ] Turtle Days
- [ ] Ulysses' Bivouac
- [ ] Undercling Bypass
- [ ] Unicorner
- [ ] Unwiped Butt
- [ ] Up to Heaven
- [ ] Urban Redevelopment
- [ ] Urine Trouble
- [ ] V Cracks
- [ ] Vogel Crack
- [ ] Volga Boat Men
- [ ] W.A.C.
- [ ] Wallaby Crack
- [ ] Walt's Solo
- [ ] We'll Get Them Little P's
- [ ] Wet Pigeon
- [ ] What
- [ ] Where Two Deserts Meet
- [ ] Which Bitch
- [ ] White Collar Crime
- [ ] Worthy of It
- [ ] Zardoz
- [ ] Zinging in the Grain

5.8+

- [ ] Bambi Meets Godzilla
- [ ] Breakfast of Champions
- [ ] Butterfingers Make Me Horny
- [ ] Continuum
- [ ] I Love Brian Piccolo
- [ ] J.B. Goes to J.T.
- [ ] Morning Star
- [ ] Mush Puppies
- [ ] My Hubby is Chubby
- [ ] Nobody Walks in L.A.
- [ ] Orange Flake
- [ ] Punked Out Porpoise
- [ ] Stains of the Stars
- [ ] Such a Poodle
- [ ] T.S. Special
- [ ] Wandering Winnebago
- [ ] Walking the Dog
- [ ] ZZZZZ

5.9

- [ ] A Farewell to Poodles
- [ ] A Last Cigarette Señor?
- [ ] Ace of Spades
- [ ] Adams Family
- [ ] Alice in Wonderjam
- [ ] All My Children
- [ ] American Express
- [ ] An Eye to the West
- [ ] Ancient Future
- [ ] Another Brick in the Wall
- [ ] Apparition
- [ ] Archimedes' Crack, Right
- [ ] Ass of Dog
- [ ] At Last
- [ ] Atomic Pile
- [ ] Autopia
- [ ] Baby Route
- [ ] Bacon Flake
- [ ] Bank Note Blues
- [ ] Barn Door, Left
- [ ] Becky's Buttress
- [ ] Beginner's Luck
- [ ] Big Boy
- [ ] Big Brother
- [ ] Birdman from Alcatraz
- [ ] Biskering
- [ ] Bitch in Heat
- [ ] Bittersweet
- [ ] Black Eye
- [ ] Blizzard
- [ ] Blood and Cuts
- [ ] Bloody Buddy
- [ ] Bloodymir
- [ ] Body Shaving for Competition
- [ ] Bolivian Freeze Job
- [ ] Bonny's Boo-Boo
- [ ] Boom Boom Room
- [ ] Boulder Dash
- [ ] Break a Leg
- [ ] Bubba's Tourist Trap
- [ ] Bush Eviction
- [ ] Buster Brown
- [ ] Buster Hymen
- [ ] Cake Walk
- [ ] Calgary Stampede
- [ ] Call of the West
- [ ] Casual
- [ ] Chalk Up Another One

5.9 *(cont.)*

- [ ] *Charlie Brown*
- [ ] *Chicken Mechanics*
- [ ] *Chocolate Chips*
- [ ] *Circus, Circus*
- [ ] *Clamming at the Beach*
- [ ] *Cling Peaches*
- [ ] *Coco-Loco*
- [ ] *Cole-Lewis*
- [ ] *Colorado Crack*
- [ ] *Controversial*
- [ ] *Convergence Crack, Left*
- [ ] *Count on your Fingers*
- [ ] *Cows in the Shade*
- [ ] *Crack B*
- [ ] *Credibility Gap*
- [ ] *Crystal Keyhole*
- [ ] *Damper*
- [ ] *Date Rape*
- [ ] *Dazed and Confused*
- [ ] *Deep Throat*
- [ ] *Defoliation*
- [ ] *Didn't Your Mama Ever Tell You ...*
- [ ] *Die Young*
- [ ] *Direct South Face*
- [ ] *Dirty Surprise*
- [ ] *DMB, The*
- [ ] *Do or Dike*
- [ ] *Don't Look a Gift Frog in the Mouth*
- [ ] *Don't Think Twice*
- [ ] *Dos Peros Negros*
- [ ] *Double or Nothing*
- [ ] *Downpour*
- [ ] *Drill Dust*
- [ ] *Drop a Frog*
- [ ] *Drop Your Drawers*
- [ ] *Duke, The*
- [ ] *Dummy's Delight*
- [ ] *El Cap*
- [ ] *Enchanted Stairway*
- [ ] *Endless Summer*
- [ ] *Enforcer, The*
- [ ] *Enter the Dragon*
- [ ] *Enterprise, The*
- [ ] *Euthyphro*
- [ ] *Excitable Boy*
- [ ] *Fiendish Fists*
- [ ] *Fighting the Slime*
- [ ] *Fishing Trip*
- [ ] *Fisting in Loveland*
- [ ] *Flakes, The*
- [ ] *Flawless Fissure*
- [ ] *Footloose*
- [ ] *For Whom the Poodle Tolls*
- [ ] *Four Car Garage*
- [ ] *Frets Don't Fail Me Now*
- [ ] *Friendly Fists*
- [ ] *Frozen Fish Fingers*
- [ ] *Full Contact Karate*
- [ ] *Gail Winds*
- [ ] *General Hospital*
- [ ] *Gladhander*
- [ ] *Glumpies*
- [ ] *Gnatty Dread*
- [ ] *Gomer Pile*
- [ ] *Good Book, The*
- [ ] *Grain and Bear It*
- [ ] *Grounder*
- [ ] *GS-5*
- [ ] *Gut Full of Suds*
- [ ] *Gypsy Queen*
- [ ] *Hairline Fracture*
- [ ] *Hand Wobler Delight*
- [ ] *Hands Away*
- [ ] *Hans Solo*
- [ ] *Head, Abdomen, Thorax*
- [ ] *Heat Wave*
- [ ] *Herman*
- [ ] *Hershey Highway*
- [ ] *High Strung*
- [ ] *Hobo Chang Ba*
- [ ] *Horny Corner*
- [ ] *Hot Crystals*
- [ ] *Hot Fudge*
- [ ] *Hunkloads to Hermosa*
- [ ] *I Can't Believe It's a Girdle*
- [ ] *I Got It*
- [ ] *Immaculate Conception*
- [ ] *In and Out*
- [ ] *Infectious Smile*
- [ ] *Innervisions*
- [ ] *Invisibility Lessons*
- [ ] *Iron Hand*
- [ ] *It*
- [ ] *Jack of Hearts*
- [ ] *Jeepers Leepers*
- [ ] *Joan Jetson*
- [ ] *Junkyard God*
- [ ] *Just a Skosh*
- [ ] *Just Another Crack From L.A.*
- [ ] *Just Another New Wave Route*
- [ ] *Just Another Roadside Attraction*
- [ ] *Kid, The*
- [ ] *Kiddie Corner*
- [ ] *Killer Bees*
- [ ] *Kippy Korner*
- [ ] *Kiss Me Where I Pee*

5.9 *(cont.)*

- [ ] *Knot Again*
- [ ] *Krakatoa*
- [ ] *La Reina*
- [ ] *Lead Us Not Into Temptation*
- [ ] *Leading Lady*
- [ ] *Lean Two*
- [ ] *Lechlinski Crack, Left*
- [ ] *Lechlinski Crack, Right*
- [ ] *Legal Briefs*
- [ ] *Letdown, The*
- [ ] *Life Without T.V.*
- [ ] *Live From Tasmania*
- [ ] *Lone Ranger, The*
- [ ] *Long-Necked Goose*
- [ ] *Looney Tunes*
- [ ] *Lunch is for Wimps*
- [ ] *Lust in the Wonderland*
- [ ] *Lust We Forget*
- [ ] *M & M's Plain*
- [ ] *Made in the Shade*
- [ ] *Magic Touch, The*
- [ ] *Manna from Heaven*
- [ ] *Mare's Tail*
- [ ] *McStumpy Sandwich*
- [ ] *Meat Wagon*
- [ ] *Midnight Dreamer*
- [ ] *Mighty Mouse*
- [ ] *Milk Run*
- [ ] *Momma Spider*
- [ ] *More Fool Me*
- [ ] *More Frozen Food*
- [ ] *Morituri te Salutamus*
- [ ] *Morning Warm-up*
- [ ] *Mr. Bunny Goes Rollerskating*
- [ ] *Mr. Bunny's Petri Dish*
- [ ] *Mrs. Paul's*
- [ ] *My First First*
- [ ] *My Laundry*
- [ ] *My Wife is an Alien*
- [ ] *NASA Crack*
- [ ] *Negasaurus*
- [ ] *New Testament*
- [ ] *Nitty Gritty*
- [ ] *No Nuts, No Huevos*
- [ ] *No Strings Attached*
- [ ] *Nobody Walks in L.A.*
- [ ] *Nobody's Right Mind*
- [ ] *North Overhang*
- [ ] *Norwegian Wood*
- [ ] *Nuke the Whales*
- [ ] *Nurses in Bondage*
- [ ] *Nuts are for Men Without Balls*
- [ ] *OK Korner*
- [ ] *Opus Dihedral*
- [ ] *Orphan*
- [ ] *Over the Hill*
- [ ] *Overseer*
- [ ] *Owl*
- [ ] *Pachyderms to Paradise*
- [ ] *Pardon Me*
- [ ] *Peabody's Peril*
- [ ] *Penalty Runout*
- [ ] *Perhaps*
- [ ] *Perverts in Power*
- [ ] *Pete's Handful*
- [ ] *Peyote Crack, Middle*
- [ ] *Pig in Heat*
- [ ] *Pinhead*
- [ ] *Poetry in Motion*
- [ ] *Pom Pom Dancer*
- [ ] *Pope and Circumstance*
- [ ] *Pope's Crack*
- [ ] *Pope's Hat*
- [ ] *Popular Mechanics*
- [ ] *Portal*
- [ ] *Prepackaged*
- [ ] *Primal Urge*
- [ ] *Progressive Lizard*
- [ ] *Prom Queen*
- [ ] *Psoriasis*
- [ ] *Psycho Groove*
- [ ] *Pterodactydl Crack*
- [ ] *Pyramid Power*
- [ ] *Quaking Has-Beens*
- [ ] *Quest for the Golden Hubris*
- [ ] *R.A.F.*
- [ ] *Rad*
- [ ] *Rattlesnake Buttress, Direct*
- [ ] *Ravens Do Nasty Things to My Bottom*
- [ ] *Reality Check*
- [ ] *Renter, The*
- [ ] *Rich and Famous*
- [ ] *Right Lizard Crack*
- [ ] *Rites of Spring*
- [ ] *Roberts Crack*
- [ ] *Rock & Roll Girl*
- [ ] *Rock Candy*
- [ ] *Roller Coaster*
- [ ] *Room to Shroom*
- [ ] *Route 182*
- [ ] *Ruffled Rooster*
- [ ] *Rush Hour*
- [ ] *Rye Not?*
- [ ] *Safety in Solitude*
- [ ] *Same As It Ever Was*
- [ ] *Sanctify Yourself*

5.9 (cont.)

- [ ] Satin Finish
- [ ] Save the Last Stance for Me
- [ ] Semisweet
- [ ] Sendero Luminoso
- [ ] Shakin' the Shirts
- [ ] Shirley MaClaine Meets Edlinger
- [ ] Shit Sandwich
- [ ] Shock the Poodle
- [ ] Short but Sweet
- [ ] Silent but Deadly
- [ ] Sine Wave
- [ ] Smithereens
- [ ] Smoke-a-Bowl
- [ ] Snow Falls
- [ ] Soft Core
- [ ] Something Heinous
- [ ] Soul Research
- [ ] South Face Center (Headstone)
- [ ] South Swell
- [ ] Sphincter Quits
- [ ] Spinal Tap
- [ ] Split Personality
- [ ] Spoodle
- [ ] Spud Overhang
- [ ] Stemulation
- [ ] Stepping out of Babylon
- [ ] Stick to What
- [ ] Strawberry Jam
- [ ] Sugar Daddy
- [ ] Sugar Daddy (L.R. Candy Mtn.)
- [ ] Sullivan From Colorado
- [ ] Sunset Strip
- [ ] Super Beak of the Desert
- [ ] Super Roof
- [ ] Tails of Poodles
- [ ] Take Two They're Small
- [ ] Tales of Brave Ulysses
- [ ] Tasgrainian Devil
- [ ] Teenage Enema
- [ ] Terminator, The
- [ ] The Harder They Fall
- [ ] Thin Air
- [ ] Thin Flakes
- [ ] Thin is In
- [ ] Thin Man's Nightmare
- [ ] Third World
- [ ] Thrash or Crash
- [ ] Throat Warbler Mangrove
- [ ] Thumbs Down Left
- [ ] Tigers on Vaseline
- [ ] Toad Crack
- [ ] Toe the Line
- [ ] Toffied Ear Wax
- [ ] Tofu the Dwarf
- [ ] Top 40 to Middle Toilet
- [ ] Totally Nuts
- [ ] Touch and Go
- [ ] Touche Away
- [ ] Trashman Roof
- [ ] Trembling Toes
- [ ] Trowel and Error
- [ ] True Democracy
- [ ] Tumbling Rainbow
- [ ] Turkey Terror
- [ ] TVC15
- [ ] Two Our Surprise
- [ ] Unbearable Lightness of Being, The
- [ ] Unconscious Obscenity
- [ ] Under the Hill
- [ ] Unnamed
- [ ] Vaino's Crack
- [ ] Voice Buddy
- [ ] Vorpal Sword
- [ ] Vulture's Roost
- [ ] Wailing Sax
- [ ] Wall Street
- [ ] Waterchute, The
- [ ] Weathering Frights
- [ ] Western Saga
- [ ] What's Left
- [ ] Which Witch
- [ ] Whips and Grains
- [ ] Whisper When You Scream
- [ ] White Line Fever
- [ ] Wild East
- [ ] Wild Gravity
- [ ] Wild Wind
- [ ] Wind Sprint
- [ ] Wise Crack
- [ ] Working Overtime
- [ ] Wuthering Heights
- [ ] X-Rated Tits
- [ ] Yei-Bei-Chei Crack
- [ ] Young Lust
- [ ] Yuppies Don't Do Offwidths

5.9 +

- [ ] *Alpentine*
- [ ] *Angular Momentum*
- [ ] *Aqua Tarkus*
- [ ] *Barn Door, Right*
- [ ] *Beam Aboard*
- [ ] *Biological Clock*
- [ ] *Chocolate is Better Than Sex*
- [ ] *Comic Book*
- [ ] *Cosmosis*
- [ ] *Crack #5*
- [ ] *Early Bird*
- [ ] *Effigy Too*
- [ ] *False Prophet*
- [ ] *Flaming Arrow*
- [ ] *Fun in the Sun*
- [ ] *Go with the Floe*
- [ ] *Grand Canyon Donkey Trail*
- [ ] *I Love Snakes*
- [ ] *Java*
- [ ] *Jumar of Flesh*
- [ ] *Marcos*
- [ ] *Misha's Madness*
- [ ] *My Senior Project*
- [ ] *Night Gallery*
- [ ] *No Holds Barred*
- [ ] *Not in Kansas Anymore*
- [ ] *Nuclear Waste*
- [ ] *Open Season*
- [ ] *Primal Flake*
- [ ] *Rich Bitch*
- [ ] *Roadside Slab*
- [ ] *Robocop Meets the Munchkins*
- [ ] *Route 1056*
- [ ] *Sidewinder*
- [ ] *Standing Ovation*
- [ ] *Stardust Memories*
- [ ] *Uncertainly Principal*
- [ ] *Wally George*
- [ ] *Wanna Bong*
- [ ] *Workout at the Y*
- [ ] *Zebra Dihedral*

5.10

- [ ] *Amoeba, The*
- [ ] *Black Todd*
- [ ] *Bolt Heaven*
- [ ] *C Sharp Roof*
- [ ] *Crack of Dark*
- [ ] *Convergence Crack, Right*
- [ ] *Cyclotron*
- [ ] *Flakey Puffs from Hell*
- [ ] *Forsaken Mein-key, The*
- [ ] *Get the Balance Right*
- [ ] *Gravity Pirates*
- [ ] *Holiday in the Sun*
- [ ] *Huevos Rancheros*
- [ ] *Major Creative Effort*
- [ ] *Moonraker*
- [ ] *More Crazy than Lazy*
- [ ] *Mosar*
- [ ] *Mustang Ranch*
- [ ] *North Dakota Big Wall Problem*
- [ ] *One Story Town*
- [ ] *Peyote Crack, Left*
- [ ] *Stainless Steel Rat*
- [ ] *Start Fumbling*
- [ ] *Stop the Presses*
- [ ] *Tomato Amnesia*
- [ ] *Two Blind Mice*
- [ ] *Unknown*
- [ ] *Walk on the Steep Side*

5.10a

- [ ] *42N8*
- [ ] *A-Jill-ity*
- [ ] *Aero Space*
- [ ] *Afternoon Shakedown*
- [ ] *Against the Grain*
- [ ] *Alligator Lizard*
- [ ] *Anty Matter*
- [ ] *Ape Man Hop*
- [ ] *Arete #1*
- [ ] *Arraignment, The*
- [ ] *Ash Gordon*
- [ ] *Axe of Dog*
- [ ] *Bad Lizards*
- [ ] *Ball Bearing*
- [ ] *Ballbearings Under Foot*
- [ ] *Ballet*
- [ ] *Baskerville Crack, Right*
- [ ] *Beafcake*
- [ ] *Beam Me Up Scottie*
- [ ] *Beef and Bean*
- [ ] *Berserk*
- [ ] *Bimbo*
- [ ] *Bird of Fire*
- [ ] *Bird on a Wire*
- [ ] *Biscuit Eater*
- [ ] *Black Slacks*

5.10a (cont.)

- [ ] Don't Think Just Jump
- [ ] Double Trouble
- [ ] Dr. Scholl's Wild Ride
- [ ] Drano
- [ ] East Face, The Stirrup
- [ ] El Rey
- [ ] Escape from the Planet Earth
- [ ] Exhibit A
- [ ] Exorcist
- [ ] Face It
- [ ] Face Race
- [ ] Face Route
- [ ] Fantasy of Light
- [ ] Feeling Groovy
- [ ] Female Mud Massacre
- [ ] Firé Glove, The
- [ ] Fist Full of Crystals
- [ ] Fists of Fury
- [ ] Flare Play
- [ ] Free Climbing
- [ ] Free Fall
- [ ] Frontal Lobotomy
- [ ] Frostline
- [ ] Frotal Logranity
- [ ] Fruit Fly
- [ ] Full Frontal Nudity
- [ ] Gait of Power
- [ ] Garden Path
- [ ] Gemstoner
- [ ] Genuine Cowhide
- [ ] Gnarly
- [ ] Gone in 60 Seconds
- [ ] Good to the Last Drop
- [ ] Good, the Bad and the Ugly, The
- [ ] Gossamer Wings
- [ ] Gripped Up the Hole
- [ ] Groove Avoidance System
- [ ] Gross Chimney
- [ ] Ground Finale
- [ ] Guardian Angels
- [ ] Gun for the Sun
- [ ] Gypsy
- [ ] Half Track
- [ ] Halfway to Paradise
- [ ] Hand Grenade
- [ ] Harvey's Bristol Cream
- [ ] Hawks Retreat
- [ ] Head Over Heals
- [ ] Block, The
- [ ] Blue Nubian
- [ ] Blues Brothers
- [ ] Bob
- [ ] Boogers on a Lampshade

- [ ] Boot Hill
- [ ] Bottle in Front of Me
- [ ] Broken Glass
- [ ] Bubba Takes a Siesta
- [ ] Buenos Aires
- [ ] C.S.Special
- [ ] Candelabra
- [ ] Captain Safe
- [ ] Caramel Crunch
- [ ] Cat in the Hat, The
- [ ] Championship Wrestling
- [ ] Cheops
- [ ] Chestwig
- [ ] Closed on Mondays
- [ ] Cole-Evans
- [ ] Cole-Lewis, The
- [ ] Coming Up Short
- [ ] Control
- [ ] Corner n' Crack
- [ ] Cornerstone, The (Touch and Go)
- [ ] Cosmic Debris
- [ ] Crack #6
- [ ] Cruelty to Animals
- [ ] Crystal Calisthenics
- [ ] Cunning Route
- [ ] Dandelion
- [ ] Dangling Woo Li Master
- [ ] Dark Ages
- [ ] Dave's Solo
- [ ] Daze of Who
- [ ] Dead Bees
- [ ] Death of a Decade
- [ ] Death on the Nile
- [ ] Deception
- [ ] Defenders of the Farce
- [ ] Defibrillation
- [ ] Deja Vu
- [ ] Desert Delirium
- [ ] Deviate
- [ ] Diamond Dogs
- [ ] Dirty Dancing
- [ ] Dodo's Delight
- [ ] Don Genero Crack
- [ ] Heart and Sole
- [ ] Heart Transplant
- [ ] Heavy Gold
- [ ] Heavy Slander
- [ ] Heavy Water
- [ ] Holy Hand
- [ ] I Get By With a Little Help From My Friends
- [ ] I Just Told You
- [ ] I Slept With L.K.

5.10a (cont.)

- [ ] Ice Climbing
- [ ] If I Only Had a Brain
- [ ] Illusion Dweller
- [ ] Immuno Reaction
- [ ] In Elke's Absence
- [ ] In the Pit
- [ ] Jack Grit
- [ ] Jamburger
- [ ] Jerry Brown
- [ ] Jersey Girl
- [ ] Jughead
- [ ] Julius Seizure
- [ ] Kachina
- [ ] Kickin' Bach
- [ ] Kid Calingula
- [ ] Kleptomania
- [ ] Knick
- [ ] KP Corner
- [ ] Ledges to Laundale
- [ ] Left Route
- [ ] Lemon Lemon
- [ ] Little Lieback
- [ ] Love Goat, The
- [ ] M & M's Peanut
- [ ] Maiden Voyage
- [ ] Mama Woolsey
- [ ] Mel Crack, Right
- [ ] Milk the Dog
- [ ] Mind Over Splatter
- [ ] Minor Detour
- [ ] Modern Warfare
- [ ] Monkey King
- [ ] Monster Mash
- [ ] More Funky Than Junky
- [ ] Mother Butler
- [ ] Moubit
- [ ] Mr. Bunny Quits
- [ ] Mr. Bunny's Refund Check
- [ ] Mud Dog
- [ ] My Favorite Things
- [ ] Negro Vortex
- [ ] New Day Yesterday
- [ ] Ninny's Revenge
- [ ] Nip in the Air
- [ ] No Calculators Allowed
- [ ] North Face of the Eiger
- [ ] Not a Hogan
- [ ] Not Forgotten
- [ ] O.W.
- [ ] Old Man Down the Road, The
- [ ] One for the Road
- [ ] Orc, The
- [ ] Ouef's Up
- [ ] Out to Grunge
- [ ] Overseer, Direct Start
- [ ] Oversight
- [ ] Pear-Grape Route
- [ ] Phineas P. Phart
- [ ] Picking up the Pieces
- [ ] Pictures at an Exhibition
- [ ] Pillar of Dawn
- [ ] Pink Thing
- [ ] Pixie Stick
- [ ] Playing Hookey
- [ ] Pocket Veto
- [ ] Polly Wants a Crack
- [ ] Poon
- [ ] Poppin' and Breakin'
- [ ] Pretty Gritty
- [ ] Prime Time
- [ ] Profundity
- [ ] Puss Wuss
- [ ] Quarantine
- [ ] Quarter Moon Crack
- [ ] Quick Draw McGraw
- [ ] Raven's Reach
- [ ] Ray's Cafe
- [ ] Red Beckey
- [ ] Reflector Oven
- [ ] Reggie on a Poodle
- [ ] Retirement
- [ ] Ride a Wild Bago
- [ ] Riders on the Storm
- [ ] Riff Raff Roof
- [ ] Roach Motel
- [ ] Rock Lypso
- [ ] Rollerball
- [ ] Roof, The
- [ ] Roofing Company
- [ ] Route 1203
- [ ] Route 152
- [ ] Sacred Cow
- [ ] Safety in Numbers
- [ ] School Daze
- [ ] Screaming Woman, The
- [ ] Second Thoughts
- [ ] Shooting Gallery Direct
- [ ] Short Cake
- [ ] Short Crack
- [ ] Short Stop
- [ ] Silent Scream
- [ ] Slanta Claus, Center
- [ ] Slip Slidin' Away
- [ ] Slushie
- [ ] Snatch, The
- [ ] Sole Food

5.10a (cont.)

- [ ] Solid Gold
- [ ] Space Slot
- [ ] Spiderman
- [ ] Spitwad
- [ ] Squeeze Play
- [ ] Squid of My Desire
- [ ] Stand By Me
- [ ] Start Trundling
- [ ] Stegasaurus
- [ ] Step'n Out
- [ ] Steppin' Out
- [ ] Stinger
- [ ] Stop Trundling
- [ ] Sublimination
- [ ] Sudden Death
- [ ] Tax Evasion
- [ ] Tax Man
- [ ] Ten Conversations at Once
- [ ] Thumbs Up
- [ ] Thunderclap
- [ ] Tidbit
- [ ] Til Death Do Us Fart
- [ ] Time to Take the Garbage Out
- [ ] Tipples in Rime
- [ ] Top Flight
- [ ] Tossed Green
- [ ] Tower of Godliness
- [ ] Trail of Tiers
- [ ] Trick of the Tail
- [ ] Tricky Move
- [ ] True Dice
- [ ] Tumbling Dice
- [ ] Two Stage
- [ ] Underwear Bandit, The
- [ ] Unknown Route, The
- [ ] Up and Down
- [ ] Upper Cow
- [ ] Use it or Loose it
- [ ] V Crack, Right
- [ ] Vaino's Renegade Lead
- [ ] Visual Nightmare
- [ ] Vortex
- [ ] Walker Spur
- [ ] Wallflower
- [ ] War Baby
- [ ] War Crimes
- [ ] War Games
- [ ] Watanobe Wall
- [ ] Weak Force, The
- [ ] What's Hannen
- [ ] Where Brownies Dare
- [ ] Where Ees De Santa Claus ?
- [ ] White Rabbit
- [ ] Yardy-Hoo and Away
- [ ] Yogi the Overbear
- [ ] Zarmog the Dragon Man
- [ ] Zen Goblins
- [ ] Zondo's Perks

5.10b

- [ ] Accelerator
- [ ] Acupuncturist, The
- [ ] Aftermath
- [ ] Ali Shuffle
- [ ] Ali Shuffle
- [ ] Aliens Ate My Buick
- [ ] An Eye for an Eye and a Route for a Route
- [ ] Ashes to Ashes
- [ ] B For Beers
- [ ] B-Movie
- [ ] B.L.T.
- [ ] Baby Blue Eyes
- [ ] Bailey's Foster
- [ ] Banana Crack, Left
- [ ] Banana Crack, Left
- [ ] Bandersnatch
- [ ] Barnie Rubble
- [ ] Baskerville Crack, Left
- [ ] Bedtime for Democracy
- [ ] Ben
- [ ] Better You Than Me
- [ ] Between a Rock and a Hard Place
- [ ] Bighorn Dihedral
- [ ] Bitchin'
- [ ] Black Ice
- [ ] Bloody Tax Break
- [ ] Blue Monday
- [ ] Blue Moon
- [ ] Bluewind
- [ ] Boogs' Route
- [ ] Book of Changes
- [ ] Brits in Drag
- [ ] Broken China
- [ ] Burn Out
- [ ] Butt Buttress, The
- [ ] Cat Paws
- [ ] Caught Outside on a Big Set
- [ ] Chemical Warefare
- [ ] Chicken Lizard
- [ ] Cholla Crack
- [ ] Clean and Jerk

5.10b (cont.)

- [ ] Clean Crack
- [ ] Cliff Hanger
- [ ] Coliseum, The
- [ ] Come-N-Do Me
- [ ] Conniption
- [ ] Crack Addiction
- [ ] Cripple Crack
- [ ] Delightful Lady
- [ ] Dialing for Ducats
- [ ] Direct Start, Pig in Heat
- [ ] Dog Day Afternoon
- [ ] Dorothy Does the Wizard
- [ ] Dyno in the Dark
- [ ] Edge of Doom
- [ ] Edge, The
- [ ] Elijah's Coming
- [ ] Energy Crisis
- [ ] Event Horizon
- [ ] Eyes Without a Face
- [ ] Fantasia
- [ ] Fall from Grace
- [ ] Far Side of Crazy
- [ ] Figures on a Landscape
- [ ] Filet of Cole
- [ ] Finger Food
- [ ] Finger Stacks or Plastic Sacks
- [ ] Fisticuffs
- [ ] Flaring Rhoid
- [ ] Flue Right
- [ ] Forbidden Paradise
- [ ] Forgotten Venture
- [ ] Foundation Crack
- [ ] Friendly Hands
- [ ] Fusion Without Integrity
- [ ] Ganado
- [ ] Georgia O'Keefe
- [ ] Get the Boot
- [ ] Grain Dance
- [ ] Grain Surgery
- [ ] Gravel Shower
- [ ] Great Unknown, The
- [ ] Gunks West
- [ ] Ham & Swiss
- [ ] Handsaw
- [ ] Hesitation Blues
- [ ] Hobbit Roof
- [ ] Hole in One
- [ ] Holy Cross
- [ ] Horror-Zontal Terror-Verse
- [ ] Howard's Horror Direct
- [ ] I Forgot to Have Babies
- [ ] Iguana Masters
- [ ] Insolvent

- [ ] Invisible Touch
- [ ] Jemiomagina
- [ ] Jet Stream
- [ ] Jody
- [ ] Judas
- [ ] Jungle Cruise
- [ ] Just Drive, She Said
- [ ] L'Chaim
- [ ] Ladder Back
- [ ] Land of the Long White Cloud
- [ ] Laura Scudders
- [ ] Leadbelly
- [ ] Lemon Head, The
- [ ] Let it all Hang Out
- [ ] Let's Get Physical
- [ ] Light Sabre
- [ ] Lips Like Sugar
- [ ] Loose Lady
- [ ] Love & Rockets
- [ ] Lower Band
- [ ] Lower Life Forms
- [ ] Magnetic Woose
- [ ] Make or Break Flake
- [ ] Maltese Falcon, The
- [ ] Math
- [ ] Matt's Problem
- [ ] Mental Bankruptcy
- [ ] Mesopotamia
- [ ] Ming Dallas, The
- [ ] Moonstruck
- [ ] Mortarfied
- [ ] Mother Lode
- [ ] Mr. Bunny Meets the Expando Flake
- [ ] Muffin Bandits
- [ ] Napkin of Shame
- [ ] Narwhal, The
- [ ] Nice and Steep and Elbow Deep
- [ ] Nipple, The
- [ ] No Biggy
- [ ] None of Your Business
- [ ] Not For Loan
- [ ] Not Just Another Pretty Face
- [ ] Nuclear Waste
- [ ] Offshoot
- [ ] On the Nob
- [ ] Ordinary Route
- [ ] Organ Grinder, The
- [ ] Out on a Limb
- [ ] Papa Woolsey
- [ ] Papillon
- [ ] Pencil Neck Geek
- [ ] Perastroika
- [ ] Peruvian Princess

5.10b (cont.)

- [ ] Pinched Rib
- [ ] Pirates of the Carabiner
- [ ] Poodle Woof
- [ ] Poodle-oids from the Deep
- [ ] Poodles Are People Too
- [ ] Pop Rocks
- [ ] Power Drop
- [ ] Power Lichen
- [ ] Pumping Ego
- [ ] Queen Crimsom
- [ ] Reach for a Peach
- [ ] Rhythm & Blues
- [ ] Rickets and Scurvy
- [ ] Rope Drag
- [ ] Run For Your Life
- [ ] Sack in the Wash
- [ ] Scare Way
- [ ] Schrodinger Equation, The
- [ ] Scope & Hope
- [ ] Search for Chinese Morsels
- [ ] Shaking Hands with the Unemployed
- [ ] Shooting Gallery
- [ ] Short and Crank
- [ ] Short but Flared
- [ ] Shovling-Cole
- [ ] Sinner's Swing
- [ ] Sitting Bull
- [ ] Six-Pack Crack
- [ ] Ski Track, Lower Right
- [ ] Slim Pickings
- [ ] Solosby
- [ ] Sound Asleep
- [ ] Space Odyssey
- [ ] Spank the Monkey
- [ ] Spread & Butter
- [ ] Statue of Elvis on Mars
- [ ] Stepping Razor
- [ ] Stinkbug, The
- [ ] Strain Gauge
- [ ] Strike it Rich
- [ ] Suffering Catfish
- [ ] Surrealistic Pillar
- [ ] Sympathy to the Devil
- [ ] Tales of Powder
- [ ] Tar Face
- [ ] Tarawassie Wiggie
- [ ] Team Scumbag
- [ ] Team Slug
- [ ] Test Pilot
- [ ] That
- [ ] Third Time's a Charm
- [ ] Tinker Toys
- [ ] TM's Terror
- [ ] Toad Warrior
- [ ] Too Loose to Trek
- [ ] Tower of Cleanliness
- [ ] Transylvania Twist
- [ ] Treinte Anos
- [ ] Tremor
- [ ] Tube, The
- [ ] Tubular Balls
- [ ] U.B. Kool
- [ ] Under a Raging Moon
- [ ] Unnamed
- [ ] Vice President
- [ ] Vicki the Visitor
- [ ] Wait Until Dark
- [ ] Walt's Frozen Head
- [ ] Waugh Crack
- [ ] Wayward Hayward
- [ ] Whatchasay Dude
- [ ] When You're Not a Jet
- [ ] Why Does it Hurt When I Pee?
- [ ] Wired
- [ ] Worth Bagly Dihedral
- [ ] Y Knot

5.10c

- [ ] A Little Bit of Magic
- [ ] A Woman's Work is Never Done
- [ ] Absolute Zero
- [ ] Against All Todds
- [ ] Albatross, The
- [ ] All Loin
- [ ] Anacram
- [ ] April Fools
- [ ] Astropoodle
- [ ] Atari
- [ ] B.A.S.E. Arrest
- [ ] Band Saw
- [ ] Bearded Cabbage
- [ ] Beginner's Twenty-Six
- [ ] Beverly Drive
- [ ] Billabong
- [ ] Birdland
- [ ] Black Plastic Streetwalker
- [ ] Black Widow
- [ ] Blonde Eyebrow Fetish
- [ ] Bongledesh
- [ ] Boulevard of Dreams
- [ ] Brief Case
- [ ] British Airways

5.10c *(cont.)*

☐ Brownian Motion
☐ Bruiser, The
☐ Brush Your Teeth With Jesus
☐ Canalizo
☐ Carnage
☐ Castrum, The
☐ Cat on a Hot Tin Roof
☐ Catch a Falling Car
☐ Ceremony
☐ Chamber of Commerce
☐ Cherry Bomb
☐ Chilly Willy
☐ Church Bazaar
☐ Chute to Kill
☐ Cleavage
☐ Cole-Gordon Offwidth
☐ Common Law Marriage
☐ Compassion of the Elephants, The
☐ Cosmic Book
☐ Crack #4
☐ Crack C
☐ Crescent Wrench
☐ Crime of the Century
☐ Cruising for Burgers
☐ Crystal Deva
☐ Cut Thin to Win
☐ Daddy Long Legs
☐ Deep, Shallow and Twisted
☐ Delusions
☐ Devil Inside
☐ Dike Da Doodad
☐ Dike, The
☐ Dirty Cat
☐ Disappearing Act
☐ Disco Sucks
☐ Disobedience School
☐ Dogleg Right
☐ Don't Dik With Walt
☐ Double Jeopardy
☐ Dunce Cap, The
☐ Dyno-soar
☐ EBGB's
☐ El Blowhole
☐ Empty Street
☐ Episcopalian Toothpick
☐ Evolutionary Throwback
☐ F.U.N.
☐ Falcon and the Snowman, The
☐ Fire or Retire
☐ First Eleven
☐ Flakes of Grasp
☐ Fool for a Pretty Face
☐ Free for a Fee

☐ Fumblers Below the Roof
☐ Goin' Down the Road Feelin' Bad
☐ Golddigger, The
☐ Good Grief
☐ Grainy Train
☐ Grandpa Gander
☐ Greenhorn Dihedral
☐ Grit Roof
☐ Gumshoe
☐ Hallow Friction
☐ Handlin' Snakeskin
☐ Harlequin
☐ Hawk Wind
☐ Heaven Can Wait
☐ Hermanutic
☐ Hintertoiser Traverse, The
☐ Holly Device
☐ Hollywood and Vaino
☐ Hour of Power
☐ Icon
☐ Importance of Being Ernest, The
☐ Indian Giver
☐ Iron Man Traverse
☐ Iron Mantle
☐ It Seams Possible
☐ Jah Loo
☐ Jedi Master
☐ Junior
☐ Kamikaze
☐ Knack
☐ Kook Book
☐ Laid Back and Doing It
☐ Land of Wonder
☐ Left Lizard Crack
☐ Legolas
☐ Life in the Fast Lane
☐ Los Tres Bovines
☐ Make That Move or Six Foot Groove
☐ Martin Quits
☐ Memorial Meowzer
☐ Mental Siege Tactics
☐ Message in a Bottle
☐ Meteorite Crack
☐ Modern Jazz
☐ Mother Board Breakdown
☐ Move to the Groove
☐ Moveable Feast
☐ Nestle Crunch
☐ No Self Confidence
☐ Nuts and Bolts of Climbing, The
☐ O'Kelley's Crack
☐ Official Route of the 1984 Olympics
☐ Oh God!

5.10c (cont.)

- [ ] One Move Leads to Another
- [ ] Orc Sighs
- [ ] Out for a Bite
- [ ] Pecking Order
- [ ] Pepo Mover
- [ ] Piggle Pugg
- [ ] Pile in the Sky
- [ ] Point of No Return
- [ ] Polytechnics
- [ ] Potato Head
- [ ] Primal Scream
- [ ] Psychotechnics
- [ ] Pullups to Pasadena
- [ ] Quantum Jump
- [ ] Rat Boy
- [ ] Raving Skinhead
- [ ] Red Sonja
- [ ] Regular Route (Plymouth Rock)
- [ ] Return of the Chuckwalla
- [ ] Rice Cake Roof
- [ ] Right Route
- [ ] Right Stuff, The
- [ ] Roark
- [ ] Rob'n the Cradle
- [ ] Route 499
- [ ] Rude Awakening
- [ ] Ruff Stuff
- [ ] Run from your Wife
- [ ] S Cracker, The
- [ ] Sandbag
- [ ] Sawdust Crack, Left
- [ ] Screaming Poodle, The
- [ ] Secret of Mother Butler, The
- [ ] Serious Fashion
- [ ] Sexy Sadye
- [ ] Shady Grove
- [ ] Shame
- [ ] Sharks in the Water
- [ ] Sharp Arete
- [ ] Shongo Pavi
- [ ] Sin City
- [ ] Sinbad the Sailor
- [ ] Skeptic, The
- [ ] Skinwalker
- [ ] Slam Dance
- [ ] Slip Skrig
- [ ] Small Town Taste
- [ ] Smear Tactics
- [ ] Software Sluts
- [ ] Solo Dog
- [ ] Solstice
- [ ] Song of the Siren
- [ ] Spaghetti Sauce Sunset
- [ ] Spiritworld
- [ ] Steps Ahead
- [ ] Still, The
- [ ] Studebaker Hawk
- [ ] Surface Tension
- [ ] Swain-Buckey
- [ ] Sweat Band
- [ ] T-N-T
- [ ] T.K.O.
- [ ] Take it for Granite
- [ ] Telegram For Mongo
- [ ] That Old Soft Shoe
- [ ] The Go-Go's on Quaaludes
- [ ] Three Best Friends Your Car Ever Had, The
- [ ] Too Thin for Poodles
- [ ] Too Wide to Trot
- [ ] Trautner-Fry
- [ ] Trespassers Will Be Violated
- [ ] Try Again
- [ ] Tube Steak
- [ ] Two Scoops Please
- [ ] Unknown
- [ ] Unknown
- [ ] Welcome to Joshua Tree
- [ ] When Lightning Strikes
- [ ] When Sheep Ran Scared
- [ ] Wide World of Sports
- [ ] Winter Wine
- [ ] Wish You Were Here
- [ ] Yabo Phone Home

5.10d

- [ ] A Cheap Way to Die
- [ ] Air Play
- [ ] Automatic Tiger
- [ ] Balance Due
- [ ] Banana Splits
- [ ] Beadwagon
- [ ] Bed of Nails
- [ ] BeeGees
- [ ] Belly Dancer
- [ ] Big Brown Eye
- [ ] Black President
- [ ] Blind Me With Science
- [ ] Bridge-It Bardot
- [ ] Casual Affair
- [ ] Cedric's Deep Sea Fish Market
- [ ] Centurion
- [ ] Child's Play
- [ ] Cinnamon Girl

5.10d *(cont.)*

- [ ] Count Dracula
- [ ] Cranking Skills or Hospital Bills
- [ ] Danny Gore
- [ ] Decompensator of Lhasa, The
- [ ] Diamonds are Forever
- [ ] Doing That Scrapyard Thing
- [ ] Dominatrix
- [ ] Don't Be Nosey
- [ ] Don't Waltz with Dick
- [ ] Dreamer
- [ ] El Brujo
- [ ] Fatty Winds His Neck Out
- [ ] Fear of Flying
- [ ] Flexible Hueys
- [ ] Foreign Legion
- [ ] Fractured Fissure
- [ ] Freeway Jam
- [ ] Fugitive, The
- [ ] Given up for Dead
- [ ] Godzilla Eats Human Sushi
- [ ] Goodbye Mr. Bond
- [ ] Gordoba
- [ ] Grain of Truth
- [ ] Grungy
- [ ] Gumbi Saves Bambi
- [ ] Hang and Swing
- [ ] Hard Rock Cafe
- [ ] Henny Penny
- [ ] Herbie's Hideaway
- [ ] Higher Yield
- [ ] Hot Knife
- [ ] Hyperventilation
- [ ] I Eat Cannibals
- [ ] Imaginary Voyage
- [ ] Invisible Touch
- [ ] It's Never Robot City
- [ ] Jack in the Crack
- [ ] Janus
- [ ] Jolly Rancher Firestix
- [ ] Kidney Stone
- [ ] Kiwi Route
- [ ] Kool Aid
- [ ] Laegar Domain
- [ ] Landlord, The
- [ ] Last Unicorn, The
- [ ] Lean and Scream
- [ ] Lemming, The
- [ ] Love Comes in Spurts
- [ ] Man from Glad
- [ ] Maneater, The
- [ ] Mel Crack, Left
- [ ] Micronesia
- [ ] Middle Band
- [ ] Midnight Lumber
- [ ] Minute Man
- [ ] Morning Thunder
- [ ] Nail 'n Gravel
- [ ] New Shoe Review, The
- [ ] No Falls
- [ ] No Perch is Necessary
- [ ] No Self Respect
- [ ] No Shirt Needed
- [ ] Oasis of Eden
- [ ] Panther Crack
- [ ] Perpetual Motion
- [ ] Petrodynamics
- [ ] Pinky Lee
- [ ] Pit Bull Attack
- [ ] Prebyterian Dental Floss
- [ ] Pussy Galore
- [ ] Rain Dance
- [ ] Raked Over the Coles
- [ ] Raker's Blaring Hat Rack
- [ ] Rat Race
- [ ] Red Red
- [ ] Rock Star
- [ ] Rockwell 41C
- [ ] Rocky Road
- [ ] Rubicon
- [ ] Scared Bare
- [ ] Semi Tough
- [ ] Shibumi
- [ ] Sketches of Strain
- [ ] Slimmer Pickens
- [ ] Squatter's Right
- [ ] Stereo in B Flat
- [ ] Such a Line
- [ ] Surrealistic Colgate
- [ ] Talking Fish, The
- [ ] Tar
- [ ] Tax Free
- [ ] Tchalk is Cheap
- [ ] Tequila
- [ ] Thunderclap Direct
- [ ] Tiers for Fears
- [ ] Time and a Half
- [ ] To Air is Human
- [ ] Too Secret to Find
- [ ] Toxic Wasteland
- [ ] Uncle Fester
- [ ] Unknown
- [ ] Wacko Placko
- [ ] Wage and Price Ceiling
- [ ] Wet Rock Day
- [ ] What's it to You
- [ ] Zion Train
- [ ] Zola Budd
- [ ] Zulu Dawn

5.10+

- [ ] Alien Life Form Arete, The
- [ ] An Unruly Camel
- [ ] Beaver Boulder Free Route
- [ ] Blue-Grass
- [ ] Brown Squeeze
- [ ] Cut to the Bone
- [ ] Dike Flight
- [ ] Fly Away
- [ ] Hands Up
- [ ] Hooterville Trolley
- [ ] Just a Dream Away
- [ ] Missing in Action
- [ ] Moonlight Crack
- [ ] One Arm Giant
- [ ] Over the Rainbow
- [ ] Peter Eater Pumpkin Eater
- [ ] Pretzel Logic
- [ ] Robbins Route, The
- [ ] Route Right of the Dumbest Climb ...
- [ ] RR Does it Again
- [ ] Sleek Beak
- [ ] Telekinesis
- [ ] Unsolved Mystery
- [ ] Unzipper
- [ ] Wild Dream
- [ ] Wonderful World of Art, The

5.11

- [ ] Absence of Malice
- [ ] Arms for Hostages
- [ ] Bridge, The
- [ ] Ceramic Bus
- [ ] Cling or Fling
- [ ] Comfortably Numb
- [ ] Crystal Voyager
- [ ] Erotic City
- [ ] Fire or Retire, Direct Finish
- [ ] Green Chile
- [ ] Gunsmoke
- [ ] High Cost of Living, The
- [ ] If it's Brown, Flush it
- [ ] Jackalope
- [ ] Mary Decker
- [ ] Mr. DNA
- [ ] Popsicle, The
- [ ] Quivering Savages
- [ ] Red Chile
- [ ] Roundup, The
- [ ] Secret Sauce
- [ ] Speculum Scrapings
- [ ] Spontaneous Human Combustion
- [ ] Spring or Fall
- [ ] Stable Girl
- [ ] Stone Hinge
- [ ] Svapada
- [ ] Tooth Decay
- [ ] Turd, The
- [ ] Viva Las Vegas
- [ ] Walk the Plank
- [ ] When You're a Sancho
- [ ] Yardarm, The

5.11a

- [ ] Abstract Roller Disco
- [ ] Acid Rock
- [ ] Adult Books
- [ ] Alf's Arete
- [ ] Amazing Grace
- [ ] Android Lust
- [ ] Archimedes' Crack, Left
- [ ] Are You Experienced?
- [ ] Arete #3
- [ ] Arete #4
- [ ] Ayatollah, The
- [ ] Baby Fae
- [ ] Bad Fun
- [ ] Battle of the Bulge
- [ ] Bebop Tango
- [ ] Bendix Claws, The
- [ ] Big Moe
- [ ] Blue Ribbon
- [ ] Break Dancing
- [ ] Breaking Away
- [ ] Breath of Death
- [ ] Brown 25
- [ ] Butterfly Crack
- [ ] California Crack
- [ ] Cast up a Highway
- [ ] Chute to Kill
- [ ] Claim Jumper
- [ ] Cleared for Takeoff
- [ ] Coarse and Buggy
- [ ] Colossus of Rhoids, The
- [ ] Comic Relief
- [ ] Congratulations
- [ ] Crazy Climber
- [ ] Cretin Bull Dancer
- [ ] Dance on Fire
- [ ] Dick Enberg

5.11a (cont.)

- [ ] Direct Wrench
- [ ] Discoy Decoy
- [ ] Dwindling Greenbacks
- [ ] Enos Mills Glacier
- [ ] Face
- [ ] Fascist Groove Thing
- [ ] Flange, The
- [ ] Flashflood
- [ ] Forgotten Galaxy
- [ ] Fowl Play
- [ ] Freckle Face
- [ ] Geometry
- [ ] Gold Hunk, The
- [ ] Goldenbush Corner
- [ ] Gravity Waves
- [ ] Great Commission
- [ ] Hey Taxi
- [ ] High and Dry
- [ ] High Interest
- [ ] History
- [ ] Hook and Ladder
- [ ] Hot Lava
- [ ] Hyperion
- [ ] I'm Pregnant With Satan's Baby
- [ ] Ignorant Photons From Pluto
- [ ] Igor's Failed Road Trip
- [ ] Jugline
- [ ] Jumping Jack Crack
- [ ] Just for the Thrill of it
- [ ] Keith's Work
- [ ] Killer Pussy
- [ ] Kilobyte
- [ ] King Pin
- [ ] Lay Back and Do It
- [ ] Layaway Plan
- [ ] Lemon Slicer, The
- [ ] Lithophiliac
- [ ] Liturgy
- [ ] Live and Let Die
- [ ] Looking for Mercy
- [ ] Loose Lips
- [ ] Manly Dike, The
- [ ] Megabyte
- [ ] Mercy Road
- [ ] Mere Illusion
- [ ] Mettle Detector
- [ ] Momento Mori
- [ ] Naked Reagan
- [ ] Natural Selection
- [ ] No Mistake or Big Pancake
- [ ] No San Francisco
- [ ] Nose to the Grindstone
- [ ] Out to Lunge
- [ ] Outsiders, The
- [ ] Pale Rider
- [ ] Peanut Gallery
- [ ] Pilgrim, The
- [ ] Poodle Smasher, The
- [ ] Popeye
- [ ] Prejudicial Viewpoint
- [ ] Preparation H
- [ ] Puzzlin' Evidence
- [ ] Quest for Fire
- [ ] Railroad
- [ ] RCA
- [ ] Red Headed Stranger
- [ ] Red Snapper
- [ ] Ripper
- [ ] Rites of Passage
- [ ] Roadrunner
- [ ] Rock Shark
- [ ] Rope Opera
- [ ] Rubberfat Syndrome, The
- [ ] S Crack
- [ ] S Crack, Middle
- [ ] Sanctuary Much
- [ ] Santa's Little Helpers
- [ ] Scar Wars
- [ ] Shooting Star
- [ ] Ski Track, Left
- [ ] Soul Kitchen
- [ ] Static Cling
- [ ] Such a Savage
- [ ] Sun City
- [ ] Super Monster Killer
- [ ] Sweet Ginger
- [ ] Swept Away
- [ ] Swift
- [ ] Taming of the Shoe, The
- [ ] Tap Dancing
- [ ] Therapeutic Tyranny
- [ ] Third Bolt from the Sun
- [ ] Traverse of no Return
- [ ] Twisted Crystals
- [ ] Unnamed
- [ ] Veucian Fece
- [ ] Washoe Crack
- [ ] Wedlock
- [ ] Weekend Warrior
- [ ] Weenie Roast
- [ ] Winds of Whoopee
- [ ] Wren's Nest
- [ ] Young Frankenstein
- [ ] Zorba

5.11b

- ☐ Adrift
- ☐ Air Voyager
- ☐ Animalitos
- ☐ Arete #2
- ☐ Atom Ant
- ☐ Banana Crack, Right
- ☐ Banana Crack, Right
- ☐ Bella Lugosi
- ☐ Catapult
- ☐ Chaos
- ☐ Charles Who?
- ☐ Chick Flakey
- ☐ Combination Locks
- ☐ Compound W
- ☐ Date Queen Corridor Crack
- ☐ Dead Man's Eyes
- ☐ Desert Song
- ☐ Dig Me
- ☐ Digitizer
- ☐ Dimp for a Chimp
- ☐ Double Trouble
- ☐ Electric Eye
- ☐ Fang, The
- ☐ Feathers
- ☐ Fingers of Frenzy
- ☐ Fingers on a Landscape
- ☐ Firefly
- ☐ Forbidden Zone
- ☐ Frat Boys in the Gym
- ☐ Friend Bender
- ☐ Gigantor
- ☐ Happy Landings, Linda
- ☐ Ho Man!
- ☐ Hot Rocks
- ☐ Inauguron, The
- ☐ Iron Curtain, The
- ☐ James Brown
- ☐ Knight in Shining Armor, The
- ☐ Laserator
- ☐ Latin Swing
- ☐ Middle Age Crazy
- ☐ Mission Impossible
- ☐ Morality Test
- ☐ More Monkey Than Funky
- ☐ Morongo Man
- ☐ Mulligan Stew
- ☐ No Options
- ☐ Overnight Sensation
- ☐ Papaya Crack
- ☐ Pat Adams Dihedral
- ☐ Poaching Bighorn
- ☐ Porky Pig
- ☐ Pretty in Pink
- ☐ Private Idaho
- ☐ Psychokenesis
- ☐ Quantum Mechanics
- ☐ R.S. Chicken Choker
- ☐ Rainy Day, Dream Away
- ☐ Right to Arm Bears, The
- ☐ Ring of Fire
- ☐ Route 1060
- ☐ Scary Poodles
- ☐ Scattered Remains
- ☐ Shifting Sands
- ☐ Sicker than Jezouin
- ☐ Silverado
- ☐ Sound of Waves, The
- ☐ Tarzan
- ☐ Time Avenger
- ☐ Twittish Empire
- ☐ Uncle Remus
- ☐ Ungawaa
- ☐ Up 40
- ☐ V Crack, Left
- ☐ Vogels are Poodles Too
- ☐ Walking Pneumonia
- ☐ Wheel of Fortune
- ☐ White Bread Fever

5.11c

- ☐ 39 Slaps, The
- ☐ A Scar is Born
- ☐ Anecdotes of Power
- ☐ Animalargos
- ☐ Animalargos
- ☐ Another Cilley Toprope
- ☐ Anti-Gravity Boots
- ☐ Black Panther
- ☐ Blind Man's Bluff
- ☐ Boogie Woogie Blues, The
- ☐ Bozo's Raindance
- ☐ Bronto's or Us, The
- ☐ Buried Treasure
- ☐ Carribean Cruise
- ☐ Castaway
- ☐ Cayenne
- ☐ Chicago Nipple Slump
- ☐ Compact Physical
- ☐ Conceptual Continuity
- ☐ Conundrum, The
- ☐ Cool But Concerned
- ☐ Digital Watch
- ☐ Euphrates
- ☐ Face to Face

5.11c (cont.)

- [ ] Famous Potatoes
- [ ] For Peter
- [ ] Frigid Dare
- [ ] Gravity Works
- [ ] Hands Down
- [ ] Hands of Fire
- [ ] Hands to Yourself
- [ ] Headbangers' Ball
- [ ] Hercules
- [ ] Hot Flashes
- [ ] Houdini Arete, The
- [ ] Human Sacrifice
- [ ] Illicit Operations
- [ ] In a Silent Way
- [ ] It's Easy to be Distant When You're Brave
- [ ] Kon-Tiki
- [ ] Let's Get Horizontal
- [ ] Magma
- [ ] Midnight Oil
- [ ] Mighty High
- [ ] Missing Persons
- [ ] Nerve Storm
- [ ] Nihilistic Pillar
- [ ] On the Back
- [ ] Orno-Necro
- [ ] Panama Red
- [ ] Pitfall
- [ ] Police & Thieves
- [ ] Predator, The
- [ ] Riddles in the Dark
- [ ] Rockwork Orange
- [ ] Rocky Vs. Rambo
- [ ] Roller Coaster
- [ ] Rule Britannia
- [ ] Safety Pin
- [ ] Secret Agent Man
- [ ] Shake, Rattle and Roll
- [ ] Shamrock Shooter
- [ ] Shin Bashers
- [ ] Simple Simon
- [ ] Snake Bite
- [ ] Son of Obsidian
- [ ] Sound of One Hand Slapping, The
- [ ] Soviet Union
- [ ] Spanish Bombs
- [ ] Spanking
- [ ] Spider Line
- [ ] Thin Line
- [ ] Tombstone, The
- [ ] Toothpick, The
- [ ] Top of the Rope
- [ ] Total Generic Package
- [ ] Triathlon
- [ ] Vector
- [ ] Wangerbanger
- [ ] Wet T-Shirt Night
- [ ] Wheat Beri-Beri
- [ ] When You're a Jet
- [ ] Whistling Sphincter
- [ ] Who'da Thought
- [ ] Wings of Steel
- [ ] Women in Cages
- [ ] Zen and the Art of Placement

5.11d

- [ ] 29 Palms
- [ ] Avante Guard-Dog
- [ ] Baby Huey Smokes an Anti-Pipeload
- [ ] Badfinger
- [ ] Blood of Christ
- [ ] Blue Velvet
- [ ] Bosch Job
- [ ] Campfire Girl
- [ ] Chicken Run
- [ ] Condor, The
- [ ] Dawn Yawn
- [ ] Destination Unknown
- [ ] Dirty Tricks
- [ ] Dynamic Panic
- [ ] Electric Blue
- [ ] Fast Track
- [ ] Flashpoint
- [ ] Functional Analysis
- [ ] Hidden Arch
- [ ] It Don't Mean a Thing ...
- [ ] Jane's Getting Serious
- [ ] Kodas Silence
- [ ] Leave it to Beaver
- [ ] Living Conjunction, The
- [ ] Meat Locker
- [ ] Micro Millenium, The
- [ ] Minor Threat
- [ ] Pox on You
- [ ] Raging Bull Dike
- [ ] Ramming Speed
- [ ] Resurrection
- [ ] Scary Monsters
- [ ] Snap On Demand
- [ ] Stone Idol
- [ ] Super Spy
- [ ] Trapeze Right
- [ ] Where Eagles Dare
- [ ] Woodshed, The
- [ ] Young Guns

5.11+

- [ ] Bell-E-Up
- [ ] Bombs Over Libya
- [ ] Cactus Flower
- [ ] Crow's Nest, The
- [ ] Elephant Walk
- [ ] Fruits of Labor
- [ ] Green Visitor
- [ ] Hollow Dreams
- [ ] Jingus Con
- [ ] My Grain
- [ ] Piledriver, The
- [ ] Puss N' Boots
- [ ] Rubicon Direct
- [ ] Rustler, The
- [ ] Shirt Heads
- [ ] Speculator, The
- [ ] Top Hat
- [ ] Toprope Conversion
- [ ] Unnamed
- [ ] Wheresabolt?

5.12

- [ ] Brown Out
- [ ] Bunnies
- [ ] Electric Birthday Party
- [ ] Flying Dutchman, The
- [ ] Good Investment
- [ ] Headbangers' Ball
- [ ] Headmaster
- [ ] Marathon Crack
- [ ] Obsidian
- [ ] Quasar
- [ ] Real McCoy, The
- [ ] Seizure
- [ ] Steep Pulse
- [ ] Thin Red Line

5.12a

- [ ] Arms Control
- [ ] Bates Motel, The
- [ ] Beautiful Screamer
- [ ] Bikini Whale
- [ ] Brain Damage
- [ ] Brain Death
- [ ] Brass Monkey
- [ ] Castles Burning
- [ ] Chief Crazy Horse
- [ ] Cross Fire
- [ ] Datura
- [ ] Dial Africa
- [ ] Emotional Rescue
- [ ] Every Which Way But Up
- [ ] Existential Decay
- [ ] Fear is Never Boring
- [ ] Fingers of Frenzy
- [ ] Glory Road
- [ ] Great Escape, The
- [ ] High Wire
- [ ] Ionic Strength
- [ ] It's Easy to be Brave From a Safe Distance
- [ ] Life's a Pitch
- [ ] Major Threat
- [ ] Middle of Somewhere
- [ ] Money for Nothing
- [ ] Nuclear Arms
- [ ] Overpowered by Funk
- [ ] Repo Man
- [ ] Riddler, The
- [ ] Slightly Ahead of Our Time
- [ ] Sole Fusion
- [ ] Spur of the Moment, The
- [ ] Stairway to Heaven
- [ ] Taxed to the Limit
- [ ] Throbbing Gristle
- [ ] Transfusion
- [ ] Trapeze Center
- [ ] Waltzing Worn
- [ ] Wavecrest
- [ ] Woodward Crack

5.12b

- [ ] 5 Crying Cowboys
- [ ] Apartheid
- [ ] Apollo
- [ ] Baby Apes
- [ ] Battering Ram
- [ ] Bikini Beach
- [ ] Chameleon, The
- [ ] Chicks for Free
- [ ] Mettle Detector
- [ ] Potato Masher
- [ ] Quickstone
- [ ] Rubik's Revenge
- [ ] Slaves of Fashion
- [ ] Talon Show
- [ ] Vanishing Point
- [ ] Walk on Water
- [ ] Warrior Eagle
- [ ] Watusi, The
- [ ] Zombie Woof

5.12c

- [ ] *A Question of Masculinity*
- [ ] *Buffalo Soldier*
- [ ] *Burning Bush*
- [ ] *Camouflage*
- [ ] *Dictators of Anarchy*
- [ ] *Love Goddess*
- [ ] *Mamunia*
- [ ] *Medusa*
- [ ] *Mind Body Problem*
- [ ] *Mohawk, The*
- [ ] *No Self Control*
- [ ] *Railer*
- [ ] *Thrill of Desire, The*
- [ ] *Trapeze Left*

5.12d

- [ ] *Acid Crack, The*
- [ ] *Equinox*
- [ ] *Moonbeam Crack, The*

5.12 +

- [ ] *Asteroid Crack*
- [ ] *Crash, The*
- [ ] *Ship Wrecked*
- [ ] *To Hold and to Have*

5.13

- [ ] *Dihedralman*
- [ ] *Persian Room, The*

5.13a

- [ ] *Book of Brilliant Things*
- [ ] *Dunce Cap*
- [ ] *Father Figure*
- [ ] *Hold Your Fire*
- [ ] *La Cholla*
- [ ] *Powers That Be, The*
- [ ] *Pumping Hate*
- [ ] *Sun Bowl*

5.13b

- [ ] *Chain of Addiction*
- [ ] *Rots O' Rock*

5.13c

- [ ] *La Machine*

5.13 +

- [ ] *Stingray*

Aid

- [ ] *North Face (Headstone Rock)*
- [ ] *Unknown Highway*
- [ ] *What is the Question?*
- [ ] *Mexican Hat of Josh*
- [ ] *Nameless*
- [ ] *Tons of Junk*
- [ ] *Rurp Romp*
- [ ] *Sacred Bear*
- [ ] *Joint Effort*
- [ ] *Off Track*
- [ ] *Perfidious*
- [ ] *Lost Lid*

INDEX